An Illustrated Guide to Civil Procedure

ASPEN COURSEBOOK SERIES

An Illustrated Guide to Civil Procedure

Fifth Edition

Michael Finch
Stetson University College of Law

Jason R. Bent
Stetson University College of Law

Michael P. Allen
Judge, United States Court of Appeals for Veterans Claims

ASPEN PUBLISHING

Cover Image: iStock/ftwitty

To contact Customer Service, e-mail customer.service@aspenpublishing.com, call 1-800-950-5259, or mail correspondence to:

Aspen Publishing
Attn: Order Department
1 Wall Street
Burlington, MA 01803

Printed in the United States of America.

1 2 3 4 5 6 7 8 9 0

ISBN 979-8-8920-7906-8

Library of Congress Cataloging-in-Publication Data
Names: Allen, Michael, 1967- author. | Finch, Michael, 1952- author. | Bent, Jason R., author.
Title: An illustrated guide to civil procedure / Michael Finch, Stetson University College of Law; Jason R. Bent, Stetson University College of Law; Michael P. Allen, Judge, United States Court of Appeals for Veterans Claims.
Description: Fifth edition. | Burlington: Aspen Publishing, 2025. |
Series: Aspen Casebook Series | Includes bibliographical references and index. |
Summary: "Coursebook for students taking a Civil Procedure course for law school students taking a Civil Procedure course"— Provided by publisher.
Identifiers: LCCN 2024040119 | ISBN 9798892079068 (Paperback) | ISBN 9798892079082 (ebook)
Subjects: LCSH: Civil procedure—United States. | LCGFT: Casebooks (Law)
Classification: LCC KF8840.A475 2025 | DDC 347.73/5—dc23
LC record available at https://lccn.loc.gov/2024040119

About Aspen Publishing

Aspen Publishing is a leading provider of legal educational content and digital learning solutions in the U.S. and around the world. Aspen provides best-in-class solutions through authoritative textbooks, written by renowned authors, and breakthrough products such as Connected eBooks, Connected Quizzing, PracticePerfect, and JD-Next.

The Aspen Casebook Series (famously known among law faculty and students as the "red and black" casebooks) encompasses hundreds of highly regarded textbooks in more than eighty disciplines, from large enrollment courses, such as Torts and Contracts, to emerging electives, like Sustainability and the Law of Policing. Study aids such as *Examples & Explanations* help law students master complex subject matter. Aspen's Paralegal, Criminal Justice, and Business Law series bring our hallmark publishing standards to undergraduate students. JD-Next is an innovative online law school prep course and admissions test that offers a realistic preview of law school, teaches underlying skills for academic success, and assesses applicants' academic readiness for law school.

Aspen Publishing is proud to be a UWorld company

Since 2003, UWorld has been a global leader in developing high-quality learning tools for students preparing for high-stakes exams. With a commitment to excellence, UWorld has helped millions of students in undergraduate, graduate, and professional programs in fields such as medicine, nursing, finance, and law achieve their academic and career goals.

Founded by Chandra S. Pemmasani, M.D., during his medical residency, UWorld began focusing on medical education and has since expanded into various academic fields, including law. In 2020, UWorld launched its Legal vertical, starting with its comprehensive Multistate Bar Exam (MBE®) Question Bank, followed by the acquisition of Themis Bar Review, which integrated resources to provide a complete bar exam preparation experience. In 2024, UWorld expanded its offerings by acquiring Aspen Publishing, enhancing its suite of legal education products.

Today, UWorld offers an unparalleled range of study materials that blend active learning methods with expert content, ensuring students and educators can access the most effective resources. From bar preparation to law school success, UWorld is committed to supporting the next generation of legal professionals. Learn more at uworld.com.

Dedication and Acknowledgments

Several people made this book possible, in all its editions. We continue to acknowledge the artistic efforts of our student Tracey Sticco, Stetson College of Law Class of 2007. Tracey drew a number of cartoons that appear in the GUIDE and put up with our (numerous) requests for revisions.

We also thank the staff at Aspen Publishers. We especially appreciate Rick Mixter, for his inspired belief that legal texts can be practical and occasionally humorous, and Eric Holt, who brought our original vision to life. We are also grateful for the editorial work of Darren Kelly and Lisa Connery of The Froebe Group on the 5th Edition.

Finally, permit us a few more personal thanks. Professor Finch thanks his wife, Lora, an exceptional wife and mother; his daughter Chloe, whose tuition at Brown has already gobbled up decades of book royalties; and Lily, whose spirit never seems to fail. And he gives his posthumous thanks to his father, mother, and brother, wherever you may be.

Professor Bent thanks his wife Shaina, whose strength continually inspires him, and his children Elianna and Jacob, who make every day an unpredictable adventure and joyous event. He also thanks his mother and his late father for their lifelong support of all his professional pursuits.

Professor Allen thanks, and dedicates the GUIDE to, his wife Debbie and his two sons, Ben and Noah. They stood (or crawled) by him throughout this effort in doing the first edition. They have equally been here for the second one. It would not have been possible to complete this project without their love and support.

We hope you learn from and enjoy our work.

Michael Finch, Jason Bent, & Michael Allen

September 2024
Gulfport, Florida

Acknowledgments

"CIV PRO MATH." © Stu Rees. www.stus.com.

"Greetings: You Are Hereby Subpoenaed to Appear. . ." © Hon. Steve Rushing.

"Kick Juror #4." *Stu's Views.* © 2002 Stu Rees. www.stus.com.

"Miss, you can't just sign up to be on the next celebrity murder jury." *Stu's Views.* © Stu Rees. www.stus.com.

"No, Jimmy, I distinctly said you can halve your allowance. . .". © Jason Love.

"Restatement of Torts. Corpus Juris. Loopholes." © Dana Fradon/The New Yorker Collection/The Cartoon Bank.

"Some people say you can't put a price on a wife's twenty-seven years of loyalty and devotion. They're wrong." © Leo Cullum/CartoonStock.

"Sympathy/Get Well/Getting Sued." *Stu's Views.* © Stu Rees. www.stus.com.

"The jury will disregard the witness's last statement." Richard Decker/The New Yorker Collection/ The Cartoon Bank.

"There is no justice in the world." © 2017 Bob Mankoff/CartoonStock.

"We made a much longer version so lawyers could understand it." © Chris Slane. www.slanecartoon.com.

"We'll apply Panama law, thereby permitting you to break our own law." © Stu Rees. www.stus.com.

"Yes we have 'general' jurisdiction." © Stu Rees. www.stus.com.

"Motion for Judgment Notwithstanding Verdict." *Motion Commotion.* © 1997 Charles Fincher. www.studiochas.com.

"Motion for Protective Orders." *Motion Commotion.* © 1997 Charles Fincher. www.studiochas.com.

"Motion to Compel." *Motion Commotion.* © 1997 Charles Fincher. www.studiochas.com.

"Say something to me in legalese." © 1979 Charles Fincher. www.studiochas.com.

Summary of Contents

TABLE OF CONTENTS

INTRODUCTION

The traditional hallmark of lawyers is their ability to navigate clients through the unfamiliar world of the court system. This special skill rests on a sound knowledge of the rules of civil procedure. You begin developing this skill during your first-year course in Civil Procedure and continue refining it as long as you are a member of the legal profession. This is just a part of the reason why we refer to our profession as the "practice of law."

Many of our former students remark that they *really* learned civil procedure when they had to use it in practice. Once students become lawyers representing clients in litigation, the importance of concepts like notice pleading, plausibility pleading, and work product becomes apparent. Practicing lawyers often discover the logic of procedural rules that eluded them in law school.

In this Guide, we hope to place you in an authentic litigation setting and assist your learning of civil procedure. We have created a hypothetical employment discrimination suit that illustrates how the rules of procedure can operate in practice. You will be privy to the procedural strategies of lawyers for both plaintiffs and defendants. You will see how these strategies take form in illustrative pleadings, motions, discovery documents, and other materials generated in a suit.

We hope you will do more than watch the case unfold. As the action develops we have formulated questions and tasks that allow you to test your working knowledge of procedural rules. You will also begin developing your legal judgment by considering tactical and strategic issues that arise in our hypothetical lawsuit. Along the way we provide a number of "tactical tips" to help you appreciate how the rules can be used pragmatically to advance a client's goals. Even if you never litigate a civil suit, we believe these tips move you closer to the law school goal of thinking like a lawyer.

A Note on the Hypothetical Case

The hypothetical case is realistic. Your authors have experience representing clients in employment discrimination suits, and we have drawn on that experience in writing and revising the Guide. At the same time, we have condensed our case presentation to emphasize the procedural rules of greatest importance to first-year law students. You will have the opportunity to refine your understanding of the litigation process in upper-level courses like Pretrial Practice, Trial Advocacy, Remedies, and Complex Litigation. We urge you to take these courses if you are interested in being a litigator.

The hypothetical case is neither artificially simple nor dauntingly complex. But it may challenge you in the beginning. An unavoidable fact of contemporary litigation is that an apparently simple case often requires that lawyers negotiate their way through a complex array of facts, substantive law, and procedural rules.

To help you manage the facts and law involved in our case, we've provided an appendix. In that appendix you will find a brief summary of (1) the parties, lawyers, and witnesses; (2) the key facts alleged in the complaint and their chronology; and (3) the legal claims the parties have asserted. Practicing lawyers often rely on such summaries to remind them of the structure of a case.

A Note on Organization and Coverage

Civil Procedure teachers and texts organize the subject in different ways. For example, two of the authors begin their course with the study of subject matter jurisdiction, personal jurisdiction, and the *Erie* doctrine and later examine the particular rules governing the litigation process. The third author begins his course with the study of these rules and defers topics like jurisdiction and *Erie* until later in the course.

Both approaches have advantages, and the Guide is suited to either approach. After introducing the dispute that underlies our hypothetical suit in Chapter One, Chapters Two through Five consider the various doctrines related to jurisdiction, venue, and the choice of law governing the dispute. If your professor begins the study of Civil Procedure by exploring these doctrines, you will likely proceed sequentially through the book.

If your professor begins the study of Civil Procedure by examining the procedural rules governing the litigation process, you will likely move directly from Chapter One to Chapter Six—where you begin studying use of those rules in the hypothetical suit. You'll continue through the remaining, rule-focused chapters, after which you'll examine the various jurisdictional doctrines in Chapters Two through Five.

The Guide is not intended to replace your textbook. For most Civil Procedure professors, the Guide is a valuable companion to one of the many excellent textbooks available from Aspen and other publishers. That said, one of the authors has used the Guide as his primary text for more than a decade—supplemented by abundant cases and secondary material posted on the class web page. Professors at other law schools have used this approach as well. Suffice it to say that we have constructed the Guide so that it can be used by Civil Procedure teachers no matter what their approach.

You should also be aware that Civil Procedure scholars have divergent views of their subject. Your professor's view of procedural law and the handling of litigation will inevitably differ from ours at times. We hope you interpret this divergence of opinion not as a sign that someone is wrong, but rather as an introduction to the inevitable ambiguity and diversity that characterizes the practice of law.

A Note on Drafting

Procedural rules give lawyers considerable discretion in drafting litigation documents. This comes as a surprise to many law students, who often come to believe that the awkward, stilted practices found in much legal writing are somehow preferred, even required, by the courts. Yet virtually everything objectionable in the writing habits of litigators is gratuitous, self-inflicted injury. Judges incessantly tell lawyers that they prefer simple language and are unimpressed by legalese.[1]

The illustrative documents in the Guide represent the authors' best efforts at writing in service of three main goals—utility, brevity, and simplicity.

By utility we mean accomplishing all that the rules permit a document to accomplish while minimizing an adversary's opportunity to make valid objections. For example, a complaint should adequately state the facts and legal claims supporting the client's suit. It should also lay a comprehensive foundation for the discovery process. At the same time, a complaint should not invite objections that could be avoided by more careful drafting. Responding to such objections causes lawyers and clients needless expense.

By brevity we mean as short as possible. It takes less time to draft a verbose document than a brief one. Lawyers sometimes flatter themselves that a longer document is more comprehensive and insightful. Occasionally this is true, but usually it is not.

By simplicity we mean, in addition to brevity, simple language. Law students understandably seek to use the specialized vocabulary they have struggled so hard to learn. Yet this is usually a mistake. The abundant formalisms found in form books ("Now comes the Plaintiff by and through his counsel and petitions this honorable Court . . .") serve no purpose and impress no one. Most always, you can satisfy procedural rules and please the court by writing in language comprehensible to a layperson.[2]

References to the Federal Rules and Relevant Law

Each chapter begins with "Rule References," in which we list all rules used in the chapter. Rules discussed in greater depth are set forth in italics. There are also numerous statutes and cases cited in the Guide. Some address procedural issues, such as statutes governing subject matter jurisdiction and venue, while others address the substantive law that governs the case, such as provisions of the Age Discrimination in Employment Act or "ADEA."

Finally, at times we have referred to the Model Rules of Professional Conduct. These are the model ethical rules developed by the American Bar Association and adopted by numerous state courts. You will study these model rules in your upper-level course in Professional Responsibility. But we believe it best to develop a casual acquaintance with rules of professionalism early in your study of Civil Procedure, since these rules can affect the litigation process as much as the rules of procedure.

---

[1] See Bryan Garner, GARNER ON LANGUAGE AND WRITING 57 (2009) ("Lawyers are notoriously poor at gauging what judges prefer in legal writing. Too many of us believe, for example, that judges expect us to use legalese.")

[2] Joseph Kimble, LIFTING THE FOG OF LEGALESE XI (2002) ("Although lawyers write for a living, most legal writing is bad and has been for centuries; most lawyers recognize this failing from what they read, but still fancy themselves to be rather good writers, thank you; likewise, most lawyers strongly prefer other writers' prose to be plainer, simpler, shorter, clearer, but they also strongly resist changing their own style.").

Finally, we have tried to inject some levity into the Guide. It has been said that studying law is like eating sawdust without butter. From time to time we have attempted to improve your digestion with legal humor, which is not always the same thing as humor. We hope you find these attempts to be a welcome distraction. Some may even help you learn Civil Procedure.

"Say something to me in legalese."

Chapter One
Origins of the Lawsuit

Rule References:[1] 5, *11*

A. The Clients Tell Their Story

Eleanor Lane practices law in Jacksonville, Florida, with her partner, Ramona Quincy. Each spent years working as a highly paid associate in a large firm before deciding that "no bosses is better than money."[2] The partnership of Lane and Quincy now specializes in employment discrimination litigation.

In December 2022, Lane met with Otis and Fiona Olman. The Olmans claimed they were victims of age discrimination during a recent corporate downsizing. Here is the Olmans' story.

1. The Olmans' Employment History

Otis Olman is 53 years old. Fiona Olman is 49 years old. They've been avid outdoor recreationists all their lives. Otis has a bachelor's degree in earth sciences from Montana State University, and Fiona has a bachelor's degree in exercise physiology from Slippery Rock State University.

---

[1] Rules in italics are discussed in greater detail than other rules. Throughout the Guide, the Federal Rules of Civil Procedure are referred to variously as "Rules" or "Federal Rules."

[2] William Least Heat Moon, *Blue Highways: A Journey into America* (1991).

The couple met shortly after graduating from college and soon married. They have two grown children.

Otis was first employed by Full Moon Sports, Inc. in 2003. Full Moon owns and operates a national chain of retail sporting goods stores. Otis began work as an assistant manager at Full Moon's store in Burlington, Vermont. He soon showed an exceptional knack for identifying and marketing high-quality sporting goods. In 2006, Otis was made manager of the Burlington store.

In 2011, Full Moon asked Otis to become manager of its store in Jacksonville, Florida. Otis was reluctant to make the transfer at first, since he and his wife loved Vermont. But when Otis visited the Jacksonville store, he saw a great opportunity to transform a mediocre business into a premier operation. Besides, his children fell in love with the ocean, which Vermont does not have.

Fiona reluctantly agreed, and the Olmans moved to Jacksonville, Florida. Within a few years, Otis transformed the store into the highly successful Full Moon Sports & Outdoor Center. At the center, customers could find top-of-the-line camping gear, outdoor clothing, and sporting equipment used in popular Florida activities like sea kayaking and scuba diving. Otis trained his sales personnel to give expert advice about the equipment they sold. In addition, the store offered instruction in sea kayaking and scuba diving and sponsored guided outdoor adventures.

In 2014, Fiona began working at the Jacksonville store. By this time, she was an accomplished sea kayaker who had guided many of the store's tours on local intracoastal waters. She became manager of the store's kayak department in 2019, when the existing department manager moved to another state.

2. New Management at Full Moon

In 2019, Full Moon was acquired by Mizar, Inc., a Delaware corporation with headquarters in St. Louis, Missouri. Mizar owns several subsidiaries engaged in a broad range of manufacturing activities. One of these is Edge Performance, Inc., which manufactures equipment for "extreme" sports like skateboarding, snowboarding, inline skating, surfing, and white-water kayaking. Full Moon was Mizar's first attempt to expand into retail sales.

When Mizar acquired Full Moon, it immediately replaced Full Moon's president. The new president, Bertie Lurch, implemented several changes in the company. First, Full Moon introduced extreme sporting goods into its stores. Prominently featured in its "extreme" line were goods produced by Edge Performance. Second, Full Moon increased television and radio advertising, with a special emphasis on extreme sports. Third, Full Moon made changes in local and regional management.

Full Moon's executive headquarters are in Atlanta, and the company is incorporated in Delaware. Because Full Moon oversees so many stores throughout the country, it has divided them into regions. The Jacksonville store is in the southeast region, encompassing the states of Florida, Georgia, North Carolina, and South Carolina. Prior to Full Moon's acquisition by Mizar, Otis worked under the oversight of Rex Ornstein, the regional manager for the southeast stores. After Mizar acquired Full Moon, Rex was transferred to the advertising department in Atlanta and replaced as regional manager by Bruce Belcher.

The new regional manager visited with Otis shortly after being hired. Belcher told Otis he was very impressed by how Otis had developed the Jacksonville store. He also told Otis that Full Moon wanted him to continue as manager. Belcher asked Otis to sign a contract with Full Moon, even though Otis had previously worked for Full Moon without a written contract. The contract had a four-year term, running from March 1, 2019 through March 1, 2023, and Otis would continue to receive his current salary of $85,000.

Otis was reluctant to sign the contract. As soon as he learned that Full Moon had been acquired by Mizar, he developed misgivings about his future with the company. Mizar had a reputation in the industry as a company that focuses on the bottom line, showing little loyalty to its employees. Otis began to explore other job options. One of these was presented by a local entrepreneur and longtime customer, Izzy Able. Izzy proposed that Otis and Fiona move to Key Largo and set up a kayak sales and rental business. Izzy offered Otis a one-half partnership interest in exchange for Otis's managing the business. Otis and Fiona gave plenty of consideration to Izzy's proposal. Key Largo was a kayaker's paradise, and they believed a business in that area might prove to be highly profitable.

Otis felt comfortable calling Rex Ornstein, his former regional manager, to discuss this important career decision. Rex counseled Otis to "do what's best for you and Fiona." Rex was not as troubled by Mizar's reputation as Otis, but he advised Otis to speak candidly with Belcher. Otis contacted Belcher, who arranged a visit with Otis at the Jacksonville store. When the two met, Belcher was surprised to hear that Otis was thinking of leaving Full Moon.

Belcher urged Otis to stay. He offered to increase Otis's salary to $100,000. He emphasized that Full Moon provided Otis "great" job security, especially compared to the speculative business venture proposed by Izzy. Although Belcher admitted he had "no room to move" on the four-year term of Otis's contract ("That's the longest term Atlanta is offering to any of its managers"), he stressed that "a guy with your track record shouldn't worry about his future with Full Moon. Jacksonville is your store as long as you want it to be. You can retire here."

Otis was reassured and signed the contract.

3. Bad News

One month after Otis signed his employment contract, Belcher introduced him to Sid Shockley. Shockley was to be the department manager for the new extreme sports section of the Jacksonville store. The Jacksonville store was going to invest big in the extreme sporting-goods business. Otis had never heard of Shockley and had an immediate aversion to him. According to Otis, "Shockley came off as a self-absorbed jock. He wore an earring and had several conspicuous tattoos. Although an expert in most 'board' sports, he showed little interest in outdoor activities like camping and sea kayaking—he said they were 'boring' and for 'old folks.'" Shockley had tested extreme sports equipment for Edge Performance prior to working for Full Moon but had no prior retail sales experience.

In their first few years, Otis and Shockley worked fairly well together. Shockley listened to Otis and largely followed his directions for running the extreme sports department. He learned the retail sporting goods business more quickly than Otis had expected. The store's extreme sporting goods sales increased to the point where they accounted for 30 percent of the store's profits. Still, Otis sensed an awkwardness in their relationship that, at the time, he thought was just a "generational difference."

In November 2022, Belcher came to Otis with bad news: Full Moon was initiating a corporate downsizing. About 20 percent of its workforce was being terminated, and Full Moon was "reshuffling" store management. What this meant for the Jacksonville store was the elimination of about 10 of the store's employees. Belcher asked Otis to consider his own career goals: "Maybe you're ready to retire, or perhaps manage another store in Florida." Otis rejected out of hand the notion that he might be ready to retire. And Otis told Belcher, "I can't imagine leaving the Jacksonville store after all the success I've had in building the business. There's still more to be done. Besides, I wouldn't feel right moving to another store and pushing out the current store manager."

Belcher promised to work with Otis to make downsizing in the Jacksonville store "as painless as possible." He also promised to "look out" for Otis and do his best to advocate Otis's retention as manager of the Jacksonville store.

In later discussions with Belcher, Otis recommended that Full Moon consider laying off newer employees. Most of these employees were lower-wage workers in their late teens and early twenties, and experience suggested that they would not stay with the company more than a few years. Otis urged that Belcher recommend retaining the store's more experienced employees who had "proved their loyalty to the store. They are better producers."

A few weeks later, Otis was dumbfounded when Belcher told him about the personnel changes coming to the Jacksonville store. His wife, Fiona, was one of the employees who would be terminated. Otis would be retained but no longer be store manager. Instead, Otis would manage the camping department, at a reduced salary of $60,000. Shockley would be the new store manager, effective upon the expiration of Otis's contract in March.

4. The Olmans Respond

Fiona stoically accepted her termination. As she said to Otis at the time, "I think they've been planning to get rid of us ever since Shockley walked into the store. I'd just as soon work someplace else." As part of her severance package, Fiona received one month's salary. In exchange, she was asked to sign a release waiving any legal rights she might have related to her employment. Fiona signed the release even though Otis urged her not to.

Otis was deeply disturbed about his demotion. He called Rex Ornstein in Atlanta. Rex expressed surprise that Full Moon was replacing Otis as store manager. Rex promised to "find out what I can," but he told Otis that "frankly, I don't have a lot of influence around here anymore." Later that day, Rex called Otis back and confirmed the bad news. Rex then tried to assuage Otis's feelings by telling him: "Otis, you and I have been with the company for a long time. The sporting-goods business has changed, and Full Moon has changed, too. The extreme generation is young. We're not. Maybe it's time to move on. I plan to retire next year." Needless to say, Otis was disappointed in Rex's advice.

In early December 2022, Otis sent a strongly worded letter to the company's president, Bertie Lurch, who worked in the corporate offices in Atlanta. Otis accused the company of "ageism" and added, "While there is still time, I hope we can resolve this dispute amicably, but if the company does not rescind its decision, I will be compelled to take legal action. Given the fact that a substantial amount of our business comes from over-40 customers, it would be bad for business if they learned of management's attitude toward them."

5. Otis Is Fired

Otis's letter got results, but not the results he expected. Two weeks after sending his letter, he was told that the offer to make him manager of the camping department was rescinded and he was fired. The termination letter, signed by Lurch, explained the company's reasons:

> Full Moon will not tolerate age discrimination in any form. But discrimination has nothing to do with our decision. As you are aware, profits in the Jacksonville store have declined in recent years, with the exception of profits from extreme line products. But for the success of Mr. Shockley in marketing the extreme line, the Jacksonville store might now be slated for closure. We had hoped you would support Mr. Shockley as new store manager, just as he has supported you. Regrettably, store employees inform us that you are openly hostile to Mr. Shockley and refuse to cooperate in the transition to new store management. It now seems inconceivable that you could work, in any capacity, with Mr. Shockley.
>
> In preparing for the transition to new management in the Jacksonville store, we have also learned that significant quantities of inventory have been reported as "lost, damaged, or unaccounted for." Legal counsel has advised us that these losses might support criminal investigation. As store manager, you are ultimately accountable for these discrepancies.
>
> With the hope that we can conclude your association with the Full Moon family on amicable terms, we are offering you six months' severance pay to enable you to pursue a new career direction and to compensate you for salary and benefits still owing under your employment contract. If our proposal is acceptable, please sign the enclosed release and return it to me at your earliest convenience. I will need a response within 10 days.
>
> Bertie Lurch
> President

Although Otis refused to sign the release sent by Lurch, Full Moon paid him the six months of salary and benefits offered in Lurch's letter. As a result, Otis had no damages for breach of his employment contract.

6. The Olmans Take Legal Action

Otis had no intention of signing the release. Otis told Eleanor Lane that, given the circumstances, he had conducted himself very professionally in his dealings with Shockley. If there was a personnel problem in the Jacksonville store, it was caused by Shockley. According to Otis,

Shockley had told several employees that Otis was "too old" to be running an extreme sports store and was being "put out to pasture" in the camping department. As soon as Shockley learned of his promotion, he immediately began behaving as if he were already store manager. This put the other employees in an awkward position. Belcher did nothing to help the situation.

As for the missing-inventory threat, Otis assured Lane that all sporting goods stores suffer a certain amount of theft and loss. He also explained that, when a store uses its own inventory for rentals and instruction, there is an unavoidable increase in lost or damaged goods. But Lurch's suggestion that a "criminal" investigation was warranted was nothing more than an attempt to intimidate Otis into signing the release.

Lane questioned Otis carefully about his story. She was especially interested in his reasons for believing that age discrimination motivated Full Moon's decision to replace him. Otis gave these reasons:

1. His replacement by Shockley was proof in itself. Shockley was in his early thirties. Shockley had learned most of his management skills directly from Otis. And the increased sales in extreme sporting goods had little to do with Shockley himself. After Mizar acquired Full Moon in 2019, the company promoted extreme lines more than conventional sporting goods. In short, Otis was being replaced by a younger manager who was less qualified—and certainly no better qualified—to run the store.

2. Regional manager Belcher (who was in his mid-thirties) had made clear to Otis that he had considerable influence over the final decision concerning Otis's retention as store manager. Yet despite Belcher's promise to "look out" for Otis during the company's downsizing, he had eventually recommended that Shockley replace Otis as store manager. And there was abundant circumstantial evidence that Belcher's recommendation was influenced by ageist views. That evidence included (1) Belcher's utterance of ageist statements, (2) Belcher's failure to censure Shockley when he expressed his belief that the Jacksonville store needed a younger manager, and (3) Belcher's final decision to recommend Otis's replacement by Shockley.

3. Older managers and employees seemed to be a primary target of Full Moon's downsizing. Of the 10 employees terminated in the Jacksonville store, six were over 40, and the store currently employed only 8 employees over 40. Further, Fiona had been replaced as manager of the kayak department by her former assistant manager, who was under 40. Otis also personally knew two older managers in other Full Moon stores who had been replaced by persons under 40, both of whom shared Otis's suspicions that older employees had been targeted by Belcher and company management.

B. Lane's First Steps

Lane asked the Olmans what they wanted from Full Moon. They were adamant about *not* returning to work for the company. The Olmans wanted Full Moon to compensate them for their losses and, if possible, they wanted to punish the company for its wrongdoing.

A Note Concerning: Remedies

Model Rule of Professional Conduct 1.2(a) emphasizes that lawyers must ultimately defer to their clients' decision concerning the "objectives" of representation. The complaint that Lane filed would demand the remedies requested by the Olmans. Federal Rule 8(a)(3) requires that a party asserting a claim expressly make "a demand for judgment for the relief the pleader seeks" and allows a party to seek more than one type of relief. Some common forms of relief sought in litigation include:

1. **Compensatory Damages:** Compensatory damages are monetary awards designed to put the plaintiff into the position she would have occupied but for the defendant's unlawful conduct. Common examples of compensatory damages include recovery of economic losses like lost wages or medical expenses, as well as recovery for noneconomic harm like pain, suffering, and other "psychic" injuries.

2. **Punitive Damages:** Unlike compensatory damages, punitive damages are designed to punish the defendant for its unlawful conduct and to deter such conduct in the future. Punitive damages are generally not available for claims like breach of contract or negligence. When recoverable, punitive damages are usually authorized by statute. They are a fairly common feature of civil rights legislation.

3. **Injunctive Relief:** An *injunction* is a court order either requiring a defendant to take an action or precluding a defendant from taking an action. Traditionally, a plaintiff is not entitled to injunctive relief unless she can demonstrate that money damages will not be adequate. An injunction is enforced by a court's power to hold a noncomplying defendant in contempt. Had the Olmans wanted to resume working for Full Moon, they would have sought injunctive relief.

4. **Ancillary Relief:** Finally, there are certain types of remedies that are categorized as ancillary or extra. Perhaps the most important ancillary remedy is an award of attorneys' fees. Absent authorization of the recovery of attorneys' fees by statute or contract, the "American rule" usually requires each party to pay their own lawyer's fee.[3]

[3] Rule 1.2(a) provides that "a lawyer shall abide by a client's decisions concerning the objectives of representation."

Lane advised the Olmans that, based on their factual representations, they appeared to have claims for age discrimination under employment discrimination laws. But she explained that the Olmans could not immediately sue Full Moon for employment discrimination. Employment discrimination laws generally require as a *precondition* of filing suit that employees first file charges with the administrative agencies that enforce these laws.[4] This provides such agencies an opportunity to attempt to resolve the dispute expeditiously out of court.

You will study the operation of administrative agencies if you enroll in an upper-level course like Administrative Law. To understand the Olmans' dispute, it is *not* important that you understand what occurred during the administrative proceedings where their charges were considered. You need only appreciate two things: (1) the Olmans' legal suit could not be filed until the administrative requirements were completed, and (2) the administrative process resulted in a few deadlines the Olmans had to satisfy to prosecute their suit.

Federal employment discrimination law is usually enforced by the U.S. Equal Employment Opportunity Commission (EEOC). The Olmans would have to file their charges against Full Moon with the EEOC or a comparable state agency. Probably nothing would come of their filing, but the Olmans had to "exhaust" this administrative remedy as a prerequisite to suing.[5] The sooner the Olmans filed their charges the better, but in no event could they file more than 300 days from the date of their termination.[6] Lane agreed to assist them in preparing charges for filing with the agency.

In the meantime, Lane would contact Full Moon and explore the possibility of settling the dispute. To guide her in these settlement discussions, Lane explored with the Olmans their financial situation, as well as the amount of money they required to settle the dispute. As was often the case, Lane's discussion of financial and other considerations in filing suit provided a check on her clients' unrealistic expectations about the costs of litigation and the prospects for recovery.

---

[4] *See* 29 U.S.C. § 626(d) (prohibiting the filing of a private Age Discrimination in Employment Act (ADEA) suit until at least 60 days after the filing of an EEOC charge). Presuit filing requirements are common. For example, many states require that, prior to suing a governmental entity, plaintiffs give the entity notice of their grievance and defer legal action until the entity has sufficient time to attempt to resolve the grievance. In the private sector, plaintiffs may be required by contract or law to pursue alternative dispute resolution mechanisms like mediation and arbitration before filing suit. The only presuit requirement applicable to the Olmans' claims was their statutory obligation to exhaust administrative procedures before suing for age discrimination or retaliation.

[5] Most grievants receive a right-to-sue letter from the EEOC authorizing them to file suit; this letter doesn't signify that the EEOC has found the grievant's claim to be meritorious. In most cases, the issuance of this letter simply means that the dispute wasn't resolved administratively and that the EEOC will not bring suit on the grievant's behalf.

[6] 29 U.S.C. § 626(d)(1)(B) (in some states, filing must occur within 180 days). "Statutes of limitation" often give clients several *years* in which to file conventional tort claims. The much shorter limitation period found in most employment discrimination laws emphasizes that clients and lawyers must act diligently when challenging unlawful behavior.

Although an attorney-client relationship can be created without a formal contract of employment, attorneys routinely enter into written contracts with their clients. The terms of such contracts specify items like: the scope of the attorney's representation, the financing of litigation costs, how the attorney will be compensated for services (developed in discussion below), the client's responsibilities, the attorney's duty of confidentiality, and how disputes between the attorney and the client will be resolved (e.g., through binding arbitration). After Lane prepared a contract and discussed it with her clients, both Lane and the Olmans signed and dated it.

C. Lane's Ethical Considerations

From the moment Lane first met the Olmans, her relationship with them was governed by rules of professional responsibility.[7] In the text box below, we identify a select but important number of Lane's ethical obligations.

A Note Concerning: Lawyers' Ethical Responsibilities to Clients

Each state adopts its own code of professional responsibility to regulate members of the bar. Most states have adopted some version of the American Bar Association's Model Rules of Professional Conduct. Some of Lane's more important responsibilities under the Model Rules included:

- *Prosecuting the suit diligently.* Model Rule 1.3. Lack of diligence through lawyer neglect or delay is the most common client grievance.
- *Communicating with the Olmans about the suit.* Model Rule 1.4. Lawyers are required to keep clients informed of the status of their suit and to respond promptly to their clients' inquiries (e.g., they must return clients' phone calls).
- *Letting the Olmans make fundamental decisions in the suit.* Model Rule 1.2(a). As mentioned earlier, clients generally set the goals of representation. Lawyers may determine the best "means" to achieve these goals after "reasonable" consultation with clients. Model Rule 1.4(a)(2). Most decisions arising under the Federal Rules of Civil Procedure are "means" decisions, which will be made by a lawyer with little if any client consultation.

[7] As a member of the Florida Bar practicing in Florida courts, Lane was subject to ethical rules promulgated by the Supreme Court of Florida. These rules are largely the same as those found in the Model Rules of Professional Conduct promulgated by the American Bar Association. References to specific ethical rules governing lawyers in Florida, such as Rule 4-1.6, parallel the Model Rules and can be found by accessing the number that follows the dash, as in "Model Rule 1.6."

- *Keeping communications with the Olmans confidential,* Model Rule 1.6(a). Lawyers owe a duty of confidentiality to both clients and *prospective* clients. Therefore, regardless of whether the Olmans retained Lane as their lawyer, their private communications with Lane were confidential.

One of Lane's first tasks was to conduct a conflicts check to verify that representing the Olmans wouldn't create a conflict of interests with former or current clients.[8] Lane confirmed that her firm had never represented any of the potential defendants. Lane also had to consider whether Otis and Fiona might have conflicting interests that could compromise her competent representation of each of them. Lane could discern no such risk, but she informed the Olmans that if one arose, they would have to address the conflict and comply with ethical rules.[9]

As you will learn in Civil Procedure, ethics are sometimes incorporated directly into the Rules themselves. The principal example is Rule 11, which we return to in later discussion. The Model Rules of Professional Conduct duplicate several of Rule 11's requirements. For example, just as the assertion of a meritless contention violates Rule 11 and can subject the offending lawyer to court sanctions, such misconduct also violates rules of professional responsibility and can subject the lawyer to sanctions by the bar.

Two other examples: Model Rule 3.1 states that a lawyer "shall not bring or defend a proceeding, or assert or controvert an issue therein, unless there is a basis in law and fact for doing so that is not frivolous, which includes a good faith argument for an extension, modification, or reversal of existing law."[10] Likewise, Model Rule 3.3 states that a lawyer shall not knowingly "fail to disclose to the tribunal legal authority in the controlling jurisdiction known to the lawyer to be directly adverse to the position of the client and not disclosed by opposing counsel."[11] Model Rules 3.1 and 3.3 complement Rule 11's mandate that lawyers not advocate legal positions unwarranted by existing law.

Still other ethical considerations governed Lane's arrangement for financing the litigation expenses of the Olmans' suit. We address the interrelated financial and ethical concerns in the following discussion.

---

[8] *See* Model Rule 1.7 (lawyer should not represent a client if responsibilities to existing or former client creates significant risk of impaired representation).

[9] Model Rule 1.7(b) permits a lawyer to continue representing two clients when a conflict arises when, among other things, the lawyer determines that she can still provide both clients competent and diligent representation and the clients give their informed consent.

[10] *Compare* Rule 11(b).

[11] *Compare id.*

D. Financial Considerations

The Olmans' principal responsibility was to cooperate with Lane and pay any expenses they were obligated to pay under their contract. The costliest element of litigation is usually attorneys' fees. Lane estimated that, if she charged the Olmans her normal hourly rate for representing them in a suit against Full Moon that proceeded to trial, the Olmans would end up with a bill exceeding $150,000. And other costs associated with litigation could also be substantial. These included (1) the cost of court reporters who would record and transcribe the testimony of witnesses both before and during trial and (2) the cost of expert witnesses who would consult with Lane and testify. Lane knew, for example, that she would have to retain an expert who was qualified to testify about the Olmans' economic losses.

Lane explained these likely expenses to the Olmans, who immediately recognized they couldn't afford them. Lane also explained that Full Moon would have no difficulty funding litigation and retaining the best attorneys money can buy. A sobering fact of contemporary litigation is that many individuals can't afford the cost of vindicating their rights in court, especially against a well-heeled defendant. And even if they file suit, litigants of lesser means will be pressured to settle for a sum that's less than what they believe they're entitled to.

This was the sobering news Lane provided the Olmans. She then leavened this news with encouraging information. Employment discrimination statutes attempt to mitigate the financial disadvantages of employees by authorizing their recovery of attorneys' fees and costs *if* they prevail at trial. Such statutes abrogate the traditional American Rule, which requires that litigants pay their own attorneys' fee even if they prevail in court.[12] Yet even these fee-shifting statutes fail to provide plaintiff-employees confident assurance that their litigation expenses will be paid by the wrongdoer. A court's award of expenses will be contingent on the extent of the plaintiff's success, the stage at which the suit is resolved, and the manner in which it is resolved.[13] Thus, the ultimate recovery of a plaintiff's attorneys' fees and other expenses was fraught with uncertainty.[14]

---

[12] Prevailing *plaintiffs* can recover their fees under 29 U.S.C. § 626(b). The ADEA does not expressly authorize fee recovery by prevailing defendants, and most courts deny such fees unless a plaintiff's suit is frivolous. *See, e.g., E.E.O.C. v. Peoplemark, Inc.*, 732 F.3d 584, 591-92 (6th Cir. 2013) (affirming an award of attorneys' fees to the defendant in a Title VII case); *Turlington v. Atlanta Gas Light Co.*, 135 F.3d 1428 (11th Cir. 1998) (vacating an award of attorneys' fees to the defendant in an ADEA case). Lane advised the Olmans of this risk and opined that it was minimal if the Olmans' story checked out during presuit investigation.

[13] *See generally Award of Attorney's Fees in Actions or Proceedings under Age Discrimination in Employment Act of 1967*, 99 A.L.R. Fed. 30 (2016).

[14] In most cases that settle short of trial, the defendant will negotiate a reduction of the plaintiff's attorneys' fee as part of the negotiation of the damages to be paid. Moreover, relatively few cases actually proceed to trial and a judicial determination of the fees to be paid to a prevailing plaintiff. For example, the percentage of civil cases resolved by trial in federal and state courts has declined from about 20 percent in the 1930s to below 2 percent in federal court and below 1 percent in state court today. *See* John H. Langbein, *The Disappearance of Civil Trial in the United States*, 122 Yale L.J. 522 (2012). *See also* Marc Galanter, *The Vanishing Trial: An Examination of Trials and Related Matters in Federal and State Courts*, 1 J. Empirical Legal Studies 459 (2004) (reporting that case resolution by trial fell from 11.5 percent

Lane proposed an arrangement she believed would best accommodate the Olmans' financial exigencies and her law firm's need to manage the risk of investing a great amount of time and money without any return. First, Lane would advance her clients most of the costs of litigation, such as filing fees, expert witness fees, and court reporter fees.[15] Ethical rules permitted Lane to do this because of the manner in which she addressed the payment of her attorneys' fees.[16] Rather than bill the Olmans based on the hours she spent on their case multiplied by her normal hourly rate, she would make recovery of her fee contingent on success.

If the Olmans recovered money from the defendants through either settlement or litigated judgment, the Olmans would pay Lane a *contingent fee,* which would equal a specific share of the Olmans' recovery, as limited by ethical rules.[17] If Lane were highly successful, she might earn a fee that appreciably exceeded the fee she would have earned by billing the Olmans at an hourly rate. While this potential bonus might appear to be a windfall for Lane, from her perspective it compensated for the risk she might eventually be paid nothing for her efforts. The potential bonus would also offset some of Lane's losses in other, unsuccessful contingent-fee cases.

Lane's contingent-fee arrangement did not prevent the Olmans from demanding in their complaint that Full Moon pay Lane's fee if they prevailed. The court-awarded fee they demanded would likely be calculated using the *lodestar* method, which emphasizes the number of hours an attorney has invested in a case and the prevailing hourly rate for attorneys of similar qualifications.[18] This fee might be more than the contingent fee Lane was entitled to under her contract, or it might be less. Knowing this, Lane was careful to keep detailed records of the time she spent working on all aspects of the case, even though she was not billing the Olmans based on an hourly rate.

Plaintiffs' lawyers often enter into contingent-fee arrangements in suits where their clients also have the right to recover their fees from the losing defendant. But the law governing how

---

in 1962 to 1.8 percent in 2002). That does not mean that all of these filed cases settled. A portion were resolved through adjudication short of trial; this includes successful motions to dismiss and motions for summary judgment, discussed later in the Guide. The precise percentage of cases ending in settlement is difficult to determine. For a discussion of the reasons for a decline in jury trials, see Shari Diamond & Jessica Salerno, *Reasons for the Disappearing Jury Trial: Perspectives from Attorneys and Judges*, 81 LA.L.REV. 1 (2020).

[15] Under Rule 54(d), the court could award "costs other than attorney's fees" to the Olmans if they prevailed. These recoverable costs are defined in 28 U.S.C. § 1920.

[16] Model Rule 1.8(e) creates an exemption from the general prohibition against lawyers providing "financial assistance to a client in connection with pending or contemplated litigation." A lawyer is permitted to "advance court costs and expenses of litigation, the repayment of which may be contingent on the outcome of the matter." The rule's other exemption permits a lawyer to pay the expenses of an "indigent client."

[17] The ethical rules governing Lane were those of the jurisdiction where she practiced and would file suit—Florida. These rules generally limited her fee to 40 percent of the Olmans' recovery if the case proceeded to trial. *See* Fla. Bar Rule 4-1.5(4)(B)(i) (contingent fee limited to 40 percent of recovery up to $ 1 million).

[18] *See, e.g., Pickett v. Sheridan Health Care Center*, 664 F.3d 632 (7th Cir. 2011).

these different fee sources are reconciled is still not settled. If an attorney's contingent share exceeds the court-awarded fee, some courts deduct from that share those monies paid by the defendant. Other courts will permit a lawyer to recover both the contingent fee and a court-awarded fee.[19]

Instead of leaving this issue for judicial resolution, Lane addressed it by devising a contract formula she believed was fair to all and acceptable to a court. She would accept as payment the greater of (1) the fee awarded by the court or (2) her contingent share of the Olmans' recovery. If her contingent share were the greater amount, she would deduct from it all monies she received from the court-awarded fee. If her contingent share were less than the court-awarded fee, she would accept the court's award as full payment.

Lane was also careful to provide details about the scope of her representation. The contingency fee arrangement described above would cover litigation of the case through settlement or trial (if it occurred) and entry of final judgment by the trial court in the district court. If an appeal or other postjudgment relief were necessary and the Olmans wanted Lane to handle that work, the agreement provided for an additional 5 percent of the Olmans' recovery to pay for the appellate work.[20]

Task 1.1

Reflect on the manner in which Lane has chosen to finance the Olmans' litigation. Does this arrangement seem (1) fair to the Olmans, (2) fair to Lane, and (3) fair to Full Moon? Why do you think that contingent fees were prohibited by ethical rules in earlier years of the nation's legal system? What potential for abuse did these earlier rules seek to avoid?

One final financial consideration before filing suit concerns the ability to actually *collect* a legal judgment from the defendant. A plaintiff might win an impressive verdict at trial, resulting in a legal judgment that's uncollectable.

A legal judgment can be collected from those assets or earnings of the judgment debtor that aren't protected from creditors' claims by law.[21] But many individuals and some businesses lack sufficient assets to satisfy a substantial judgment.[22] In some cases, liability insurance provides

[19] *Compare id. with Ross v. Douglas County, Neb.*, 244 F.3d 620 (8th Cir. 2001).

[20] *See* Fla. Bar Rule, 4-1.5(f)(4)(B)(i)(d).

[21] Each jurisdiction has appreciable power to determine which assets of a judgment debtor can be recovered to satisfy a judgment. In many states, for example, a debtor's homestead is partially or fully protected from the claims of general creditors. And federal law limits a judgment creditor's ability to garnish the wages of a debtor or to reach certain assets such as retirement accounts.

[22] One practitioner estimates that 80 percent of civil money judgments are never enforced. *See* Joe Dickerson, *Why Do 80% of Judgments Remain Uncollected?*, ABAJ (April 2, 2020).

a source of recovery, at least to the extent of policy limits.[23] And sometimes the defendant/debtor that currently lacks assets may acquire them in the future through, for example, labor or inheritance. In most states, a domestic judgment is enforceable for 20 years, which means that a judgment may eventually be collectible.[24] To paraphrase a common quip, while you can't get blood out of a turnip, the defendant may not always remain a turnip.

Another risk to plaintiffs is that the judgment debtor will seek protection in bankruptcy court and ask to have the judgment—which is ultimately just another form of debt—discharged. A judgment debtor willing to surrender its assets to the bankruptcy court for distribution to creditors can thus reduce the ultimate value of the judgment.[25] One of the principal limitations on such discharge is that judgments based on "willful and malicious injury" inflicted by a defendant can't be extinguished.[26] According to the U.S. Supreme Court, this means that a judgment debtor can have the judgment discharged unless the debtor *intended to injure* the plaintiff.[27] This means that a judgment debtor that acted intentionally, but without intent to cause the injury suffered by the plaintiff, can have the judgment discharged.[28]

Lane was confident that Full Moon would have sufficient assets to satisfy its liability to the Olmans, and it might even have insurance coverage of their claims—something she would be permitted to discover soon after filing suit against the company.[29] And she did not fear that a thriving company like Full Moon would resort to bankruptcy in the imaginable future. But it was less clear whether Bruce Belcher could satisfy a judgment against him or might seek to discharge any judgment in bankruptcy court. As you later review the legal claims alleged by the Olmans, consider whether the claims against Belcher alleged that he inflicted "intentional and malicious injury" that might prevent a discharge in bankruptcy.

Finally, Lane also felt obligated to warn the Olmans about the intangible costs of filing a lawsuit. As Lane explained, once the Olmans filed suit, they would be subject to various demands of the court and the defendants and would surrender an appreciable amount of personal privacy. They could, among other things, be compelled to attend depositions, hearings, and trial. These

---

[23] For example, all states require that licensed drivers contract for liability coverage. But a large fraction of drivers either fail to obey the law or insure for the relatively small amount required by law. As a consequence, state laws usually require that insurers offer their policy holders "uninsured" or "underinsured" motorist coverage. When an insured driver or passenger is entitled to such "UM" benefits, the insurer steps into the liability shoes of the uninsured tortfeasor and pays the insured party damages up to the policy limits of the contract.

[24] *See, e.g.*, Fla. Stat. § 95.11 (domestic judgments can be enforced within 20 years of their issuance).

[25] The defendant in an employment discrimination suit can also seek to have the suit stayed or adjudicated in bankruptcy court once a bankruptcy petition is filed. *See generally* Joanne Gelfand, *The Treatment of Employment Discrimination Claims in Bankruptcy: Priority Status, Stay Relief, Dischargeability, and Exemptions*, 56 U. Miami L. Rev. 601 (2001).

[26] *See* 11 U.S.C. § 523(a)(6).

[27] *See Kawaauhau v. Geiger*, 523 U.S. 57 (1998).

[28] *See* Gelfand, *supra* note 23 at 635.

[29] The Rule authorizing discovery of insurance coverage is discussed in Chapter Nine.

events might, or might not, be scheduled at a time convenient for the Olmans. They might also be required to answer questions and produce personal records that they considered private (e.g., their income tax returns). Virtually no party enjoys the litigation process, and many parties come to strongly dislike it. On this point, Lane shared the observation of one of the twentieth century's leading jurists, Judge Learned Hand, about litigation: "After now some dozen years of experience I must say that . . . I should dread a lawsuit beyond almost anything else short of sickness and death."[30]

E. Preparing to File Suit

After the Olmans left her office, Lane began work on their case. She immediately took several steps that would make litigation more organized and efficient. First, she dictated a summary of the notes she had taken during the initial interview. These notes would be a useful reminder of the Olmans' basic story, as well as a valuable check to determine if the Olmans' story changed down the road. Lane also prepared a chronology of events and a "cast of characters" to which she would periodically refer. These are included in the Appendix. Finally, she copied and organized the various documents she obtained from the Olmans. These documents included Otis's employment contract with Full Moon, the release Fiona signed, the release Otis refused to sign, and the letter to Otis from Full Moon's president. These documents could prove critical to the case, and Lane wanted to make sure she knew exactly where they could be found.

Lane then began the factual and legal investigation required by her professional code and the Rules of Civil Procedure.

[30] Learned Hand, 3 Lectures on Legal Topics, Association of the Bar of the City of New York 106 (Macmillan, 1926).

1. Investigating the Facts

Lane had heard her clients' version of the facts and had no specific reason to question their credibility. She knew, however, that clients' memories are imperfect and some clients are less than forthright with their lawyers. Under Rule 11, when Lane filed suit, she would be personally certifying to the court that (1) she had made "inquiry reasonable under the circumstances," and (2) the allegations in the complaint had "evidentiary support" or, so long as such allegations were specifically identified in the complaint, would "likely have evidentiary support after a reasonable opportunity for further investigation or discovery." Because the Olmans' own testimony would be evidentiary support, could Lane reasonably rely solely on what the Olmans had told her?

Based on judicial interpretation of Rule 11[31] and good sense, Lane knew she should at least investigate other sources of evidence readily available to her. Therefore, she would review any important documents to which she had access. As explained earlier, Lane had already obtained some of these documents from the Olmans. These included the Olmans' employment contracts and the releases they had been asked to sign. Lane had also asked the Olmans for copies of any communications they had had with Full Moon related to the dispute (e.g., letters and emails). In addition, Lane would try to obtain copies of the Olmans' employment records from Full Moon.

Lane would also attempt to speak to some of the key witnesses identified by the Olmans and perhaps take witness statements.[32] She might search the internet for useful information or even use a private investigator to gather information. By conducting such an investigation, Lane would satisfy her professional responsibility under Rule 11 and her professional code.[33] She would also be in a much better position to draft a good complaint. Finally, economic self-interest supported a sound investigation of the facts. Because Lane and Quincy would be paid for their time only if the Olmans recovered monies by settlement or judgment, the lawyers would be invested in the suit.

2. Determining the Applicable Law

When Lane signed the Olmans' complaint, she would be certifying under Rule 11 that their claims were "warranted by existing law" or a plausible argument for changing the law. Lane could not rely on the Olmans or anyone else to make this certification. She would use her

---

[31] *See, e.g., Worldwide Primates, Inc. v. McGreal*, 87 F.3d 1252 (11th Cir. 1996) (a lawyer who failed to conduct inquiry into truth of client's allegations was subject to sanctions under Rule 11 when he had time to conduct an inquiry and did not have to rely on client).

[32] Under Model Rule 4.2, Lane could not speak about the suit with parties or persons already represented by a lawyer without the lawyer's consent. Consequently, Lane would communicate with Full Moon through its lawyer.

[33] Model Rule 3.1 largely reiterates Rule 11's prohibition of filing legal claims that lack factual or legal support.

acquired knowledge and legal research skills to determine what legal claims she could fairly allege in the complaint. To some extent, Lane would be doing the same thing she had done on law school exams when asked to determine the legal rights of a hypothetical plaintiff.

a. Sources and Types of Law

To properly research the Olmans' legal claims, Lane needed to consider all possible *sources* of law. She knew that the principal sources governing employment discrimination were federal and state law.[34] Federal and state lawmakers have overlapping powers in the field of civil rights, which includes employment discrimination. Although Congress has passed laws to remedy age discrimination in the workplace, most state legislatures have supplemented those laws. The principal limit on states is that they may not contradict or undermine the protections given by Congress.[35]

Lane also needed to consider the various *types* of federal and state law. Among the more commonly used types of law are (1) constitutions, (2) statutes, (3) administrative regulations, and (4) common law. She was aware that neither the U.S. Constitution nor the Florida Constitution regulates workplace discrimination in the private sector. She was aware, however, that both federal and state statutes prohibit age discrimination in private employment. Federal statutory law is found in the Age Discrimination in Employment Act (ADEA);[36] and applicable state law is found in the Florida Civil Rights Act (FRCA).[37] The Olmans would probably want to assert claims under both statutes.

Lane also considered whether administrative regulations might apply in the Olmans' suit. Administrative regulations are a type of legal rule issued by governmental agencies that have responsibility for interpreting and enforcing particular statutes. The EEOC has responsibility for the ADEA. Lane knew from past experience that EEOC regulations would be important in processing the Olmans' employment discrimination claims in the administrative proceedings.

Finally, Lane considered whether common law—judge-made law—might apply to the Olmans' suit. Lane knew what first-year law students learn during their study of the *Erie* doctrine: federal courts have very little authority to make common law.[38] State courts, by comparison, have extensive common lawmaking authority. In the Olmans' suit, state common law might provide the Olmans rights or remedies in addition to those found in federal and state statutes prohibiting employment discrimination.

---

[34] Local government (cities and counties) may also share lawmaking authority with the United States and the states. Neither the city nor the county in which the Olmans had been employed had laws prohibiting age discrimination by private employers.

[35] Under the Supremacy Clause of Article VI of the U.S. Constitution, federal law preempts inconsistent state law. Preemption may also exist when federal law "occupies" a subject area and preempts state law, whether or not inconsistent with federal law. *See Metropolitan Life Ins. Co. v. Taylor,* 481 U.S. 58, 63-64 (1987).

[36] 29 U.S.C. § 621.

[37] Fla. Stat. §§ 760.01-760.11.

[38] *See* Chapter Five.

"You seem to know something about law. I like that in an attorney."

To sum up, Lane needed to consider numerous sources and types of law to properly research and prepare the suit. She had a professional obligation to be competent in all this law, or to develop such a competence, before proceeding too far with the case.[39]

b. Federal Law Applicable to the Olmans' Dispute

(1) The Olmans' Claims for Discriminatory Treatment

Evidence indicated that Full Moon management may have had ageist motives for replacing Otis and laying off Fiona. If management's hostility toward, or false stereotypes about, older employees played a determinative role in its decisions,[40] the Olmans would have a *prima facie* case of discrimination under the ADEA.[41]

[39] Lawyers are not prevented from representing a client simply because they lack expertise in a particular area of law. Model Rule 1.1 only requires that a lawyer *become* competent in that area of law in sufficient time to adequately represent a client's interests. Lawyers, particularly new lawyers, frequently learn an area of law while representing clients.

[40] *See Hazen Paper Co. v. Biggins,* 507 U.S. 604, 610 (1993) (discrimination occurs when an employee's age "play[s] a role . . . and [has] a determinative influence on the outcome"). *See also Gross v. FBL Fin. Servs.,* 557 U.S. 167, 176 (2009) ("To establish a disparate-treatment claim under the plain language of the ADEA, therefore, a plaintiff must prove that age was the "but-for" cause of the employer's adverse decision.").

[41] Age discrimination differs historically from discrimination based on race or national origin. Age discrimination is based less on animosity toward older workers than on false stereotypes about their ability. An employer who takes job action against an employee because of false stereotypes about age violates the ADEA even though the employer lacks animosity toward older workers. *See, e.g., Hazen Paper Co. v. Biggins,* 507 U.S. 604, 610 (1993) ("It is the very essence of age discrimination for an older employee to be fired because the employer believes that productivity and competence decline with old age.").

Tactical Tip ✍

List the Elements of Each Potential Claim

When you are considering whether a given set of facts supports a claim, it is useful to make a checklist of the *elements* of the claim. You can use the checklist for many purposes during litigation, including (1) assessing whether you have evidentiary support for each element of the claim as required by Rule 11; (2) verifying that you have adequately alleged the elements of a claim in your complaint, *see* Rule 8(a)(2); and (3) framing your plans for discovery, summary judgment, and trial.

Lane made a list of the elements of a claim under the ADEA.[42] They are:

1. The plaintiff-employee is age 40 or over;
2. The employer took an adverse job action against the employee;
3. The employer took the adverse job action "because of" the employee's age; and
4. The employee suffered damages.

Task 1.2

Determine whether, under Rule 11(b)(3), Lane has sufficient evidentiary support to allege ADEA claims on behalf of both Otis and Fiona Olman. Be sure to identify all evidence supporting *each* element of an ADEA claim.

(2) Otis's Claim for Retaliation

Evidence indicated that when Otis complained to the company president about age discrimination, Full Moon responded by terminating him. This suggested to Lane that Full Moon might be liable for retaliation. A claim of retaliation consists of the following elements:[43]

1. The employee engaged in statutorily protected activity;
2. The employee suffered adverse employment action; and
3. The adverse action was causally related to his protected expression.

---

[42] Lists of the elements constituting the parties' claims are found in the Appendix. Statutes typically fail to enumerate the specific elements of a cause of action. The elements of a cause can usually be found, however, in either case law or a text discussing the subject area. *See, e.g.*, Andrew J. Ruzicho, et al., Litigating Age Discrimination Cases (2015).

[43] 29 U.S.C. § 623(d).

Otis's retaliation claim might succeed even if his age discrimination claim did not. A retaliation claim didn't require that Otis prove he was the victim of discrimination. Instead, the claim required that he show that he had engaged in "statutorily protected activity" that caused Full Moon to terminate him. As is often the case with legislation, elaboration of the meaning of the ADEA's retaliation protections had been left by Congress to the courts.

Lane's research revealed the complexity of the seemingly simple concept, "statutorily protected activity." An employee's activity is protected by the ADEA when he has either (1) participated in an investigation or proceeding related to age discrimination (protected "participation") or (2) opposed an unlawful practice of the employer (protected "opposition").[44] To show that an employee has engaged in protected opposition, the employee must present evidence establishing (1) that he engaged in an act of opposition, such as sending a letter to the employer complaining of discrimination; and (2) he "*subjectively* (that is, in good faith) believed that his employer was engaged in unlawful employment practices . . . [and] his belief was *objectively* reasonable in light of the facts and record presented" (emphasis added).[45]

This meant that Lane had to assess whether Otis had an objectively reasonable basis for believing that Full Moon had engaged in age discrimination at the time he complained to Lurch. His subjective belief that Full Moon had discriminated was not enough. And even if Lane later uncovered evidence of discrimination during discovery, that evidence was irrelevant unless Otis knew of it when he complained to the company's president.

Task 1.3

Determine whether, under Rule 11(b)(3), Lane has sufficient evidentiary support to allege a claim for retaliation on behalf of Otis. Be sure to identify all evidence supporting *each* element of a retaliation claim. Consider the evidence identified earlier in this chapter and speculate whether that evidence gave Otis an "objectively reasonable" belief that Full Moon engaged in age discrimination.

(3) Federal Law Remedies

The Olmans sought monetary relief. Obviously, Lane wanted to demand all types of damages to which the Olmans were entitled. Many civil rights statutes permit plaintiffs to recover full *compensatory* damages, which include economic losses, as well as damages for "psychic" injuries like emotional distress and humiliation. Typically, these statutes also permit the recovery of *punitive* damages if the defendant's wrongdoing is sufficiently egregious.[46]

---

[44] *Id.*

[45] *See, e.g., Weeks v. Harden Mfg. Corp.*, 291 F.3d 1307, 1312 (11th Cir. 2002).

[46] For example, employees alleging racial or ethnic discrimination under Title VII may recover both compensatory damages and punitive damages. *See* 42 U.S.C. § 1981A(a)(1).

The law of damages under the ADEA, however, was more limited. The Olmans could recover back pay. They could also recover future pay and earnings for the jobs they had lost. But the Olmans could *not* recover compensatory damages for their emotional distress and humiliation. This reduced the economic value of their suit considerably.[47]

Nor could the Olmans recover punitive damages per se. Instead, if they proved that Full Moon acted in "reckless disregard" of their rights, their award of back pay (not future pay) would be doubled.[48] This doubling of back pay under the ADEA is called "liquidated damages." But under the Eleventh Circuit's interpretation of the ADEA, even if a jury believed Full Moon deserved greater punishment than double back pay, it could not award additional damages.

The Olmans' inability to recover punitive damages under the ADEA illustrates an important aspect of litigation in federal court: Interpretation of federal law often varies from circuit to circuit. Had the Olmans filed suit in a circuit that authorized recovery of punitive damages under the ADEA,[49] their potential recovery would have been enhanced. But the Olmans' suit would be governed by Eleventh Circuit precedent—which is why that precedent will be frequently cited throughout the Guide.

Lane was aware of another limit to ADEA remedies. While Full Moon as an employer could be sued under the ADEA, its *employees*—even employees like Shockley and Belcher, who may have been the worst culprits—could not be sued personally. Under the ADEA, the employer alone is liable for workplace discrimination.[50] Consequently, if the Olmans wanted to sue Shockley or Belcher for their role in Full Moon's discriminatory action, they would have to base their claims on state law (if it existed).

In addition, it would be very difficult to sue Mizar, Inc., even though Mizar owned Full Moon and probably had considerable influence over its subsidiary. Federal law honored the distinct legal identities of Full Moon, Inc. and Mizar, Inc. In essence, Full Moon's status as a corporation served as a warning to the world that it—and not its parent corporation, officers, or shareholders—was liable for its wrongdoing. Although the corporate veil can be pierced in certain circumstances, Lane knew that Mizar's mere ownership of and influence over Full Moon were not enough to justify joining Mizar as defendant.[51]

---

[47] *See* Andrew J. Ruzicho, et al., 1 Litigating Age Discrimination Cases §§ 5:2, 5:5 (2015).

[48] *See id.* § 5:6.

[49] *See, e.g., Moskowitz v. Trustees of Purdue Univ.*, 5 F.3d 279 (7th Cir. 1993) (stating that punitive damages are recoverable in a suit alleging retaliation under the ADEA).

[50] Similarly, Title VII prohibiting employment discrimination based on race or gender authorizes suit against the employer, but not against individual managers or employees.

[51] *See, e.g., Wellman v. Dupont Dow Elastomers L.L.C.*, 414 Fed. Appx. 386 (3d Cir. 2011) (presumption that parent company is not liable for its subsidiary's violations of employment discrimination law unless the two companies are substantially interrelated and integrated in their activities, labor relations, and management).

c. State Law Applicable to the Olmans' Claims

Because remedies available to the Olmans under the ADEA were limited, state law might be important in their suit. Lane considered whether the following state law claims should be included in the complaint.

(1) Statutory Claims for Age Discrimination and Retaliation

The FCRA prohibits age discrimination in employment, as well as retaliatory action. In fact, Florida courts interpret the FCRA such that it prohibits essentially the same actions prohibited by the federal ADEA.[52] Florida law, however, provided the Olmans additional remedies.

Most important, the FCRA allowed the Olmans to recover full compensatory damages,[53] which would include psychic damages like emotional distress and humiliation that could substantially increase the jury's verdict. The FCRA also authorized the award of punitive damages up to $100,000.[54] This monetary punishment might exceed the "double back pay" punishment provided under the ADEA.

But like the ADEA, the FCRA failed to provide the Olmans with a remedy against individual employees like Shockley or Belcher. To sue them, Lane would have to find a remedy in state common law.

(2) State Common Law Claims

Lane knew that Florida common law provided no remedy for age discrimination in the workplace per se. So she considered whether the facts suggested some other common law cause of action.

Lane considered, and rejected, breach-of-contract claims. First, like many other states, Florida is an "employment-at-will" jurisdiction, and courts will not infer unwritten employment obligations.[55] Fiona had no written contract with Full Moon and consequently had no contract claim. Otis, on the other hand, had been a party to a four-year contract. But Lane discovered that Otis's contract gave him no right of renewal. At worst, Full Moon had terminated Otis's contract a few weeks prematurely. Because Full Moon had paid Otis for the weeks remaining on the contract, he suffered no damages as a result of his premature termination.[56]

---

[52] *See Florida State Univ. v. Sondel*, 685 So. 2d 923, 925 n.1 (Fla. Dt. Ct. App. 1997).

[53] Fla. Stat. § 760.11(5).

[54] *Id.*

[55] *See, e.g., Smith v. Piezo Technology and Professional Adminstr.*, 427 So. 2d 182, 184 (Fla. 1983) (employment relationship that is either discretionary or for indefinite term can be terminated for any reason). *See generally* Wrongful Discharge of At-Will Employee, 31 Am. Jur. Trials 317 (2016).

[56] Rule 8(a)(2) requires that a plaintiff allege a "statement of the claim showing that the pleader is entitled to relief," and Rule 8(a)(3) requires that a plaintiff demand the "relief sought." Unless Otis could allege that Full Moon's breach entitled him to some remedy, he could not allege a viable claim for breach of contract.

Lane next considered possible tort law remedies. She recalled that in 2019, Belcher had told Otis that he had job security if he stayed with Full Moon and could "retire" as manager of the Jacksonville store. In relying on Belcher's representation, Otis had passed up a potentially lucrative partnership with Izzy Able in Key Largo and, instead, signed a four-year contract with Full Moon. Otis felt Full Moon had lured him into staying with the company through fraud. The elements of a common law fraud action under Florida law are:

1. The defendant (or its agent) made a false representation of fact;
2. The defendant knew the representation was false when made;
3. The defendant made the false representation to induce the plaintiff to rely; and
4. The plaintiff justifiably relied on the false representation to his detriment.[57]

Further, Otis could assert his fraud claim against *both* Full Moon and the actual agent of fraud, Belcher.[58]

As mentioned earlier, when Lane filed the complaint, she would be certifying that all claims were "warranted by existing law or by a nonfrivolous argument for the extension, modification, or reversal of existing law."[59] Consider the following problem related to Otis's fraud claim.

Question 1.1

Assume that Lane discovers a Florida Supreme Court decision issued in 1978 stating that a fraud claim cannot be based on a promise that contradicts the terms of a written contract. Lane believes that the Court's position is both harsh and obsolescent and also believes that Otis's complaint presents a compelling case for changing precedent. However, she can discover no precedent signaling the Supreme Court is ready to recede from its older decision.

1. Will Lane violate Rule 11 if she asserts the fraud claim in the complaint? Why or why not?
2. Must Lane point out this adverse precedent to the trial court in her complaint? To answer this question, consider Model Rule of Professional Conduct 3.3(a):

[57] *Gandy v. Trans World Computer Technology Group*, 787 So. 2d 116 (Fla. Dt. Ct. App. 2001).

[58] *See, e.g., Salit v. Ruden, McClosky, Smith, Schuster & Russell*, 742 So. 2d 381 (Fla. Dt. Ct. App. 1999) (employer liable for intentional torts of employee committed within the scope of employment).

[59] Fed. R. Civ. P. 11(b)(2).

> A lawyer shall not knowingly . . . fail to disclose to the tribunal legal authority in the controlling jurisdiction known to the lawyer to be directly adverse to the position of the client and not disclosed by opposing counsel.
>
> 3. Regardless of Lane's legal obligation to notify the court of this adverse precedent, can you think of a strategic reason why she might want to?

Lane next considered the implications of the letter terminating Otis, in which Full Moon's president insinuated Otis might be connected to criminal acts involving missing store inventory. Lane's research revealed that the common law tort of libel generally requires:

1. A written statement;
2. Made by the defendant;
3. Containing false and defamatory statements of fact concerning the plaintiff; which are
4. Communicated to a third party.

> **Task 1.4**
>
> Review Otis's letter of termination and Otis's discussion of the comments made in that letter. See *supra* page 10. Why, in light of her obligations under Rule 11(b)(3), might Lane decline to assert a claim for libel? Make sure you focus on the specific elements constituting libel and the evidence presently available to Lane.

For reasons you will have recognized when considering Task 1.4, Lane concluded she lacked a good faith basis for alleging a claim of libel. That meant she would draft a complaint alleging statutory claims of age discrimination and retaliation, as well as a common law claim for fraud. To complete her factual and legal research, Lane prepared the following table summarizing the claims she intended to allege against each of the defendants in the Olmans' complaint:[60]

[60] This same type of table of parties and claims is also valuable when, in your study of civil procedure, you have to apply the rules to a complex set of facts. For example, a table is helpful when applying the rules of claim and party joinder, and when determining whether there is a jurisdictional basis for multiple claims and parties. Lane also had to address the issue of "joinder" when deciding which parties and claims might be included in the Olmans' suit. We have deferred discussion of joinder to Chapter Ten. If you are interested in how the joinder rules permitted Lane to assert all these claims in one complaint, feel free to preview these materials.

Plaintiff	Defendant	Claim
Otis Olman	Full Moon	Discrimination under ADEA
Otis Olman	Full Moon	Retaliation under ADEA
Otis Olman	Full Moon	Discrimination under FCRA
Otis Olman	Full Moon	Retaliation under FCRA
Otis Olman	Full Moon and Bruce Belcher	Common law fraud
Fiona Olman	Full Moon	Discrimination under ADEA
Fiona Olman	Full Moon	Discrimination under FCRA

F. Final Considerations

Having fulfilled her obligation to investigate the Olmans' claims, Lane felt confident she could draft a sound complaint. But she had three final decisions to make before drafting and filing the complaint. First, she had to decide upon the best geographic locale for the suit. Should she bring suit in Full Moon's home state of Georgia, where employment decisions affecting the Olmans had been made, or in the Olmans' home state of Florida, where they had worked? Second, Lane had to decide whether to file suit in a federal or state court. Third, she had to determine the proper time to file the suit.

1. Determining Jurisdiction and Venue

In selecting the geographic locale for the suit, Lane had to consider issues of *personal jurisdiction* and *venue*. In deciding whether to file suit in federal or state court, she had to consider the issue of *subject matter jurisdiction*. Lane's analyses of these issues can be found in Chapters Two through Four. Those of you who have already studied the topics of personal jurisdiction, venue, and subject matter jurisdiction are ready to examine the material in these chapters. Those of you whose professors begin their course with an examination of the Federal Rules governing the litigation process can move ahead to Chapter Six and return later to Chapters Two through Four.

For reasons explored more fully in Chapters Two through Four, Lane chose to sue in a federal court located in Jacksonville, Florida, where the Olmans had been employed by Full Moon and where they currently lived. Specifically, she chose to file suit in the "United States District Court for the Middle District of Florida, Jacksonville Division."

2. Determining When to File Suit

The final question Lane needed to consider was *when* to file the Olmans' suit. As mentioned earlier, the Olmans had to "exhaust" their administrative remedies before suing Full Moon for employment discrimination.[61] On Lane's advice, the Olmans had previously filed claims with the governmental agencies that administer employment discrimination laws.[62] The administrative process was now complete, and the Olmans' age discrimination claims were ripe for filing in federal court.[63] Notice that Otis had not been required to exhaust any administrative proceeding or other presuit requirement before filing his state law claim for fraud. As is typical of most common-law tort claims, Otis was permitted to file suit for fraud once he was injured. But Lane had sensibly deferred filing Otis's fraud claim until *all* the Olmans' claims were ready for filing and she could join them in one complaint.

The other time limit applicable to the Olmans' suit was the relevant statute of *limitations.* A *statute of limitations* typically gives an aggrieved party a specific period of time after wrongful conduct has occurred in which to file suit. In the case of most legal claims, this window of opportunity extends for several years. For example, the statute of limitations governing Otis's fraud claim gave him four years after he was defrauded to file suit. However, a lawyer *cannot* assume that the relevant statute of limitations provides the luxury of waiting years before filing suit. Federal employment discrimination laws vividly illustrate how short statutes of limitations can be. According to federal law, the Olmans had only 90 days in which to file suit once administrative proceedings were exhausted.[64] This 90-day limitation began to run on the date when the federal agency considering the Olmans' claims issued them a "right-to-sue" letter.[65] Lane had recently received a copy of this right-to-sue letter and needed to file suit expeditiously.

---

[61] Federal law required that the Olmans file administrative charges within 300 days of the time Full Moon took adverse action against them. 29 U.S.C. § 626(d)(1).

[62] As mentioned earlier, the federal agency in charge of the Olmans' age discrimination claims is the EEOC. Federal law also required that the Olmans file their charges with the state agency charged with enforcing state law prohibiting age discrimination, which in this case was the Florida Commission on Human Relations. *See* 29 U.S.C. § 633(b).

[63] Based on Rule 9(c), discussed in Chapter Six, Lane would allege in her complaint that these "conditions precedent" had been satisfied.

[64] 29 U.S.C. § 626(e).

[65] When the EEOC issues a right-to-sue letter, it means that (1) the agency has declined to file suit against an employer and (2) the employee is now free to file his own suit. A right-to-sue letter does not mean the EEOC has determined that an employee's charge has or does not have merit. For a variety of reasons, the EEOC files suit in only a small fraction of the complaints it considers. When the EEOC does occasionally elect to sue an employer, it is usually because the issue raised by the employee has important policy implications.

A Note Concerning: **Sources of Procedural Law**

As the Olmans' case illustrates, a lawyer must litigate with numerous sources and types of law in mind. We have already identified the substantive law underlying the Olmans' dispute, including statutory provisions, administrative rules, and common law. But lawyers also have to juggle numerous sources of *procedural* law. In a federal court suit, applicable procedural law may include:

- Federal constitutional provisions (e.g., the due process clause requirements);
- Federal statutory provisions (e.g., jurisdictional and venue statutes);
- Federal rules of civil procedure;
- Federal rules of evidence (to be discussed later); and occasionally;
- Judge-made procedural law. *See, e.g., Chambers v. NASCO, Inc.*, 501 U.S. 32 (1991) (recognizing trial court's inherent power to assess sanctions for bad faith conduct during litigation).

To all these must be added two other sources of procedural law that can be important in litigation. First, there are local rules of civil procedure. Federal Rule 83 states that "each district court . . . may . . . make and amend rules governing its practice." *See also* 28 U.S.C. § 2071 (recognizing the right of local district courts to prescribe additional procedural rules). According to Rule 83, these local rules must be "consistent with" the federal rules. Second, many federal judges adopt standing orders for civil cases that set out procedures unique to those judges. Such standing orders also should be consistent with the federal rules. A lawyer should *always* become familiar with both the local rules in the district in which a case is filed and any standing orders of the individual judge assigned to the case.

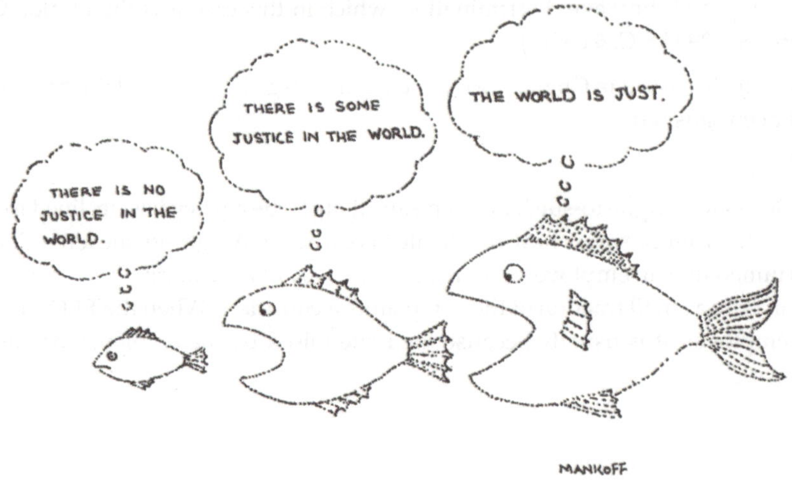

Chapter Two
Selecting the Locale for Litigation

Chapter Rule References: 3, 4, 5

In Chapter One, we discussed Eleanor Lane's preparation for filing suit. As mentioned, once Lane completed her investigation of the facts and the law, she had to decide upon the best geographic locale for the suit. This choice turned on which courts had *personal jurisdiction* over the defendants she intended to sue. Once Lane decided which court would serve as the locale for the Olmans' suit, she had to *serve process* on the defendants and thus invoke the chosen court's jurisdictional power. We consider these topics in this chapter.

A. Personal Jurisdiction

In the federalist system of government in the United States, numerous independent court systems may have the power to adjudicate a dispute. These systems—or *jurisdictions*—include the courts of the United States (i.e., federal courts), as well as those of the states and territories. When a suit involves parties or events related to more than one jurisdiction, the plaintiff has the first (and often the final) choice as to which jurisdiction will hear the suit. For example, the Olmans' suit concerned the loss of their employment at a retail store in Jacksonville, Florida, but it also involved decision making by Full Moon's officers in Atlanta. Both locales might serve as a forum for litigation, depending on jurisdictional law.

Lane had strong reasons to file suit in a court near Jacksonville, Florida. The Olmans lived in Jacksonville. Lane's law offices were located in Jacksonville, and she knew most of the judges in the area. In addition, Lane was licensed to practice law only in Florida.[1] Further, northeast Florida was where many of the witnesses to the dispute resided, and Lane hoped to call them to testify at trial. Finally, because the alleged employment discrimination and fraud had occurred in Florida, Florida law would likely apply in the suit.[2]

In short, from the perspective of the Olmans and Lane, almost all the relevant considerations pointed to the wisdom of filing suit in the greater Jacksonville area. But Lane knew that, as a matter of law, she needed to assess jurisdiction from the *defendants'* perspective as well as that of the plaintiffs. Did Full Moon and Belcher have sufficient contacts with Florida to make the state a fair location for litigation? It is the defendants' perspective that is ultimately determinative when applying jurisdictional statutes and the U.S. Constitution.

---

[1] If suit were filed in a court located in another state (of whose bar Lane was not a member), Lane would probably have to seek admission *pro hac vice* to appear in that court. Such admission usually requires that the lawyer associate with co-counsel already admitted in the jurisdiction. Lane wants to avoid sharing either the responsibility for the case or her fee.

[2] This choice-of-law issue is discussed more fully in Chapter Five.

1. Whose Law Governs Personal Jurisdiction?

Lane intended to file a complaint containing claims based on both federal and state law. For reasons we examine later in this book when we address the topic of subject matter jurisdiction, Lane had the right to sue in either federal or state court. So a preliminary question Lane had to address was whether the law governing personal jurisdiction might vary depending on whether she filed in federal or state court.

A *state* court's personal-jurisdictional power is defined in the first instance by state law. Each state has authority to define that power, subject to constitutional limits we discuss later in this chapter. Had Lane chosen to file suit in a Florida state court, for example, she would use Florida's statutes and rules to determine whether the state court had jurisdictional power over Full Moon and Bruce Belcher.

If Lane filed in *federal* court, federal law would naturally determine the scope of the court's jurisdictional power. The United States, like individual states, has the power to define who can be sued within its own courts. One possible source of jurisdictional law might be federal statutes, in particular the ADEA, under which the Olmans were suing for age discrimination. But the ADEA contains no provision detailing the scope of a federal court's power of personal jurisdiction. The ADEA, like most federal statutes, is silent on the issue of personal jurisdiction.

The most important source of jurisdictional power for federal courts is usually Federal Rule 4.[3] This rule can be challenging to interpret since it addresses a variety of subjects, including the contents of a summons, the means for serving process, and personal jurisdiction. Our focus at this point is personal jurisdiction. Rule 4(k)(1)(A) affirms an important source of a federal court's jurisdictional power: a federal court may exercise the same power exercised by the state courts of the state in which the federal court is located.[4] In other words, a federal court "borrows," in a sense, the personal jurisdictional power of the state where it is located. This means that, if the Olmans' suit were filed in a federal court in Florida, the court could exercise the same jurisdictional power exercised by Florida state courts.[5]

The consequence of Rule 4 is that, in many civil suits between private parties, the federal court's jurisdictional power is functionally the same as that of local state courts. Plaintiffs seeking to invoke a federal court's jurisdictional power over defendants usually engage in the same analysis they would use if they had chosen to file suit in state court instead.[6]

---

[3] In Chapter Three, we consider Federal Rule 82, which states that the rules themselves "do not extend . . . the jurisdiction of the district courts." This reference to "jurisdiction" means subject matter jurisdiction, not personal jurisdiction. Rule 4 clearly does affect the personal jurisdiction of district courts.

[4] This principle is also affirmed by other provisions like Rules 4(e)(1) and 4(h)(1)(A).

[5] The rule authorizes the borrowing of the jurisdictional power of state courts of "general jurisdiction." For present purposes, you can assume this refers to the state's civil courts that handle most litigation—thus excluding state courts that handle limited, special forms of litigation.

[6] There are circumstances where a plaintiff may have to rely on federal jurisdictional law because local state law does not extend to the defendants being sued. For example, Rule 4(k)(2) authorizes jurisdiction

2. Common Bases for Exercising Personal Jurisdiction

Lane's task in assessing which courts had personal jurisdiction over her intended defendants was now simplified. She would consult state jurisdictional law for any state where she might want to file suit, and it did not matter whether she chose to file in a federal or state court in that locale.

Today, most state law converges on several grounds for exercising jurisdictional power. Here is a brief summary of the principal bases for jurisdictional power, all of which you will likely examine in detail in your Civil Procedure course:

- *Presence in the state.* Most states authorize the exercise of jurisdiction over defendants that are present in the state when service of process is made. For example, if Belcher visited friends in Florida and was served with process while in the state, he would usually be subject to suit in Florida state courts.[7] Matters are more complicated when the defendant is an entity like a corporation. One common form of corporate "presence" exists when the corporation carries on substantial activity within a state.[8]

- *Domicile in the state.* Most states authorize the exercise of jurisdiction over defendants that are domiciled in the state—sort of the price that one pays for calling the state "home." In the case of entities like corporations, the term "domicile" may have different meanings. One traditional form of corporate domicile exists when a business has incorporated under the laws of a particular state. For example, some 68 percent of Fortune 500 companies are incorporated in Delaware, meaning that suits against such companies are often filed in that state.[9] Among the reasons why businesses often choose to incorporate in Delaware are: tax benefits, corporate law that facilitates a business's operation, and the existence of a specialized court, the Delaware Court of Chancery, which has resulted in well-developed and predictable legal precedent.

- *Consent to suit in the state.* Most states authorize the exercise of jurisdiction over defendants that consent to be sued in the state. Consent may be *express*, as when a corporation consents to suit in a state's courts when obtaining authorization to

over a defendant in cases arising under federal law when "the defendant is not subject to jurisdiction in any state's courts of general jurisdiction." But in most domestic litigation, the plaintiff will identify some state court that does have jurisdictional power over the desired defendants.

[7] In Civil Procedure, you will consider exceptions to this generalization. For example, many states grant immunity from service of process when a person enters the state to participate in court proceedings. And many states refuse to exercise jurisdiction when a person has been fraudulently induced to enter the state for the purpose of effecting service.

[8] *See, e.g.*, Fla. Stat. § 48.193(2) (2016) (conferring jurisdiction over a defendant carrying on "substantial and not isolated" activity).

[9] *See Why Incorporate in Delaware? Benefits and Considerations*, found at www.forbes.com/advisor/business/incorporating-in-Delaware/ (Feb. 15, 2024).

do business there, or when two parties enter into a contract containing a "choice of forum" clause. Or consent may be *implied*, as when state law provides that persons operating a vehicle on state roads impliedly consent to suit in the state if their operation results in an accident.

- *Procedural waiver*. Most procedural rules authorize the exercise of jurisdiction over defendants that fail to object to personal jurisdiction in a timely fashion. *See, e.g.*, Rule 12(h)(1).
- *Long-arm jurisdiction*. All states authorize the exercise of jurisdiction over defendants whose contacts with, or activities within, a state give rise to a dispute.

Question 2.1

As mentioned in Chapter One, Full Moon is a Delaware corporation whose main headquarters are in Georgia. Full Moon operates retail stores in all 50 states and, you may assume, has properly registered to do business in all states. Finally, recall that Full Moon and Otis Olman entered into an employment contract that expired in 2023, but Otis has not asserted a claim under the contract. In light of these facts, and based on the brief jurisdictional summary above, consider the following questions about personal jurisdiction:

1. What facts might support asserting jurisdiction over Full Moon in a Florida court based on (1) presence, (2) domicile, or (3) consent? What additional information would Lane need in considering these grounds?
2. Assume that Otis's contract with Full Moon contained a choice-of-forum clause stating, "It is agreed by . . . the parties all disputes arising under this contract ***shall*** be litigated . . . in and before a Court located in the State of Georgia." What argument might Lane make if Full Moon invokes this contract clause in an attempt to defeat a Florida court's personal jurisdiction?
3. Based on the information Lane has concerning Full Moon's operations, which states other than Florida might have personal jurisdiction over Full Moon? What about jurisdiction over Belcher, who as you will learn in Chapter Seven, has moved to Connecticut?

As you have learned in Civil Procedure, the exercise of jurisdiction over nonresident, nonconsenting defendants has led to many of the important U.S. Supreme Court decisions addressing the proper bounds of personal jurisdiction. The question essentially has two parts: analysis of statutory long-arm jurisdiction and consideration of the constitutional limits imposed on jurisdiction. In some states, long-arm statutes grant state courts jurisdictional power as broad as the U.S. Constitution permits. In such states, the issue of statutory jurisdiction is the same as that for constitutional jurisdiction. We will shortly consider that constitutional power in the context of the Olmans' suit.

Other states, like Florida, define their courts' long-arm jurisdiction in elaborate detail. A plaintiff invoking long-arm jurisdiction in such a state must first attempt to fit the claims she alleges into the statutory detail. This means that some claims—like claims for discrimination and retaliation—must be pigeonholed into statutory language not clearly suited for those claims. For example, a plaintiff may have to use a statutory provision governing common-law, tortious conduct as the vehicle for asserting a claim for statutory wrongdoing like discrimination.

Recall that Otis wants to sue Full Moon for employment discrimination, retaliation, and fraud, and wants to sue Belcher for fraud. Recall also that his wife, Fiona, wants to sue Full Moon for employment discrimination. In researching Florida jurisdictional statutes, Lane discovers the following long-arm provisions:[10]

State Long-Arm Statute:

(a) A person, whether or not a citizen or resident of this state, who personally or through an agent does any of the acts enumerated in this subsection thereby submits himself or herself and, if he or she is a natural person, his or her personal representative to the jurisdiction of the courts of this state for any cause of action arising from any of the following acts:

1. Operating, conducting, engaging in, or carrying on a business or business venture in this state or having an office or agency in this state.

2. Committing a tortious act within this state.

* * * *

6. Causing injury to persons or property within this state arising out of an act or omission by the defendant outside this state, if, at or about the time of the injury, either:

    a. The defendant was engaged in solicitation or service activities within this state; or

    b. Products, materials, or things processed, serviced, or manufactured by the defendant anywhere were used or consumed within this state in the ordinary course of commerce, trade, or use.

7. Breaching a contract in this state by failing to perform acts required by the contract to be performed in this state.

One thing you may notice about these provisions is that they confer *specific jurisdiction* over particular types of claims (or "causes of action"). Jurisdiction is claim specific. Section (a) creates jurisdiction "for any cause of action *arising from*" various activities that occur within the

[10] Fla. Stat. § 48.193(1) (2024).

state of Florida. These activities include business, tortious conduct, and the failure to perform contracts. In light of your reading of these long-arm provisions, answer the following question:

Question 2.2

Which long-arm provisions, if any, might be used by Lane to invoke jurisdiction over the specific claims the Olmans intend to assert against Full Moon? Against Belcher? Although the long-arm provisions do not refer to job discrimination as an activity giving rise to jurisdiction, which of the provisions seems most analogous to discrimination?

3. Constitutional Limitations on Personal Jurisdiction

Lane was confident Florida law provided a basis for asserting personal jurisdiction over Full Moon and Belcher in a court located in Florida. But even if she could satisfy state law requirements, she still needed to assess whether jurisdiction was consistent with the Due Process Clauses of the Constitution.[11]

As you will learn in Civil Procedure, the relevant constitutional standard may vary depending on whether jurisdiction is based on presence,[12] consent,[13] purposeful activity connected with the forum state,[14] or some other ground. In the case of suit against Full Moon, Lane had no doubts about the constitutionality of suing it in a Florida court. By the way, which Supreme Court decisions gave Lane such assurance? She also felt confident that a Florida court had constitutional power to exercise jurisdiction over Belcher. Again, which Supreme Court decisions gave Lane this confidence?

The Olmans' suit against Full Moon and Belcher based on activities centered in the State of Florida typifies much civil litigation. That is, in many suits, a particular state is the obvious focal point for events giving rise to litigation. For example, a particular state may be the place where a tortious injury occurred or an employment or business relationship was centered. Because the defendant will have far more than "minimum contacts" with such a state, the plaintiff's choice of this state as the forum will raise no real constitutional issues.

But let's vary the situation. Assume the Olmans moved to Georgia after losing their jobs with Full Moon. They retain counsel in their new home state and want to sue in Georgia. Because

---

[11] The Constitution contains two Due Process Clauses. The one in the Fifth Amendment applies to the federal government, and the Fourteenth Amendment's Due Process Clause applies to the states.

[12] *See, e.g., Burnham v. Superior Court*, 495 U.S. 604 (1990).

[13] *See, e.g., Carnival Cruise Lines, Inc. v. Shute*, 499 U.S. 585 (1991); *Mallory v. Norfolk Southern Railway Co.*, 600 U.S. 122 (2023).

[14] *See, e.g., World-Wide Volkswagen Corp. v. Woodson*, 444 U.S. 286 (1980).

Georgia is the location of Full Moon's corporate headquarters, a Georgia court plainly has jurisdictional power over the company.[15] Belcher, however, presents a complication.

Assume further that, while serving as the regional manager for Full Moon,[16] Belcher lived in Greenville, South Carolina. His job required that he regularly meet with store managers in all four states of his region. He occasionally visited Full Moon's headquarters in Atlanta, but for the most part, he dealt with headquarters by phone, email, and similar electronic means.

As far as Belcher's dealings with the Olmans, they all took place through visits to the Jacksonville store or by electronic means. The allegedly fraudulent statements that he made to Otis in 2019 were made while Belcher was visiting the Jacksonville store.

Finally, assume that Belcher quit working for Full Moon in 2022 and moved to Connecticut. He no longer has any connection with Full Moon or with the State of Georgia.

Question 2.3

After being sued in our hypothetical suit, Belcher hires a lawyer to object to the Georgia court's personal jurisdiction. Belcher's argument centers on his constitutional objection that (1) he lacks minimum contacts with Georgia and, (2) jurisdiction in a Georgia court offends principles of "fair play and substantial justice." Belcher's lawyer emphasizes that Belcher will be severely inconvenienced if he has to defend himself in a Georgia court; that Georgia has "little interest" in litigating a dispute that primarily arose in Florida; and that the Olmans have selected a Georgia forum purely for their personal convenience.

Based on your study of constitutional standards governing jurisdiction, is Belcher's challenge likely to succeed?

[15] In *Daimler AG v. Bauman*, 571 U.S. 117 (2014), the Supreme Court affirmed that the "paradigm all-purpose forums for general jurisdiction are a corporation's place of incorporation and principal place of business." Thus, even if events related to the Olmans' suit had not occurred in Georgia, a federal court in Georgia could assert general jurisdiction over Full Moon in that state.

[16] As explained in Chapter One, this region encompassed the states of North Carolina, South Carolina, Georgia, and Florida.

B. Service of Process

As mentioned, Lane was confident that a Florida court could exercise personal jurisdiction over Full Moon and Belcher and adjudicate the Olmans' claims. But to *invoke* the jurisdictional power of a court in Florida, Lane had to either "serve process" on the defendants or ask them to waive service. This process typically consists of (1) the plaintiff's complaint (which we explore in Chapter Six) and (2) a summons directing the defendant to appear and defend itself.[17]

We have already learned that Rule 4(k) authorizes the borrowing of state jurisdictional law, with the consequence that Florida law could be used to acquire jurisdiction over Full Moon and Belcher regardless of whether suit was filed in federal or state court. A similar borrowing of state law is authorized (although not required) by Rule 4 when the plaintiff is serving process.[18] This means that a plaintiff invoking the jurisdictional power of a court in Florida—whether federal or state—can serve process as authorized by state law.[19] As well, Rule 4 states several specific means of serving process in a federal court suit.[20] So Lane might have many options for serving process, some based on state law and others on Rule 4.[21]

1. The Mechanics of Service

In most law firms, service of process is viewed as a mechanical exercise and is often left to office employees or professional process servers. In routine litigation, the lawyer representing a party need not get involved in these mechanics, but the lawyer still has final responsibility for seeing that process is properly served and, if a harmful error occurs, may be liable for malpractice. Given the large number of published opinions in suits where error has occurred, a lawyer needs to take this responsibility seriously.

Lane had to serve process on a corporate defendant, Full Moon, and an individual defendant, Belcher. There is no substitute for reading the applicable rules governing service. But there are several conventional methods used to serve such defendants, which are generally described below:

---

[17] *See* Rule 4(a).

[18] *See, e.g.,* Rule 4(e)(1), (h)(1)(A).

[19] This borrowing of state law includes the borrowing of the law of a state where process is served when that state differs from the state where suit has been filed. *See, e.g.,* Rule 4(e)(1), (h)(1)(A).

[20] *See, e.g.,* Rule 4(e) (serving individuals); Rule 4(f) (serving individuals in a foreign country); and Rule 4(h) (serving corporations).

[21] Although service of the initial complaint (along with the summons) and service of witness subpoenas is governed by more formal, exacting procedures, service of subsequent documents is less formal. *See* Rule 4.1 ("serving other process"). As explained in Chapter Seven, service of such documents often occurs automatically when a document is filed with the trial court using an electronic filing system.

Individuals:

- Individuals can be served process by personally delivering it to them.
- Individuals can be served by delivering process at their home to someone of suitable maturity, a method often called "abode service."[22]
- Individuals can be served by delivering process to their agents. An "agent" may be someone specifically appointed as an agent by the individual (e.g., in a contract) or someone appointed as a matter of law (e.g., state law may dictate that a public official serves as the individual's agent).[23]

Corporations:

- Corporations may be served directly by delivering process to a designated corporate official like an officer or managing agent.[24]
- Corporations may be served by delivering process to its agent, which may include an agent appointed by the corporation as a condition of doing business within a state.[25]

Process is usually served by a professional process server, and the cost is minor (at least in comparison to a lawyer's fees!). In some states, the process server must be specifically licensed under state law. But the federal rules dispense with such licensing and permit service by anyone "who is at least 18 years old and not a party [to the suit]."[26] After process is served, the server typically signs a statement affirming service and the plaintiff later files a "proof of service" with the court.[27] This provides the court with assurance that the defendants have proper notice of the pending suit, as well as assurance that the court has power to proceed with the suit.

Rule 4(m) gives a plaintiff until 90 days after the complaint is filed with the court to serve process on the named defendant. But the rule is indulgent about time limits and states that a court "must" give a plaintiff additional time to serve when the plaintiff shows "good cause" for not serving within the 90-day period.

---

[22] *See, e.g.,* Rule 4(e)(2)(B).

[23] *See, e.g.,* Rule 4(3)(2)(C). For example, when a person operates a vehicle on a state's roads, state law often dictates that an official like the secretary of state becomes that person's agent for serving process in a suit alleging that the person operated the vehicle negligently.

[24] *See, e.g.,* Rule 4(h)(1)(B).

[25] *See, e.g., id.*

[26] *See* Rule 4(c)(2).

[27] *See* Rule 4(l).

In most cases, a plaintiff need only file the complaint to satisfy the time limits found in a statute of limitations. But that does not mean the plaintiff lacks incentive to serve process on a defendant. As we learn in a later chapter, the Rules impose no obligation on a defendant to respond to a suit until he has been served with process. So, to move the litigation along, the plaintiff will want to serve all defendants as soon as practicable.

One aspect of service law sometimes strikes law students as odd. In many cases where defendants challenge a plaintiff's failure to comply with the technicalities of service law, the defendant is not actually complaining that he lacks notice of the suit. The defendant may have received actual notice of the suit and even have a copy of the complaint in hand. But actual notice of the suit may not be sufficient. Defendants have the right to insist that they be brought into litigation through compliance with service law. If the plaintiff fails to comply strictly with the law's technical requirements, the defendant may challenge the lawfulness of the suit.[28] The plaintiff runs the risk that technical oversight or noncompliance can defeat an otherwise meritorious suit.

2. Waiving Formal Service of Process

A major innovation in the federal rules is found in Rule 4(d), which authorizes waivers of service. The rule permits a plaintiff to mail the complaint, along with various forms, to a defendant and request waiver of service. If the defendant agrees to execute the waiver documents, he receives additional time to respond to the complaint (usually 60 days) but does not surrender other challenges that he might have to personal jurisdiction or venue. If the defendant does not cooperate and lacks "good cause" for noncooperation, the plaintiff recovers all costs incurred in formally serving process, including attorneys' fees.

One innovation not yet authorized in federal court is service of original process by electronic means. While Rule 5(b)(2)(E) generally permits the parties to consent to electronic service of other pleadings and papers once litigation is under way, the rule does not encompass service of the complaint and summons.

So Lane had two primary options for invoking a court's jurisdictional power over Full Moon and Belcher. She could formally serve the defendants under federal or state law, or she could request they waive service.

How would Lane choose which path to follow? As with any choice, context matters. She might want to send a message to a defendant concerning the seriousness of litigation. This might lead to a decision to use formal service. On the other hand, she might want to send a conciliatory message, which could make proceeding under Rule 4(d) the better option. The point

[28] *See, e.g., Armco Inc. v. Penrod-Stauffer Bldg.*, 733 F.2d 1087, 1089 (4th Cir. 1984) ("When there is actual notice, every technical violation of the rule or failure of strict compliance may not invalidate the service of process. But the rules are there to be followed, and plain requirements for the means of effecting service of process may not be ignored."). In Chapter Seven, we consider how defective service of process might be challenged by a motion or in the defendant's pleadings.

is that the rules provided Lane with options; she would have to use her strategic and tactical instincts to actually make the decision.

Lane had several options for serving Full Moon if she filed suit in a federal court in Florida. First, the company had properly registered to do business in Florida, and in so doing had appointed a statutory "agent" for service of process. This agent was a lawyer in Orlando, and Lane could serve process on him under Rule 4(h)(1)(B). Second, she could "borrow" state law for serving process under Rule 4(h)(1)(A).[29] Third, Lane could use Rule 4's waiver-of-service provisions and ask Full Moon to cooperate. In the context of this case, she considered that the third avenue was most advantageous. After contacting Full Moon's corporate counsel, she learned that Full Moon would waive service.

Belcher was more of a problem. As discussed later in this book, Belcher no longer worked for Full Moon and now resided in Connecticut. Lane tried to phone Belcher, but he failed to return her calls. As far as she knew, Belcher had no lawyer that she could contact. In light of Lane's inability to contact Belcher, consider her options for bringing Belcher into a suit filed in Florida.

Question 2.4

Briefly discuss Lane's options for serving process on Belcher in Connecticut. What method of service will be more economical?

3. The Constitutionality of Service Methods

Service of process rules, like rules governing personal jurisdiction, are subject to the requirements of due process.[30] But lawyers filing suit seldom need to address those requirements. The main reasons seem to be that (1) federal and state rules governing service have been refined to ensure that they comply with the Supreme Court's interpretations of due process; and (2) most defendants who are worth suing can usually be found and served through conventional methods. Due process concerns are more likely to arise, for example, when a defendant cannot be found or is attempting to evade service; when it is unclear what interests a potential defendant has in pending court proceedings; or when the plaintiff (particularly a governmental plaintiff) is suing to determine its rights in property.[31]

---

[29] According to Rules 4(h)(1)(A) and 4(e)(1), Lane could use either the state law of Florida (where the federal court "is located") or the state law of the place where Full Moon had a person who could be served on its behalf ("where service is made"). For example, because most of Full Moon's officers were located at its Atlanta headquarters, Lane could use Georgia law authorizing service on such an officer.

[30] *See, e.g., Mullane v. Central Hanover Bank & Trust Co.*, 339 U.S. 306 (1950).

[31] *See, e.g., Jones v. Flowers*, 547 U.S. 220 (2006) (discussing what notice is required when government seeks to foreclose on real estate to recover unpaid property taxes); *Lehr v. Robertson*, 463 U.S. 248 (1983) (discussing what notice is required to putative father when mother commences adoption proceedings).

Suffice it to say that the Olmans' suit did not present the uncommon situation where attempts to serve process run up against constitutional constraints. Full Moon had waived formal service. Provided Lane carefully followed applicable law in serving Belcher, she could proceed with the Olmans' suit with confidence.

Chapter Three
Choosing Between State and Federal Court

Chapter Rule References: 8, 82

Select Statutory References: 28 U.S.C. §§ 1331, 1332, 1367, 1441

In Chapter Two, we discussed Eleanor Lane's choice of a place (i.e., a state) in which to file suit. In this chapter, we consider another question concerning the forum for litigation—whether Lane could file in a federal court, a state court, or either. As we learned, Lane had a decision to make. And that decision was dictated by the law of *subject matter jurisdiction,* as well as a host of pragmatic concerns.

A. Courts and the Judicial Power in the United States

1. The Allocation of Judicial Power

Many civil litigators never handle a case in federal court. Sometimes this reflects litigators' inexperience with federal procedure and their desire to stay in the more familiar, and often less formal, atmosphere of state court. But in larger part, this reflects the allocation of judicial power between federal and state courts. Most of the civil suits that lawyers handle in state court cannot be filed in federal court because they do not come within the federal court's subject matter jurisdiction.

As you will learn in Civil Procedure, the framers of the U.S. Constitution did not agree on the need for federal trial courts to handle the nation's litigation. Failing to agree, they compromised and gave the U.S. Congress the power to create federal courts and a limited power to confer jurisdiction on them.[1] A plaintiff seeking to invoke a federal court's subject matter jurisdiction always carries the burden of showing the court that it has the power to hear a case. And as we learn later in Chapter Six, Rule 8(a)(1) requires that the plaintiff recite at the outset of her complaint the basis for the federal court's subject matter jurisdiction.

Under our federalist scheme of judicial power, federal courts are courts of *limited jurisdiction.* State courts, in contrast, presumably have *general jurisdiction* to handle any civil litigation. Even when a case is based on federal law—like the Olmans' case, based in part on federal employment discrimination law—the presumption is that state courts can hear the case.[2] Thus, in most cases that fall within the federal courts' limited jurisdiction, state courts share a *concurrent jurisdiction* to hear the case. As we discuss below, the principle of concurrent jurisdiction means that Lane had a choice of whether to file in federal or state court.

---

[1] *See generally* Finch, Roberts, and Allen, Federal Courts: Context, Cases, and Problems (4th ed. August 2024) (discussing the Madisonian Compromise that led to Article III of the Constitution).

[2] The most common exception occurs when a federal statute places jurisdiction of litigation exclusively in the federal courts. This is called *exclusive jurisdiction.*

Among the types of cases that can be heard in federal (and usually state) court, are (1) those that "arise under" federal law, and (2) those that involve diverse citizens. These are the leading forms of jurisdiction invoked when private parties litigate in federal court. Each, as we learn, provided a basis for filing the Olmans' suit in federal court.

2. Reasons for Invoking the Federal Courts' Jurisdiction

Before examining the law of subject matter jurisdiction, let's briefly consider what factors might influence a plaintiff's choice to file in federal or state court when such a choice exists. There are many. And different factors may come into play in different cases, making generalizations difficult. But here are some of the factors that may influence the choice.

First, lawyers know that the litigation process is often different in federal court. In federal court, a judge will manage the suit much more closely than will most state court judges. Shortly after the suit is filed, the lawyers meet to develop a plan for completing key matters like conducting discovery, filing dispositive motions, and holding the trial. The court usually confirms this plan in an order.[3] This plan remains fairly firm throughout the pretrial process and puts the parties on a timetable that could result in a trial within a year. By comparison, in most state courts, the trial judge largely leaves it up to the parties to schedule the litigation process and the trial date. This can delay the date of the trial substantially. In many cases, years pass between the time a suit is filed in state court and the trial.

Second, there is a lot more paperwork in federal court, which consumes more of the lawyers' time. Until trial, virtually every request the lawyers make of a federal court is made by a written motion supported by a legal memorandum.[4] These motions and supporting memoranda need to be well drafted and well researched, as they are scrutinized closely by the judge or the judge's clerks. In many federal districts, motions are decided without an actual hearing before the judge. In many state courts, by comparison, motions are orally argued in open court during a *motions session.* Further, written motions and memoranda in state court—if any—are usually briefer. As a consequence, a lawyer's skill in oral advocacy may play a greater role in the pretrial process in state court.

Lane, unlike some trial lawyers, was not intimidated by the more formal and time-consuming legal writing required in federal court. She was both a good researcher and a careful writer. At the same time, she knew that her opponent might use the paper-intensive litigation process to her disadvantage. Lane had observed that some defense lawyers file an excessive number of motions in federal litigation. A few unscrupulous defense lawyers even boast of "papering the plaintiff to death," meaning that they use motion practice to place demands on a plaintiff's time and money. Even though Federal Rule 11(b)(1) prohibits filing a motion "for any improper purpose," it may be difficult to prove this rule has been violated.

---

[3] This meeting and the resulting court action in the Olmans' suit are discussed in Chapter Eight.

[4] *See* Rule 7(b) (applications for court orders, other than motions made during a hearing or at trial, "must be in writing," must "state with particularity the grounds for seeking the order," and must "state the relief sought").

A third difference between federal and state court concerns the judges and their supporting personnel. In federal court, judges are appointed by the President of the United States and confirmed by the U.S. Senate, and thus they are subject to more rigorous screening. They also have lifetime tenure. In contrast, some state trial judges (like those in Florida) are elected by the voters in campaigns that disclose very little about the judges' philosophy or competence, and they have to stand for office every four years.

Although Lane knew that federal judges are not necessarily more capable or fair-minded than state judges, they have certain advantages over the typical state judge. For one thing, federal judges are far more likely to have experience presiding over cases involving federal law. The judge assigned to the Olmans' case would probably have handled federal employment discrimination cases and, if she had not, she would draw upon the research support of highly credentialed judicial clerks to educate her about the law. Any particular state court judge, on the other hand, is less likely to have experience with federal employment discrimination laws. State judges frequently rotate among divisions, where they spend their time judging cases limited to particular subjects like probate and criminal law. And state judges often lack the support of a team of law clerks.

In addition, Lane recognized that the composition of the jury pool in federal court can differ from that in state court. If she filed the suit in Florida state court, the jury would be drawn from residents of the county where Jacksonville is located. On the other hand, if she filed in federal court, the jury would be drawn from a larger pool, including several counties in the eastern part of the Middle District of Florida. The demographic composition of the jury might vary widely between state and federal court.

But in the final analysis, Lane knew that the most important factor in choosing a court was unknown: to which *particular* federal or state judge would the Olmans' case be assigned (which is random)? This could prove a critical difference in the conduct of the litigation and the outcome, but it was beyond the parties' prediction or control. The Olmans' case would be randomly assigned to a judge by the clerk when it was filed. In the past, this random assignment was done by spinning a wheel or picking a name out of a box. Today, it is usually done by computer. No matter the method used in assigning the case, Lane would have to wait and see which judge would try the case.

After considering those factors she could reliably forecast, Lane knew she wanted to sue in federal court. She believed the Olmans' case posed some challenging issues of federal-law interpretation, and she had greater confidence that a federal judge with experience in employment discrimination litigation would do a better job at resolving those issues. And because Lane had litigated several employment discrimination cases in federal court in recent years, she was comfortable with her knowledge of federal procedure.

Lane now had to consider the law of federal subject matter jurisdiction and determine whether some or all of the claims she intended to assert on behalf of the Olmans could be heard by a federal court. It was important that she identify sound bases for a federal court's subject matter jurisdiction at the start of the suit. Lane knew that doubts about subject matter jurisdiction can be raised "at any time," and a court "must dismiss" a suit if it determines that subject matter jurisdiction is lacking.[5] Lane does not want to invest time and money in litigation if there are realistic doubts about a federal court's power to hear a case.

B. Federal Jurisdiction and Claims Arising under Federal Law

1. Arising under Jurisdiction

Most cases filed in federal district court today base jurisdiction on 28 U.S.C. § 1331,[6] which grants these courts "original jurisdiction of all civil actions arising under the Constitution, laws, or treaties of the United States."[7] This language largely mirrors language found in Article III, § 2 of the Constitution. The reference to actions "arising under" federal law has generated appreciable controversy in the U.S. Supreme Court. You will explore some of this controversy in Civil Procedure and later, in courses like Federal Courts.

Fortunately for Lane and most civil litigators, the scope of "arising under" jurisdiction—or "federal question" jurisdiction, as it is also called—can be reliably estimated in the majority of cases. Among the guidelines the Court has given for deciding whether a claim arises under federal law are these:

- Jurisdiction must be determined by examining the plaintiff's "well-pleaded complaint," and the content of the defendant's answer is usually irrelevant.[8]

- A count in the plaintiff's complaint typically arises under federal law when federal law creates the *cause of action* alleged in the count;[9] stated differently, when federal law provides both the right and remedy alleged in the count, it arises under federal law.[10]

---

[5] *See* Rule 12(h)(3).

[6] *See* Federal Courts, *supra* note 1.

[7] You will often see other jurisdictional statutes referred to in cases based on federal law. For example, 29 U.S.C. § 216 confers jurisdiction over claims filed under the ADEA. These specific jurisdictional grants frequently duplicate 28 U.S.C. § 1331, and plaintiffs commonly allege both specific and general jurisdictional power.

[8] *See Louisville & Nashville Railroad Co. v. Mottley*, 211 U.S. 149 (1908).

[9] The terms "claim," "cause of action," and "count" are sometimes used interchangeably, even though they do not always mean the same thing. We will keep things simple for our discussion. The terms "claim" and "cause of action" are used to refer to the combined right and remedy given the plaintiff under applicable law. For example, the ADEA gives Otis Olman the right to be free of age discrimination in employment and provides him with a remedy if this right is violated. Thus, Otis has a "claim" or "cause of action" under the ADEA, which takes the form of a "count" when it is alleged in his complaint.

[10] *See Merrell Dow Pharmaceuticals, Inc. v. Thompson*, 478 U.S. 804 (1986) (observing that the "vast majority" of cases that arise under federal law do so because federal law creates "the cause of action.").

Applying these guidelines, Lane readily confirmed that the Olmans' counts alleging age discrimination and retaliation arose under the ADEA within the meaning of section 1331.[11] In particular, 29 U.S.C. § 623 gives employees like the Olmans the right not to be terminated because of their age, as well as the right not to suffer retaliation for complaining about age discrimination. And 29 U.S.C. § 626 provides them monetary and equitable remedies if those rights are violated by an employer. Because these federal "causes of action" would be asserted in the Olmans' well-pleaded complaint, these claims satisfied the requirements of arising under jurisdiction.

Notice that arising under jurisdiction focuses on *specific legal claims* in the plaintiff's complaint. Lane could be confident that the Olmans' claims under the ADEA qualify for jurisdiction under section 1331. But what about the other claims that the Olmans wished to assert? Recall that the Olmans also want to allege that (1) Full Moon violated their rights under *Florida* statutory law, which gives them largely the same rights and remedies given by the ADEA; and (2) Full Moon committed fraud against Otis under Florida common law.

Question 3.1

Do the Olmans' claims under state statutory and common law satisfy the cause-of-action standard for determining if they arise under federal law? Does it matter that (1) the Olmans will assert these claims in their well-pleaded complaint; and (2) the claims under Florida statutory law provide largely the same rights and remedies provided by federal law? Would it matter if the Florida legislature expressly stated that its age-discrimination statutes "should be interpreted and applied in the same manner as the federal Age Discrimination in Employment Act"?

As you can see, the standard used in the "vast majority" of cases does not go far enough for plaintiffs that want to allege all their claims—federal and state—in one suit. Of course, plaintiffs like the Olmans do have an option if they want to allege all their claims in one suit: they can sue in state court. Recall that state courts presumably have concurrent jurisdiction to hear federal claims. This means that plaintiffs like the Olmans could consolidate all their claims in a single state court action. But at what cost? As discussed earlier, Lane saw several reasons to file suit in federal court, and one important reason was her belief that a federal judge may have greater competence in the adjudication of federal age discrimination claims. In authorizing broad jurisdiction over federal claims, would Congress have wanted to force plaintiffs like the Olmans to choose between (1) invoking their right to a federal forum and (2) litigating all their claims in one state-court action?

[11] You might find it helpful to refresh your memory about the legal claims the Olmans intend to assert; *see* Chapter 1.

2. Supplemental Jurisdiction[12]

The solution for plaintiffs like the Olmans came first from the Supreme Court, and it was later codified by Congress. In *United Mine Workers v. Gibbs*,[13] the Court affirmed that federal courts may hear state claims, provided that they have a sufficient relationship to federal claims. The Court's famous articulation of the standard for relatedness is found in this passage, to which we have added emphasis:

> The state and federal claims must derive from a *common nucleus of operative fact*. But if, considered without regard to their federal or state character, *a plaintiff's claims are such that he would ordinarily be expected to try them all in one judicial proceeding*, then, assuming substantiality of the federal issues, there is power in federal courts to hear the whole.[14]

Congress eventually affirmed the *Gibbs* standard when it authorized exercise of "supplemental jurisdiction" in 28 U.S.C. § 1367.[15] And Congress also affirmed that supplemental jurisdiction can be used when a party seeks to add *another* party to the suit, provided that the claim against that new party satisfies the relatedness test.[16]

Section 1367 is a complex statute applicable to a wide array of claims and parties. We limit our examination of supplemental jurisdiction to the problem faced by the Olmans—how to invoke a federal court's jurisdiction over the state claims that they wished to assert against Full Moon and Bruce Belcher. You will no doubt explore other uses of § 1367, as well as its procedural mechanisms, in Civil Procedure.

Question 3.2

Recall that Lane would like to assert these state claims on behalf of the Olmans: (1) Statutory claims against *Full Moon* for age discrimination and retaliation based on the Florida Civil Rights Act, which largely duplicates the protections given by the ADEA and (2) a state common-law fraud claim against *Full Moon and Belcher* based on allegedly fraudulent statements made to Otis by Belcher when he renewed his contract with the company in 2019.

---

[12] Section 1367(b) affirms that supplemental jurisdiction can also be used when the primary basis for jurisdiction is diversity of citizenship, but this use is limited in important respects. Because the combined use of supplemental and diversity jurisdiction poses some very challenging issues, and because those issues were not relevant to the suit that Lane intended to file, we limit our discussion of § 1367 to the case where § 1367 is used in connection with federal claims.

[13] 383 U.S. 715 (1966).

[14] *Id.* at 725.

[15] Section 1367(a) extends supplemental jurisdiction to claims outside the federal courts' original jurisdiction when they are "so related to claims in the action . . . that they form part of the same case or controversy under Article III."

[16] *See* § 1367(a) ("Such supplemental jurisdiction shall include claims that involve the joinder or intervention of additional parties.").

1. Can the Olmans successfully argue that their state statutory claims share a "common nucleus of operative fact" with their federal statutory claims?

2. Can Otis successfully argue that his state fraud claim shares a "common nucleus of operative fact" with *some* federal claim already asserted against Full Moon? What will Full Moon likely argue in response?

3. Recall that the *only* claim asserted against Belcher is the state fraud claim. Does this mean that Belcher cannot be added to the complaint using supplemental jurisdiction under § 1367 because no federal claim has been alleged against him to which the state claim can be "supplemental"?

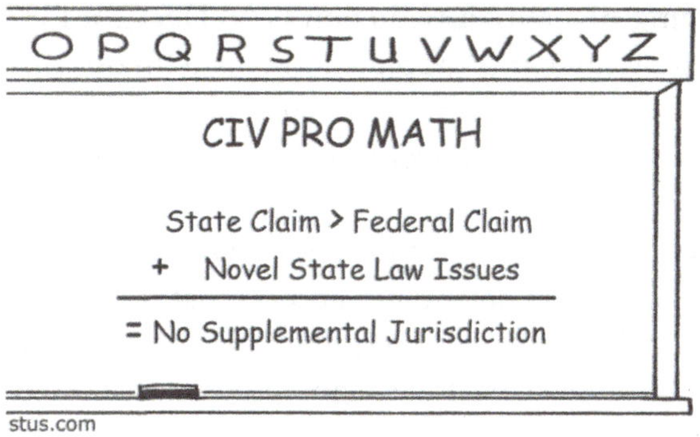

As you can see in attempting to answer Question 3.2, analysis of subject matter jurisdiction is *claim specific*. That is, the plaintiff must break down the claims she wishes to assert and ask whether *each* claim has a jurisdictional basis. For example, as we have explored thus far, jurisdiction will extend to claim that either (1) itself arises under federal law, or (2) has a sufficient factual relationship to *another* alleged claim that arises under federal law. In short, arising under jurisdiction is built one claim at a time.

Later, in Chapter Ten, we explore the procedural rules governing the joinder of individual claims and parties. These rules dictate what claims and parties might be added to the suit by both plaintiffs and defendants. As we will learn, the *rules themselves* do not create subject matter jurisdiction to adjudicate additional claims or parties.[17] So a party adding additional claims or parties to a suit will need to assess (1) what procedural rules permit her to do and (2) what is permissible under jurisdictional law. For the time being, be content with your understanding of the jurisdictional requirements for joining claims.

[17] *See* Rule 82 ("These rules do not extend or limit the jurisdiction of the district courts.").

C. Diversity of Citizenship Jurisdiction

A plaintiff invoking federal jurisdiction need show only one basis for the court's jurisdiction over each claim in the suit. For example, if the Olmans could show the district court that some of their claims arise under federal law and the remaining state claims qualify for supplemental jurisdiction, they need not show the court that it also has jurisdiction based on other potential grounds. But good lawyering suggests the wisdom of addressing alternative grounds for jurisdiction when they are available—especially when the plaintiff foresees a possible challenge to the original basis for jurisdiction.[18]

We have seen that arising under jurisdiction focuses on the nature of the claims asserted by the plaintiff. Diversity of citizenship jurisdiction, by contrast, focuses on the nature of the *parties*, particularly their citizenship. Based on her understanding of basic diversity principles, Lane believed that diversity provided an alternative basis for invoking a federal court's jurisdiction over her suit against Full Moon and Belcher.

The main statute governing diversity jurisdiction is 28 U.S.C. § 1332. Section 1332 is a long and complex statute with highly varied applications. As with our discussion of arising under jurisdiction, our discussion of diversity jurisdiction is limited. We focus on how section 1332 might be used as a basis for jurisdiction over the claims in the Olmans' lawsuit.

Section 1332 typically requires that a plaintiff show two things:[19] (1) that the citizenship of the plaintiff differs from that of the defendant; and (2) that the plaintiff satisfies the statutory "amount in controversy," which currently requires that the plaintiff seek more than $75,000 from the defendant. The Supreme Court has elaborated on the law of diversity and affirmed several guidelines:

Complete diversity: All plaintiffs must be of diverse citizenship from all defendants.

Rules of citizenship: Select rules governing a party's citizenship include:

- When a suit is originally filed in federal court, a party's citizenship is determined at the time of filing.

- The citizenship of a natural person is based on his domicile, which is determined by (1) his physical presence in a state when combined with (2) his intent to make his "home" in that same state. A person has only one domicile at a time and keeps that domicile until a new one is established by the combination described above.

---

[18] Based on the prior discussion of arising under and supplemental jurisdiction, what jurisdictional challenge might Lane anticipate?

[19] Again, we emphasize that this discussion focuses on the case the Olmans wish to allege in their complaint. Some of the textual generalizations may not apply, or may apply differently, in other types of litigation.

- The citizenship of a corporation consists of both (1) its state of incorporation and (2) its principal place of business.

- When a corporation carries on appreciable business in several different states, its "principal place of business" is usually "the place where a corporation's officers direct, control, and coordinate the corporation's activities," often styled its corporate "nerve center."[20]

Amount in controversy: To satisfy the amount-in-controversy requirement, the plaintiff need only allege in good faith a demand for more than $75,000 from the defendant. The fact that the plaintiff ultimately fails to recover that amount does not affect the court's jurisdictional power. If one plaintiff satisfies this requirement, the federal court may hear the claims of additional plaintiffs who seek less than $75,000, provided their claims are factually related to those of the plaintiff satisfying the amount-in-controversy requirement.[21]

Based on these guidelines for diversity jurisdiction, Lane believed that the Olmans' suit came within a federal court's diversity jurisdiction. Here are the facts known to Lane, most of which are found in Chapter One. First, the Olmans had made Jacksonville, Florida, their home, and they continued to reside there. Second, Full Moon is incorporated in Delaware and operates numerous retail stores throughout the country. Full Moon directs its retail operations from its executive headquarters in Atlanta. Belcher, you may assume, resided in Florida during the time that he served as the regional director for the region encompassing the Jacksonville store. But shortly after the Olmans were terminated, Belcher quit working for Full Moon and moved to Connecticut.

Under federal age discrimination law, each of the Olmans is entitled to recover from Full Moon past and future lost earnings, as well as attorneys' fees. Under state age discrimination law, the Olmans may also recover for the emotional distress and humiliation resulting from their wrongful termination, and they may recover up to $100,000 in punitive damages. Based on reported case law, Lane is confident that each of the Olmans can allege in good faith damages easily exceeding $100,000. As for Otis's fraud claim, Lane also believes that his damages potentially exceed $100,000.

In light of these factual assumptions, consider the following questions about diversity jurisdiction:

---

[20] *Hertz Corporation v. Friend*, 559 U.S. 77 (2010).

[21] This guideline is derived from supplemental jurisdiction under § 1367. *See Exxon Mobil Corp. v. Allapattah Serv., Inc.*, 545 U.S. 546 (2005).

Question 3.3

As Lane works through her analysis of diversity jurisdiction, she considers each of the following issues. Discuss how she will resolve them.

1. What are the states of citizenship for the Olmans, Full Moon, and Belcher? Can Lane satisfy the "complete diversity" requirement? Explain.

2. If, at the time Lane files suit, Belcher has taken a new job and moved to Atlanta, will complete diversity be destroyed?

3. Assume for the purposes of this question that Lane concludes that Otis could recover no more than $50,000 under his fraud claim. What effect would this have on Otis's ability to rely on diversity jurisdiction in suing Full Moon? Belcher?

D. Removal Jurisdiction

Lane's analysis led her to the conclusion that the Olmans could sue Full Moon and Belcher in federal court. But the ADEA did not require her to sue in federal court; state courts share concurrent jurisdiction over ADEA litigation.

An appreciable amount of litigation based on federal law in fact occurs in state court. For a variety of reasons, plaintiffs' lawyers may conclude that state court provides the best forum for litigating the suit.

When a plaintiff files in state court a suit that might also have been filed in federal court, a defendant often has the power to veto the plaintiff's choice. The defendant exercises this veto by removing the state suit to federal court. The most commonly used federal removal statute is 28 U.S.C. § 1441.[22] According to section 1441(a), a defendant may remove a case to federal court "any civil action brought in a State court of which the district courts of the United States have original jurisdiction."

This right of removal initially requires that a defendant perform the same jurisdictional analysis that the plaintiff has performed. If the plaintiff could have filed a suit in federal court originally, the defendant can trump the plaintiff's choice of state court and remove it to the local federal court. But the right of removal is subject to several restrictions that defendants must consider:

[22] There are other federal removal statutes that might apply to particular forms of litigation. Our discussion is limited to removal under § 1441.

- In the case of suits that might have been originally filed in federal court based *only* on diversity of citizenship grounds, removal is generally not permitted if one of the defendants "is a citizen of the State in which such action is brought."[23]

- Usually all defendants must consent to removal of the suit filed against them in state court.[24]

- Defendants must act quickly in exercising their right of removal. In most cases, they must remove within 30 days of receiving notice (e.g., through service of the complaint) that the case is removable.[25]

- If the defendants remove a case to federal court over which the court lacks jurisdiction, or if the defendants commit procedural error in removing the case (e.g., removal is untimely) and the plaintiff timely moves to remand, the federal court will remand the case back to state court.[26]

---

[23] 28 U.S.C. § 1441(b)(2). This rule is often called the "forum defendant rule."

[24] 28 U.S.C. § 1446(b)(2)(A).

[25] 28 U.S.C. § 1446(b)(2)(B).

[26] 28 U.S.C. § 1447(c) authorizes remand at any time if subject matter jurisdiction is lacking. A party seeking remand based on any other defect must move to remand the case within 30 days of removal.

To assess your understanding of some of the statutory rules governing removal, consider the following questions:

Question 3.4

Assume that Lane had chosen to file suit in state court in Florida. Her suit includes the same federal and state claims and the same defendants already discussed in this chapter. Assume, in answering the questions below, that Belcher is a citizen of Connecticut at the time of the litigation. Based on the removal principles summarized above, how would you resolve the following issues?

1. Does the citizenship of either Full Moon or Belcher negate their right to remove the suit to federal court? Would your answer change if, instead of suing the defendants in a Florida state court, Lane had filed suit in a Georgia state court?

2. Assume that Full Moon wants to remove the suit to federal court, but Belcher simply fails to respond to its request to join in removal. Finally, some 35 days after suit is filed in Florida state court, Full Moon decides to act unilaterally and removes the suit to federal court. Can Lane move to remand the case to state court? How much time does she have to seek remand?

3. Assume that Lane decides that the Olmans can obtain full recovery from the defendants simply by asserting claims under state law. She files a complaint in Florida court that relies *solely* on Florida law. Can the defendants remove the Olmans' suit to federal court? What if Lane files suit in a Georgia state court and again relies solely on state law. Can the defendants remove the Georgia suit to federal court?

Chapter Four
Venue: A Final Decision about the Forum

Chapter Rule References: 12

Select Statutory References: 28 U.S.C. §§ 1391, 1404, 1406, 1631

A. Forum Selection and Venue

Eleanor Lane had now determined that (1) both Full Moon and Bruce Belcher were subject to the personal jurisdiction of a court in Florida; and (2) both federal and state courts shared concurrent subject matter jurisdiction in the Olmans' suit. So Lane could follow her preference and sue the defendants in a federal district court in Florida.

But *which* federal district court? As you can imagine, no single federal court could efficiently handle all the litigation that takes place in the United States. So federal statutes break down the federal trial-court system into numerous "districts." At least one federal district court is located in each state, but in most states, there are two or more districts.[1] These districts, in turn, are usually divided further into separate "divisions." Our principal focus is the federal district.

On the next page is a map of the federal court system showing the breakdown of district courts,[2] as well as the breakdown of the federal circuits (which are numbered) that handle appeals from these districts. As you can see, there are three federal districts in Florida, reflecting the fact that the state stretches some 833 road miles from Key West to Pensacola.

Lane wanted to file the Olmans' suit as close to Jacksonville, Florida, as possible. Jacksonville, it turns out, is located in the U.S. District Court for the *Middle* District of Florida. This is a large district stretching more than 300 miles from Jacksonville on the east coast to Ft. Meyers, Florida, on the west. (The fainter dotted lines in the map below show how federal circuits are divided into districts.) The Middle District is further broken into divisions (not shown on the

[1] *See, e.g.*, 28 U.S.C. § 132 (showing the breakdown of district courts within each state).

[2] Because states with smaller populations have only one federal district (e.g., Connecticut and Montana), the boundaries of the district are co-extensive with state borders. More populated states like New York, California, Texas, and Florida have several districts within their borders, and these are identified on the map with broken lines. For example, federal trial courts in Florida are broken into the Northern, Middle, and Southern districts. Note that, although most district courts are identified by the name of the state within which the court is located, these courts are not part of the state government.

Federal circuits, which serve as appellate courts, are distinguished by different shadings and are numbered 1 through 11. Not shown on this map are the U.S. Court of Appeals for the District of Columbia Circuit and the U.S. Court of Appeal for the Federal Circuit, which are also located in the District of Columbia and handle specialized appeals in disputes involving patents and other legislatively designated matters.

map), with Jacksonville found in the Jacksonville Division. Lane's preference, then, was to file suit in the U.S. District Court for the Middle District of Florida, Jacksonville Division.

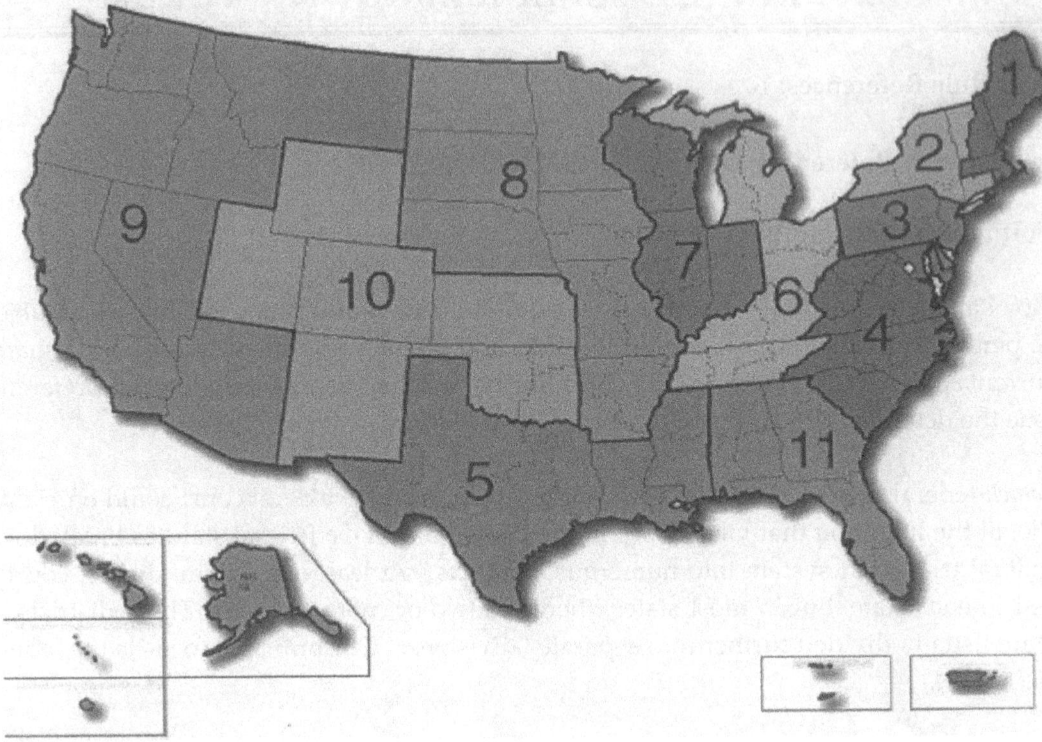

There are *hundreds* of federal statutes governing venue for particular types of cases, but the statute governing most private civil litigation is 28 U.S.C. § 1391, the "general" venue statute. This is the statute that would guide Lane's choice of a venue for the Olmans' suit.

Section 1391(b) authorizes venue based on two provisions, either of which can be used by the plaintiff. The plaintiff can choose:

- A judicial district in which any defendant resides, if all defendants are residents of the State in which the district is located; or

- A judicial district in which a substantial part of the events or omissions giving rise to the claim occurred, or a substantial part of property that is the subject of the action is situated.[3]

Note that the "residence" provision can be used only if *all* defendants reside in the same state. In the case of individuals like Belcher, residence is usually easy to determine, but corporate residence is not so straightforward.

[3] Section 1391(b)(3) is a rarely applicable default provision that applies only when venue does not properly lie in any district under either of the two main provisions; it authorizes venue in "any judicial district in which any defendant is subject to the court's personal jurisdiction with respect to such action."

Section 1391(c) gives a special definition of corporate residence for venue purposes.[4] A corporation is said to "reside" in any judicial district where it is "subject to the court's personal jurisdiction with respect to the civil action in question." In the case of states having several federal districts (like Florida and most other states), a corporation is said to "reside" in the specific districts in which its contacts with that district "would be sufficient to subject it to personal jurisdiction if that district were a separate State." In other words, the corporate residence provision requires that one imagine that a district is the equivalent of a state, and then determine whether the corporation has "sufficient contacts" with that district. As if minimum contacts doctrine were not difficult enough!

Try your hand at determining which district or districts in Florida have venue over the Olmans' suit. Recall that Florida contains three federal districts, one of which—the Middle District—encompasses Jacksonville, where the Olmans were once employed. You may assume that Full Moon operates retail stores throughout Florida in all three of its federal districts. You may also assume that, at the time the suit is filed, Belcher resides in Connecticut.

Question 4.1

1. According to section 1391, what is the most obvious basis for asserting venue in the Middle District? Why?
2. Why does the residence provision of section 1391 *not* authorize venue in the Middle District?
3. Assume, for this question only, that Belcher still lived in Jacksonville, Florida, at the time the Olmans filed suit. Under the residence provision of section 1391, in what federal districts in Florida would venue be proper?

Let's briefly consider an alternative venue for the Olmans' suit. As you will explore more fully in later chapters, much of the decision making leading to the Olmans' termination took place in Atlanta, at Full Moon's corporate headquarters. Atlanta is located in the U.S. District Court for the Northern District of Georgia. Assume, again, that Belcher resides in Connecticut at the time the Olmans file suit.

[4] This section also applies to other forms of entities that have the capacity to sue or be sued in a common name and defines residence for still other types of defendants, including aliens admitted for permanent residence in the United States.

Question 4.2

1. Which provision of section 1391 provides the best ground authorizing venue in the Northern District of Georgia?

2. Even if venue is proper in the Northern District of Georgia, do you see another reason why suit in that district might be challenged by at least one of the defendants?

B. Challenging the Plaintiff's Choice of Venue

Where events underlying a dispute occur in different states, plaintiffs often have a choice of locales for litigation. For example, events leading to the Olmans' termination occurred both in Florida and Georgia. If Belcher were sufficiently involved in the corporate decision making that occurred at Full Moon's Atlanta headquarters, a court in Georgia might be a proper place for litigation under principles of personal jurisdiction and venue. In fulfilling her obligation to represent the Olmans competently and zealously, Lane would need to consider the strategic value of filing suit in Georgia. If suit in Georgia were in the best interests of her clients, Lane should strongly consider filing suit there—or handing the case over to a lawyer who could handle litigation in Georgia. Such "forum shopping" is a legitimate part of client representation.

When alternative forums are available, the plaintiff has the first choice of venue. But that choice can be challenged by the defendant. Under federal rules and statutes, at least three grounds for challenging the plaintiff's choice are recognized:

- A defendant may argue that it is not subject to personal jurisdiction in the state chosen by the plaintiff.[5]

- A defendant may argue that the plaintiff has chosen a district where venue is improper under the governing statute.[6]

- A defendant may argue that the plaintiff has chosen a district where personal jurisdiction and venue are proper, but where litigation will be highly inconvenient for the parties or witnesses.[7]

If the plaintiff has chosen a forum where either personal jurisdiction or venue is improper, the court may dismiss the suit.[8] But federal statutes provide the court another option—the court can transfer the case to a federal district where jurisdiction or venue is proper.[9]

---

[5] *See* Rule 12(b)(2).

[6] *See* Rule 12(b)(3); 28 U.S.C. § 1406.

[7] *See* 28 U.S.C. § 1404.

[8] *See, e.g.*, Rule 12(b)(2), (3); 28 U.S.C. § 1406.

[9] *See* 28 U.S.C. § 1406 (curing venue defects); 28 U.S.C. § 1631 (curing defects in personal jurisdiction).

If the plaintiff has chosen a forum where jurisdiction and venue are proper but highly inconvenient for the parties or witnesses, the defendant may ask the court to transfer the suit to another district where jurisdiction and venue are also proper.[10] In other words, the defendant contends that the plaintiff had a choice among several forums but chose one that is highly inconvenient for the defendant. Section 1404 identifies three broad factors that courts should consider in deciding whether to transfer venue—the convenience of the parties, the convenience of witnesses, and "the interest of justice." But leading procedural authorities confess that the issue of transfer is too case specific to justify easy generalizations:

> The three statutory factors—convenience of parties, convenience of witnesses, and the interest of justice—are broad generalities that take on a variety of meanings in the context of specific cases. Further, the statute gives no hint about how these broad categories are to be weighed against each other. Accordingly, courts through the decades have recognized that each case must turn on its particular facts, and the trial court must consider and balance all the relevant factors to determine whether the litigation would proceed more conveniently and whether the interests of justice would be better served by transfer to a different forum.[11]

Although section 1404 gives courts fairly broad discretion in ruling on motions to transfer, courts typically defer to the plaintiff's initial forum selection.[12] This places a fairly heavy burden of proof on the party seeking to transfer. Moreover, the party seeking transfer must also show that the case could have been properly filed in the district to which that party seeks to transfer the case.[13] Thus, venue must be proper in that district, and the defendants must be subject to personal jurisdiction there.[14]

When suit has been filed in a federal district court, the party seeking to transfer to another locale in the United States has one advantage over a party sued in state court. Because the U.S. district courts are part of one court system, interdistrict transfer is feasible and permitted. That is, one district court of the United States can transfer a suit to another district court of the United States. But when suit has been filed in a state court, there is seldom any procedural mechanism for *interstate* transfer.[15] For example, if the Olmans filed suit in a Florida state court, Full Moon could not seek a "transfer" of the case to a Georgia state court. In such circumstances, a party arguing that another state court is a better forum typically uses the doctrine of *forum non conveniens*.[16] The result is that the state court suit is dismissed and the plaintiff refiles the suit in another state.

---

[10] *See* 28 U.S.C. § 1404.

[11] *See* Charles Allen Wright & Arthur R. Miller, Federal Practice and Procedure § 3847 (2024).

[12] *See, e.g., In re Apple, Inc.*, 602 F.3d 909, 913 (8th Cir. 2010).

[13] *See* 28 U.S.C. §§ 1404(a), 1406.

[14] The U.S. Supreme Court has held that the defendant seeking transfer cannot consent to personal jurisdiction to facilitate transfer. The relevant issue is whether there would be personal jurisdiction over the *nonconsenting* defendant in the transferee district. *See Hoffman v. Blaski*, 363 U.S. 335 (1960).

[15] Occasionally, there are federal statutes, uniform laws, or interstate agreements that provide for state-to-state transfer.

[16] For example, Florida Rule of Civil Procedure 1.061 permits a state court to dismiss a suit when litigation is more "conveniently sought" outside Florida.

Chapter Five
Choosing the Law That Governs a Suit

Chapter Rule References: *8*

A. Choice of Law in Litigation

As explained in Chapter One, Eleanor Lane had to consider numerous sources and types of law when drafting the Olmans' complaint. She eventually decided to allege claims under both federal and Florida state law. Some claims were based on statutes, while others (namely, Otis's fraud claims) were based on common law. By asserting a variety of legal claims, Lane best ensured that the Olmans would recover the greatest compensation for their losses.

The federal court that would hear the Olmans' suit potentially faced some challenging issues. These issues stemmed from the fact that the federal court would be asked to interpret and apply state law.[1] In this chapter, we briefly discuss some of those issues, including:

- When interpreting state common law, how free is a federal court to *modify* state-court precedent? And what interpretive guides should the court use in deciding what state law means?

- When a suit arises from events that occurred in different states, how does a federal court decide *which* state's law to apply? In the Olmans' suit, for example, is it possible that Georgia law should apply because that is where Full Moon is headquartered and where it made key downsizing decisions that led to the Olmans' termination? What choice-of-law rule would the federal court consult in deciding which state's law to apply?

- To what extent does state law governing *procedural* issues apply when a federal court is adjudicating a state claim? When adjudicating state claims in the Olmans' suit, did the federal court have to apply state law restrictions governing recovery of punitive damages? Or did some other law—like the federal rules—require that state law be displaced?

These are not easy issues to resolve. While some are addressed in Civil Procedure, others may require an understanding of legal doctrine studied in more advanced courses, like Federal Courts and Choice of Law. Our treatment of these issues is necessarily limited. But we believe that a basic appreciation of how a court goes about deciding these issues is important to your understanding of the suit of *Olman v. Full Moon*. So, here goes.

[1] As to the federal claims, the U.S. Constitution's Supremacy Clause dictates that federal law will apply.

B. State Common Law in Federal Court

In Chapter Three, we saw that federal courts regularly acquire subject matter jurisdiction over state claims in two ways. A state claim may come within the court's supplemental jurisdiction because it is sufficiently factually related to a federal claim. Or a state claim may be presented in a suit between diverse citizens.

The Olmans' complaint would allege two forms of state claims—those based on Florida employment discrimination statutes and those based on Florida common law of fraud. As you learn in Civil Procedure, a dispute concerning the federal courts' obligations when adjudicating common-law claims underlies the U.S. Supreme Court's famous decision in *Erie Railroad Co. v. Tompkins*, 304 U.S. 64 (1938). *Erie* announced important principles concerning a federal court's adjudication of common-law claims. First, *Erie* states that, outside of certain, specialized areas, federal courts cannot "make" common law. This means that, in the Olmans' suit, the federal court lacked power to develop a federal common-law rule to govern Otis's fraud claim. The federal court would *have* to apply state common law in adjudicating whether Otis could recover for fraud under *Erie*, and it would also have to apply state law concerning the state statutory claims.[2]

Another principle related to the *Erie* doctrine is that federal courts must follow the lead of state courts when interpreting a state's law (both statutory and common law). In other words, a federal court cannot reshape state common law based on its own sense of policy or justice. According to the Supreme Court, a federal court must put itself in the shoes of a state's supreme court when interpreting that state's law. This means that "the federal court must determine issues of state law as it believes the highest court of the state would determine them, not necessarily (although usually this will be the case) as they have been decided by other state courts in the past."[3]

When preparing to draft Otis's fraud claim, Lane was aware that Florida state court precedent was critical. But Lane's research indicated that there was no Florida Supreme Court decision *directly* on point. As she saw it, Otis's case presented a very specific issue: Can an employee be defrauded by an employer's oral promise to give him lifetime employment when the employee eventually signs a contract limiting his employment to four years? Lane could find no Florida Supreme Court decision addressing this specific issue. Unfortunately, she found numerous decisions by lower state courts broadly stating that a person has no claim for fraud based on an oral promise that contradicts the terms of a signed, written contract.[4] None of these decisions specifically addressed the employer-employee situation, but the lower courts' pronouncements were so categorical that Lane was concerned.

---

[2] *See* 28 U.S.C. § 1652 (the "Rules of Decision Act").

[3] *See* Charles Allen Wright & Arthur R. Miller, Federal Practice & Procedure § 4507 (2024).

[4] We develop this issue more fully in Chapter Seven.

In the face of adverse state court precedent, Lane had to consider Otis's prospects for circumventing that precedent. Lane believed that a federal court *might* be more prone to err on the side of employee protection and to scrutinize harsh state law precedent. At the same time, Lane knew that the federal court would have to rationalize any departure from lower court precedent by "predicting" that the Florida Supreme Court would decide in the same way.

While Lane faced an uphill battle, she was somewhat better off in federal court than she would have been in a Florida state court. Florida trial courts lack the power to modify precedent based on their prediction that the state supreme court would so act. Instead, state trial courts must hew even to bad precedent and await a change in that precedent by the state supreme court. A federal district court, by comparison, is not disabled from anticipating a change in state law when adjudicating a dispute at the trial level.

Such were the implications of *Erie* for Otis's common law fraud claim.

C. Choosing Which State's Law to Apply

Till this point, we have assumed that Florida state law governs all issues in the Olmans' suit not governed by federal law. But why? Does Florida law govern because the federal court where Lane intends to file suit is located in Florida? Does Florida law govern because the Olmans are Floridians, or because they formerly worked for Full Moon at its Jacksonville store?

The reasons a federal court would likely apply Florida state law are complicated. You will better understand them after taking a course in Choice of Law. But we present an abbreviated, necessarily sketchy explanation of why a federal court would likely conclude that Florida law applies.

When suit is filed in a state court, the court proceeds on the presumption that its own state's law governs issues in the suit.[5] This means that, had Lane filed suit in Florida state court, the trial judge would assume that Florida law governed all legal issues (like the issues of common law fraud) not otherwise governed by federal law. But in appropriate circumstances, this presumption can be rebutted and the forum court may choose—or even be required—to apply the law of some *other* state.

When asked to displace local law and apply that of some other state, a trial court will consider the forum's *choice-of-law* principles. Choice-of-law principles are usually developed by the courts, although occasionally they are enacted legislatively. These principles guide a court when it is asked to determine which state's law applies to a dispute that involves several states. For example, the dispute between the Olmans and Full Moon clearly involved persons and events in the state of Florida; but it also involved corporate decisions made in Atlanta by a defendant whose principal offices are in Georgia. If Full Moon believed it had a viable

[5] But as observed above, if *federal* law governs the rights and duties of the parties, it must be applied under the command of the Supremacy Clause of the Constitution. The present discussion focuses on issues that are properly governed by state law.

argument that Georgia law should apply, it would use choice-of-law principles to make the argument.

Here is where things can become complicated. Congress rarely enacts national choice-of-law principles that govern suits involving events or parties in several states. With few exceptions, choice-of-law doctrine is developed by each state's Supreme Court to govern suits filed in local courts. This means that, if the Olmans sued Full Moon in a Florida state court, the court would apply choice-of-law doctrine developed by the Florida Supreme Court to determine whether to apply Florida substantive law or Georgia substantive law.

What happens when suit is filed in federal court? This takes us back to the *Erie* doctrine. *Erie* tells us that, in the absence of federal statutes or the like, federal courts must apply state law—including state common law. After *Erie*, in the case of *Klaxon v. Stentor Electric Manufacturing Company*,[6] the Supreme Court affirmed that state choice-of-law doctrine is itself part of the state law that federal courts must apply. As a consequence, a federal court in Florida that is applying state law (based on diversity or supplemental jurisdiction) looks to local choice-of-law doctrine to determine which state's law to apply. So if a Florida state court would construe its choice-of-law doctrine to apply Florida employment discrimination and fraud law in the Olmans' suit, a federal court is required to do likewise. The federal court will have to predict how a Florida state court would interpret state choice-of-law doctrine in the same manner that it has to predict how a Florida state court would interpret its common law of fraud.

Got that?

In sum, if Full Moon wanted a federal trial court in Florida to apply Georgia law to govern the parties' rights and duties, it would have to (1) argue using local (i.e., Florida) choice-of-law doctrine;[7] and (2) explain how that doctrine requires the application of Georgia substantive law.

Full Moon's prospects for getting a federal court to apply Georgia law were poor. Florida's choice-of-law principles accord great weight to the fact that the Olmans were Floridians who had been employed in Florida and suffered their injuries in Florida.[8] Because Florida had an obvious interest in applying its law to occurrences centered in the state, a Florida court was highly unlikely to choose Georgia law. As a consequence, a federal court in Florida would likely reject application of Georgia law as well.

---

[6] 313 U.S. 487 (1941).

[7] If the Olmans had chosen to sue in a federal court in Georgia, the federal court would apply Georgia choice-of-law doctrine.

[8] Florida, like most states, has adopted some of the choice of law principles set forth in the RESTATEMENT (SECOND) OF CONFLICT OF LAWS, which generally requires that the law of the state having the more "significant relationship" to the parties and the occurrence be applied.

D. The Potential Impact of State Law on "Procedural" Issues

The Olmans' complaint would allege claims under the "substantive" law of the United States and Florida. A federal court would be guided by federal statutes and federal precedent when interpreting the ADEA; and it would be guided by Florida statutes and state precedent when interpreting the Florida Civil Rights Act and Florida common law. This much seems straightforward.

In contrast to the way in which substantive issues are treated, *all* procedural issues arising in the Olmans' suit would be litigated using the applicable Federal Rules of Civil Procedure.[9] According to *Hanna v. Plumer*,[10] a federal court must apply lawfully adopted Federal Rules of Civil Procedure regardless of whether the procedural issue concerns a federal or state claim. As developed in later chapters, the Olmans and Full Moon would rely on the Federal Rules in drafting their pleadings and motions, in conducting discovery, and in litigating the merits of their positions.

But the Olmans' suit presented one of the atypical situations where the substance/procedure distinction is not altogether clear. This uncertainty arises from the fact that Otis Olman intended to seek punitive damages from Full Moon based on his claim that Full Moon defrauded him. Under Florida common law, this misconduct supports a demand for punitive damages. Yet Florida law also restricts a plaintiff's right to demand punitive damages in the complaint.[11] A plaintiff may not allege punitive damages in the initial complaint. According to Florida Statutes § 768.72, a plaintiff seeking punitive damages must *first* produce evidence supporting the demand, after which the trial court may permit an *amendment* of the complaint to allege those damages:

> In any civil action, no claim for punitive damages shall be permitted unless there is a reasonable showing by evidence in the record or proffered by the claimant which would provide a reasonable basis for recovery of such damages. The claimant may move to

[9] *See, e.g., Hanna v. Plumer*, 380 U.S. 460, 465 (1965) (courts in diversity actions "apply state substantive law and federal procedural law").

[10] 380 U.S. 460 (1965).

[11] This statutory limit doesn't apply to claims under the Florida Civil Rights Act. Fla. Stat. § 760.11(5).

> amend her or his complaint to assert a claim for punitive damages as allowed by the rules of civil procedure. The rules of civil procedure shall be liberally construed so as to allow the claimant discovery of evidence which appears reasonably calculated to lead to admissible evidence on the issue of punitive damages. No discovery of financial worth shall proceed until after the pleading concerning punitive damages is permitted.

Lane, who had experience litigating punitive damages claims in state court, knew that she would not be able to allege punitive damages for fraud in her original complaint had she filed in a Florida state court. A defendant like Full Moon would quickly move to strike such a demand. But did the restriction on pleading found in the Florida Statutes apply in federal court? Lane wanted to allege a demand for punitive damages in her original complaint. Among other things, the potential threat of punitive damages provided her a certain amount of negotiating leverage.[12] Even if she could later provide evidence supporting punitive damages and amend her complaint, she preferred to introduce her demand for punitive damages at the outset of the case and possibly induce an early settlement.

Lane apparently faced issues governed by the *Erie* doctrine. If Full Moon moved to strike the Olmans' demand for punitive damages, the federal court would have to consider two questions:

- Did a Federal Rule of Civil Procedure permit the Olmans to allege a demand for punitive damages in their original complaint without first presenting supporting evidence and obtaining the trial court's permission? In other words, did a Federal Rule conflict with Florida law?

- If no Federal Rule conflicted with Florida law, was the federal court required to follow state law because failure to do so would lead to different outcomes in state and federal court and result in inequitable administration of the laws or forum shopping?[13]

As Lane read the Federal Rules of Civil Procedure, Rule 8(a)(3) gave her the right to plead punitive damages for fraud in her initial complaint without seeking court permission. That rule explains that a pleading like the complaint must state "a demand for the relief sought, which may include relief in the alternative or different types of relief." Nothing in the Federal Rules required her to receive the court's approval before demanding punitive damages. Because Florida law appeared to conflict with Rule 8(a)(3), Lane believed Florida law was inapplicable.[14]

---

[12] Not only would the threat of recovering punitive damages provide Lane negotiation leverage, she might also have the right to conduct discovery concerning Full Moon's financial situation. For example, the state of Full Moon's finances would be relevant in determining how much of a penalty they should pay for their wrongdoing. And if Full Moon preferred to keep its financial information private, it might be willing to "pay" for its privacy by negotiating a settlement more favorable to the Olmans.

[13] *See generally Hanna v. Plumer*, 380 U.S. 460, 465 (1965) (describing the steps a court must take when assessing whether state law must apply in litigating state claims).

[14] Notice that there was no question that the substantive basis on which punitive damages could be awarded was governed by Florida law. The issue related to what rules of pleading applied when seeking such relief.

If Lane were mistaken and there was no conflict between Rule 8(a)(3) and Florida law, she would have to persuade the court that discarding Florida law would not be "outcome determinative" and lead to forum shopping and inequitable differences in federal and state court practice. According to *Hanna,* the "outcome-determinative" effect of a state-court rule turns on "whether application of the rule would make so important a difference to the character or result of the litigation that failure to enforce it would unfairly discriminate against citizens of the forum State, or whether application of the rule would have so important an effect upon the fortunes of one or both of the litigants that failure to enforce it would be likely to cause a plaintiff to choose the federal court."[15]

The two *Erie* questions raised by Florida's statute governing punitive damages are challenging. Based on your study of the *Erie* doctrine, try your hand at resolving these questions:

Question 5.1

1. Does Federal Rule 8(a)(3) conflict with Florida law concerning the pleading of punitive damages? Is there any way a conflict can be avoided? If there is a conflict, must the federal court apply Rule 8(a)(3)?

2. Assume, for the purposes of this question, that a federal court finds that the Federal Rules do *not* conflict with Florida law. Must the federal court now apply Florida law restricting the pleading of punitive damages? Why or why not? Is there other information that would help you in resolving this question?

3. Assume that a federal court finds that Federal Rule 8(a)(3) precludes application of Florida law limiting a party's right to plead a demand for punitive damages. Thus, the plaintiff is permitted to allege a demand for punitive damages in the initial complaint. The court is later asked to apply another feature of the Florida statute that precludes discovery of a party's financial worth until the movant proffers evidence supporting the demand for punitive damages. (As you learn when studying the topic of discovery, a party is usually limited to discovering relevant information, and a party's financial worth is usually not relevant when only compensatory damages are demanded.) The movant argues that the federal court should not apply Florida's limit on discovering financial worth because Federal Rule 26(d) permits discovery any time after the parties have conducted an initial discovery conference under Rule 26(f). If such a conference has occurred, should the court permit the plaintiff to seek discovery of the defendant's financial worth?

These *Erie*-related issues eventually produced numerous, conflicting opinions in the federal district courts asked to reconcile the Federal Rules and Florida law. For the Eleventh Circuit's

[15] *Hanna,* 380 U.S. at 468 n. 9.

ultimate resolution of question 5.1(1), read *Cohen v. Office Depot*, 184 F.3d 1292 (11th Cir. 1999). *See also Porter v. Ogden, Newell & Welch*, 241 F.3d 1334 (11th Cir. 2001). As for question 5.1(3), read the conflicting rulings in decisions like *Pantages v. Cardinal Health 200, Inc.*, 2009 WL 1011048 (M.D. Fla. April 15, 2009) and *Gallina v. Commerce and Industry Insurance*, 2008 WL 3895918 (M.D. Fla. August 15, 2008).

Chapter Six
Commencing the Lawsuit

Chapter Rule References: *3, 8, 9, 10, 11,* 15, 26, 38, 54

A. The Complaint

Federal rules governing how a complaint should be drafted appear to be fairly indulgent—or at least they were prior to a few decisions by the U.S. Supreme Court in 2007 (discussed below). Rule 8 literally requires a "short and plain" statement of the court's subject-matter jurisdiction, a "short and plain" statement of the plaintiff's claims, and a demand for relief. Rule 10 sketches a format for the complaint that requires little more than a standard heading at the beginning, followed by numbered paragraphs containing the plaintiff's allegations. This approach is called *notice* pleading. The plaintiff need only give the defendant general notice of the events prompting the suit, the legal claims the plaintiff intends to assert, and the remedy sought. There is no requirement that a plaintiff allege specific legal theories or all the elements of a claim.[1] And as Rule 8 reminds the courts, "Pleadings must be construed so as to do justice."[2]

As well, official forms promulgated by the Court illustrated a quite liberal approach to pleading a case.[3] For example, the specific language in form 11 indicated that a plaintiff could allege a routine personal injury action in just a few paragraphs:

> 2. On [date] at [place], the defendant negligently drove a motor vehicle against the plaintiff.
>
> 3. As a result, the plaintiff was physically injured, lost wages or income, suffered physical and mental pain, and incurred medical expenses of [$__].
>
> Therefore, the plaintiff demands judgment against the defendant for [$__] plus costs.

Note that this complaint form does not specifically allege all the elements of the tort of negligence (e.g., duty, breach, causation, and injury). It doesn't even allege what the defendant did that was negligent: Was he speeding, intoxicated, or driving against a red light?

---

[1] *See Kirksey v. R.J. Reynolds Tobacco Co.,* 168 F.3d 1039, 1041 (7th Cir. 1999) ("the courts keep reminding plaintiffs that they don't to have to file long complaints, don't have to plead facts, don't have to plead legal theories"); *Sparrow v. United Air Lines, Inc.,* 216 F.3d 1111, 1113 (D.C. Cir. 2000) (a plaintiff does not have to "make out a prima facie case of discrimination" in his complaint).

[2] Rule 8(e).

[3] The former Rule 84 confirmed that these sample forms were "sufficient under the rules and [were] intended to indicate the simplicity and brevity of statement which the rules contemplate." Along with the forms, Rule 84 was abrogated effective December 2015.

Had Lane relied on form 11 for guidance, she could probably have stated the Olmans' case in less than a page.[4] The gist of Otis's discrimination claim seems to be as follows: Otis, who was 53 at the time, lost his management position in the Jacksonville store when Full Moon replaced him with a younger employee who was no better qualified than Otis. When Otis complained of perceived age discrimination, Full Moon retaliated by firing him days later.

Lane could also have relied on Court precedent affirming the modest amount of detail required to allege a claim of age discrimination. In *Swierkiewicz v. Sorema N.A.*, the Court found that an ADEA plaintiff satisfied his pleading burden by alleging "events leading to his termination . . . relevant dates [and] the ages . . . of at least some of the relevant persons involved with his termination." This was sufficient to give the defendant "fair notice of what [plaintiff's] claims are and the grounds upon which they rest."[5]

But form 11 was removed from the rules in 2015. And more recent Supreme Court decisions have interjected a note of uncertainty into federal pleading. In *Ashcroft v. Iqbal*,[6] the Court refused to accept "conclusory" allegations of racial and religious discrimination, even though Rule 9(b) permits a pleader to allege "intent" generally. And in *Bell Atlantic Corp. v. Twombly*,[7] the Court stated that a pleader must allege sufficient detail to show that claims are factually "plausible" and not "speculative."

Since *Iqbal* and *Twombly*, lower courts have struggled when applying this new "flexible plausibility" standard of pleading.[8] Courts surmise that the relaxed pleading standard suggested by earlier Court precedent is no longer in effect, although they express some uncertainty about how much detail in pleadings is now required. Further, courts and lawyers can no longer rely on those official forms promulgated by the Court—as of December 2015, these forms have been abrogated.

Lane suspected that Full Moon would rely on *Iqbal* and *Twombly* to challenge the sufficiency of the complaint no matter what she alleged. But she was confident she could withstand these challenges by following the guidance of recent ADEA precedent. Courts continue to affirm that, in a "straightforward case" of discrimination like Otis Olman's, a plaintiff's burden of pleading is relatively light.[9] As these courts have held, *Iqbal*'s requirement of "plausible" factuality in pleading is satisfied by alleging that (1) the plaintiff was at least forty years old; (2) his

---

[4] *See, e.g.*, *Bennett v. Schmidt*, 153 F.3d 516, 518 (7th Cir. 1998) (an employment discrimination complaint alleging, "I was turned down for a job because of my race" would seem to satisfy federal notice pleading).

[5] 534 U.S. 506, 514 (2002).

[6] 556 U.S. 662, 686 (2009).

[7] 550 U.S. 544, 555-56 (2007).

[8] *See Boykin v. Keycorp*, 521 F.3d 202 (2d Cir. 2008) (opinion of Sotomayor, J.).

[9] *Swanson v. Citibank, N.A.*, 614 F.3d 400, 404 (7th Cir. 2010) ("[I]n many straightforward cases, it will not be any more difficult today for a plaintiff to meet [his] burden than it was before the Court's recent decisions.").

"performance was satisfactory or better" and he "received consistently good performance reviews"; (3) he was demoted or discharged; and (4) a younger employee replaced him.[10] Lane would allege these elements of a *prima facie* claim of age discrimination and be prepared to defend their sufficiency.

Here is the complaint Lane filed on behalf of the Olmans:

[10] *See, e.g., Sheppard v. David Evans and Assoc.*, 694 F.3d 1045, 1049 (9th Cir. 2012); *Rhodes v. R&L Carriers, Inc.*, 491 Fed. Appx. 579, 584 (6th Cir. 2012).

IN THE UNITED STATES DISTRICT COURT
FOR THE MIDDLE DISTRICT OF FLORIDA
JACKSONVILLE DIVISION

Rule 10(a) requires that the complaint contain this introductory information, e.g., the court's name, the litigants' names, and the type of pleading.

OTIS AND FIONA OLMAN,

Plaintiffs,

v. Case No. ______________

The case would be assigned a number by the clerk.

FULL MOON SPORTS, INC.,
& BRUCE BELCHER

Defendants.

COMPLAINT AND DEMAND FOR JURY TRIAL

Preliminary Allegations

1. This is an action based upon the Age Discrimination in Employment Act, 29 U.S.C. § 621 *et seq.* ("ADEA"), the Florida Civil Rights Act, Fla. Stat. § 760.01 *et seq.*, and Florida common law.

2. The court has jurisdiction of all ADEA claims under 28 U.S.C. § 1331 and 29 U.S.C. § 216, and supplemental jurisdiction of all state law claims under 28 U.S.C. § 1367. The court also has jurisdiction based on 28 U.S.C. § 1332. The Plaintiffs are both citizens of Florida, Defendant Full Moon is incorporated in Delaware and has its principal place of business in Georgia, and Defendant Bruce Belcher is a citizen of Connecticut. Each of the Plaintiffs seeks more than $75,000 in damages, exclusive of interest and costs, from each of the Defendants.

Rule 8(a)(1) requires a statement of the court's subject matter jurisdiction.

Rule 9(c) permits a plaintiff to allege "generally" that all conditions precedent have been satisfied.

3. The Plaintiffs have satisfied all conditions precedent to bringing this action under the ADEA and the Florida Civil Rights Act. Specifically, Plaintiffs filed timely claims with the EEOC and the Florida Human Relations Commission on December 20, 2022, and the EEOC subsequently issued Plaintiffs a right-to-sue letter on February 3, 2023.

Parties

While no rule requires a detailed explanation of the parties, this is a good idea when there are several plaintiffs and defendants.

4. Otis Olman ("Olman") is the former manager of the Full Moon Outdoor Center, a retail sporting goods store located in Jacksonville. Olman served as store manager from 2011 to 2022. At the time of his termination, Olman was 53 years old.

5. Fiona Olman ("Fiona Olman") is the wife of Otis Olman. She was employed by Full Moon at the Jacksonville store from 2014 through 2022. From 2019 through 2022 she served as manager of the store's kayak department. At the time of her termination, Fiona was 49 years old.

6. Full Moon Sports, Inc. ("Full Moon") is a Delaware corporation that owns and operates retail sporting goods stores throughout the United States. It is a wholly owned subsidiary of Mizar, Inc., and its principal place of business and executive headquarters are in Atlanta, Georgia.

7. Bruce Belcher ("Belcher") was employed by Full Moon as regional manager of all retail stores located in the states of Florida, Georgia, North Carolina, and South Carolina from 2019 through early 2023.

Rule 10(c) states that allegations in a pleading are to be made in "numbered paragraphs," and that each paragraph "shall be limited as far as practicable to a statement of a single set of circumstances." As you will see later, this enumeration of allegations in separate paragraphs is useful when the parties or the court needs to refer to specific allegations. For example, defendants usually respond to each numbered allegation when answering the complaint, as illustrated in Chapter Seven.

General Allegations

8. Olman began working for Full Moon in 2003, when he became assistant manager for its store in Burlington, Vermont. Olman was promoted to store manager in 2006.

9. In 2011, Full Moon asked Olman to become manager of its store in Jacksonville, Florida. At the time, the Jacksonville store was a marginally profitable business.

One approach to pleading, not set forth in the rules, is "to tell the plaintiffs' story" in an introductory section. Ask yourself: Does this section tell a compelling story? Does it provide sufficient detail? Too much detail?

10. Olman accepted the manager's position at the Jacksonville store.

11. Under Olman's management, the Jacksonville store became a highly profitable store which featured high-end sporting goods, instruction in popular activities like sea kayaking, and guided outdoor adventures.

12. In 2014, Fiona Olman began working for the Jacksonville store. In 2019, she became manager of the store's kayak department when its existing manager moved to another state.

13. In 2019, Full Moon was acquired by Mizar. Mizar made numerous changes in Full Moon's management and began advertising and selling "extreme" sporting goods in many Full Moon stores.

14. In 2019, defendant Belcher was made regional manager of Full Moon's southeast region, which included the Jacksonville store.

15. When Belcher first met Olman in August, 2019, he admitted to being very impressed by Olman's work at the Jacksonville store. Belcher asked Olman to sign a four-year contract to continue as store manager.

16. In prior years as store manager for Full Moon, Olman had no formal contract with the company.

17. At the time Belcher proposed the contract, Olman was considering a business offer from a local entrepreneur. The entrepreneur offered Olman a one-half partnership interest in a new business to be located in Key Largo, Florida, a proposal Olman believed would be highly profitable.

18. Olman told Belcher of his interest in the Key Largo business partnership.

19. With the intent of inducing Olman to remain as manager for the Jacksonville store and decline the Key Largo partnership offer, Belcher promised Olman "great" job security and also promised that he could "retire" as manager of the Jacksonville store at his will.

20. In reliance on Belcher's promise of job security, Olman agreed to remain as store manager, executed a four-year employment contract with Full Moon, and declined to join in the Key Largo partnership.

21. Shortly after Olman agreed to remain as manager of the Full Moon store, the company opened an extreme-sports department in the Jacksonville store. To run the department, Full Moon hired Sid Shockley, an extreme-sports athlete with no retail sales experience.

22. From 2019 to 2022, Olman trained Shockley in retail sales and management skills.

23. In November 2022, Belcher informed Olman that Full Moon intended to implement a corporate downsizing. As part of this downsizing, Full Moon's overall workforce would be reduced by 20%, and the Jacksonville store would terminate 10 employees. Belcher sought Olman's advice in implementing the downsizing. Belcher also asked Olman if he was interested in managing some other Full Moon store.

24. Olman recommended to Belcher that the company retain its most experienced employees because of their greater productivity and loyalty to the store. Olman also advised Belcher he was not interested in managing another Full Moon store.

25. In December 2022, Belcher informed Olman that Full Moon had decided to terminate many of its more experienced employees at the Jacksonville store, including several employees over the age of 40. One of these terminated employees was Fiona Olman.

26. Belcher also informed Olman that he was being reassigned to the position of manager of the camping department, and his salary would be reduced from $100,000 to $60,000. Belcher stated that Full Moon intended to replace Olman with Sid Shockley, the 32-year-old manager of the extreme-sports department.

27. Olman immediately contacted his former regional manager for advice. This advisor was now employed in Full Moon's executive headquarters. Olman was told that "Full Moon has changed," the market for extreme sporting goods required "younger" employees, and it might be time for Olman to "move on."

28. Olman protested Full Moon's discriminatory downsizing decisions in a letter to company president, Bertie Lurch, dated December 10, 2022. That letter, a copy of which is attached to this complaint and adopted by reference, told Lurch he would take legal action if Full Moon did not cease its practice of age discrimination. Two weeks later Olman received a letter of termination from Lurch, which is also attached to this complaint and adopted by reference. The letter offered severance pay to Olman if he would sign a release. Olman refused to sign.

29. Immediately prior to Olman's termination, newly designated store manager Shockley told store employees that Olman was "too old" to be running the store and that he was being "put out to pasture" through his demotion to the store's camping department. Regional manager Belcher was aware of Shockley's improper behavior but did nothing to correct it.

30. Since their termination by Full Moon, Otis and Fiona Olman have obtained other employment in the Jacksonville area but have suffered a substantial reduction in compensation and other employment benefits.

Rule 10(b) recommends that "each claim founded upon a separate transaction or occurrence" be stated in a "separate count." But in practice, most lawyers plead separate counts for each *legal* cause of action, even if these separate counts arise out of the same transaction or occurrence.

COUNT ONE:
Disparate Treatment under the ADEA
(Otis Olman v. Full Moon)

Rule 10(c) permits a party to "adopt by reference" matters alleged in another part of a pleading. Notice how Lane simplifies the pleading of specific counts by adopting prior allegations in the introductory fact section.

31. Plaintiff Otis Olman re-alleges paragraphs 8-30.

32. At the time of Full Moon's corporate downsizing, Olman was 53 years of age, highly qualified for retention as store manager, and was interested in remaining as store manager.

33. Notwithstanding Olman's qualification and interest, he was replaced by a 32-year-old assistant manager and eventually terminated.

34. Olman was informed that his demotion was prompted by Full Moon's desire to reduce the cost of management salaries, yet Olman was never asked to continue serving as manager at a reduced salary consistent with Full Moon's economic goals.

35. Full Moon's decision to demote and terminate Olman was motivated by age-discriminatory animus and stereotypes, including those of assistant manager Shockley and regional manager Belcher, whose recommendations to final decision makers for Full Moon played an important role in downsizing decisions.

Notice how Lane qualified this allegation. Can you see how this qualification responds to Lane's obligation under Rule 11(b)(3)?

36. Based on plaintiff's good-faith belief as to evidence that will be discovered upon further information and discovery, Full Moon's discriminatory action against Olman was part of a pattern and practice of age discrimination affecting company-wide downsizing.

37. Full Moon's discriminatory treatment of Olman was in reckless disregard of his rights under the ADEA.

Therefore, Plaintiff Otis Olman demands of Full Moon back pay, future pay and lost earnings, liquidated damages of double back pay, prejudgment interest, costs, attorneys' fees, and any other relief the court deems appropriate.

COUNT TWO:
Retaliation under the ADEA
(Otis Olman v. Full Moon)

Take a moment to review the elements of a cause of action for retaliation under the ADEA. Has Lane alleged all elements?

38. Plaintiff Otis Olman realleges paragraphs 8-30.

39. Upon learning of his demotion from store manager and other downsizing decisions in violation of the ADEA, Olman objected to Full Moon's discriminatory actions in a letter to the company's president.

40. Olman's protest was made in good faith based on objectively reasonable information indicating Full Moon was violating the ADEA in the course of its downsizing.

41. In direct response to Olman's good-faith objection, Full Moon terminated him.

Therefore, Plaintiff Otis Olman demands of Full Moon back pay, future pay and lost earnings, liquidated damages of double back pay, prejudgment interest, costs, attorney's fees, and any other relief the court deems appropriate.

Notice how Counts One and Two demand specific remedies authorized by the ADEA. These remedies are discussed in greater detail in Chapter One.

COUNT THREE:
Disparate Treatment under the Florida Civil Rights Act
(Otis Olman v. Full Moon)

42. Plaintiff Otis Olman realleges paragraphs 8-30.

43. The previously described discriminatory action of Full Moon against Olman violates the Florida Civil Rights Act, Fla. Stat. § 760.01 *et seq.*

Therefore, Plaintiff Otis Olman demands of Full Moon compensatory damages, punitive damages, prejudgment interest, costs, attorney's fees, and any other relief the court deems appropriate.

Again, notice how the demand for relief in Count Three reflects the remedies authorized by applicable state law. Can you identify the difference in remedies authorized by federal law in Count One and state law in Count Three?

COUNT FOUR:
Retaliation under the Florida Civil Rights Act
(Otis Olman v. Full Moon)

44. Plaintiff Otis Olman realleges paragraphs 8-30.

45. The previously described retaliatory action of Full Moon against Olman violates the Florida Civil Rights Act, Fla. Stat. § 760.01 *et seq.*

Therefore, Plaintiff Otis Olman demands of Full Moon compensatory damages, punitive damages, prejudgment interest, costs, attorney's fees, and any other relief the court deems appropriate.

COUNT FIVE:
Common Law Fraud
(Otis Olman v. Full Moon and Belcher)

46. Plaintiff Otis Olman realleges paragraphs 8-30.

47. In August 2015, Bruce Belcher, acting as regional manager and agent of Full Moon, promised Olman he could remain as manager of the Jacksonville store until he retired. These promises were made for the purpose of inducing Olman to remain as store manager and dissuading Olman from entering into the business partnership in Key Largo, Florida.

48. At the time Belcher made these promises, he knew that neither he nor Full Moon had any intention of honoring them.

49. Belcher made these promises with the intent that Olman rely on them.

Paragraphs 47 through 49 allege defendant Belcher's intentions. What is Lane's factual basis for imputing intention? Are these allegations consistent with Lane's Rule 11 obligations?

The allegations of fraud in Count Five must satisfy the more demanding pleading requirements of Rule 9(b). Do they?

50. Olman reasonably relied on Belcher's promises.

51. As a result of Olman's reliance, he forfeited the opportunity to be a partner in a successful business venture.

Therefore, Plaintiff Otis Olman demands of Full Moon and its agent, Bruce Belcher, compensatory damages, punitive damages, prejudgment interest, costs, attorney's fees, and any other relief the court deems appropriate.

COUNT SIX:
Disparate Treatment under the ADEA
(Fiona Olman v. Full Moon)

52. Plaintiff Fiona Olman realleges paragraphs 8-30.

53. At the time of Full Moon's corporate downsizing, Fiona Olman was 49 years of age, qualified for retention as manager of the store's kayak department, and interested in remaining in that position.

54. Notwithstanding Fiona Olman's qualifications and interest, she was replaced by a subordinate employee aged 28.

55. Full Moon's decision to demote and terminate Fiona Olman was motivated by age-discriminatory animus and stereotypes.

56. Based on plaintiff's good-faith belief as to evidence that will be discovered upon further information and discovery, Full Moon's discriminatory action against Fiona Olman was part of a pattern and practice of age discrimination affecting company-wide downsizing.

57. Full Moon's discriminatory treatment of Fiona Olman was in reckless disregard of her rights under the ADEA.

Therefore, Plaintiff Fiona Olman demands of Full Moon back pay, future pay and lost earnings, liquidated damages of double back pay, prejudgment interest, costs, attorney's fees, and any other relief the court deems appropriate.

COUNT SEVEN:
Disparate Treatment under the Florida Civil Rights Act
(Fiona Olman vs. Full Moon)

58. Plaintiff Fiona Olman realleges paragraphs 8-30.

59. The previously described discriminatory action of Full Moon against Fiona Olman violates the Florida Civil Rights Act, Fla. Stat. § 760.01 *et seq.*

Therefore, Plaintiff Fiona Olman demands of Full Moon compensatory damages, punitive damages, prejudgment interest, costs, attorney's fees, and any other relief the court deems appropriate.

Jury Demand

Rule 38(b) permitted Lane to demand a jury trial in her complaint. If she failed to do so, would she have forfeited the right to a jury trial?

Plaintiffs Otis and Fiona Olman demand a jury trial on all claims.

Respectfully submitted,

____

Eleanor Lane
Lane & Quincy, P.A.
Trial Counsel for Plaintiffs
Fla. Bar No. 937402
100 Cook Street
Jacksonville, Florida 32210
(904) 555-1111
Elane@yahoo.com

Dated: March 1, 2023

Before we examine Lane's reasons for drafting the complaint as she did, consider the following advice about drafting pleadings. It might be useful when you are asked to make your first attempts at drafting legal documents.

A Drafting Tip ✍

Relying on Form Books or "Model" Complaints

Whatever your philosophy of pleading, it's best not to rely uncritically on "model" pleadings drafted by others. There are many sources for model pleadings, including commercial form books, pleadings developed by other attorneys, and increasingly, pleadings found in electronic databases of actual court filings. These pleadings can provide useful guidance when you are considering what claims and remedies to allege, and can also provide valuable clues to drafting. But there are significant shortcomings to relying on these sources. First, they will seldom be tailored to the specific facts and legal issues presented in your case. Second, too often they are poorly drafted and perpetuate undesirable writing practices.

If you have access to high-quality forms (e.g., those provided by an experienced lawyer with writing skill), you are fortunate. If not, develop your own. While it may take a bit of courage in the beginning, try to draft pleadings that convey the law and the facts in a straightforward manner. Use simple language to write short, clear sentences that a layperson could understand. Writing expert Bryan Garner has remarked on how novices lacking confidence employ legalese as a sort of "secret handshake" indicating to others that they are bona fide members of the legal guild. But to lawyers and judges who appreciate good writing, such gestures convey a less complimentary message.

B. Lane's Goals in Drafting the Complaint

Could Lane have drafted a simpler, shorter complaint and still satisfied her obligation under the "flexible plausibility" standard articulated in recent Court opinions? Probably. Some lawyers prefer a more minimalist approach to pleading and might allege less detail in an age-discrimination complaint. There are sound arguments for following this approach, particularly when the facts of a dispute are unclear. First, it might be unwise to commit to a detailed version of the facts in the complaint before discovery is completed. Allegations in a complaint are treated as a plaintiff's "admissions," which can be used against the plaintiff unless the court permits their amendment. Second, detailed factual allegations can unintentionally provide fodder for pretrial challenges and discovery disputes. Third, lawyers must always keep in mind their obligation to plead in good faith under Rule 11. This good-faith obligation takes precedence over the desire to tell a compelling story in the complaint.

Lane drafted a more detailed complaint because she believed it served more purposes than simply giving the defendants "notice" of the plaintiffs' dispute. In addition to the notice function served by pleadings, Lane drafted with these goals in mind:

- Preparing for the defendants' anticipated responses;
- Preserving the opportunity to fully litigate the plaintiffs' case, at a minimum of procedural cost;
- Preserving clients' legal rights;
- Pinning down the defendants;
- Telling a "good story" to the court, the defendants, and (perhaps) the public; and
- Complying with a lawyer's ethical obligations.

Let's briefly examine each of these considerations. To do this, we need to think ahead to aspects of the litigation process that you'll study more fully in later chapters.

1. Preparing for the Defendants' Anticipated Responses

A useful approach to drafting a complaint is to consider how you would respond to it if you represented the defendant. Lane was aware that defendants in civil rights suits commonly file a Rule 12(b)(6) motion seeking to dismiss one or more of the plaintiff's counts[11] because they fail "to state a claim upon which relief can be granted." As we will see in Chapter Seven, a Rule 12(b)(6) motion enforces Rule 8(a)'s requirement that the complaint allege a "claim showing the pleader is entitled to relief." Lane was also aware that some courts seem to require "heightened pleading" in civil rights suits, even though there's no basis for this in the Rules.

Anticipating a possible Rule 12(b)(6) motion, Lane alleged greater detail than might be required by notice pleading, even as that concept is understood after *Iqbal* and *Twombly*. She alleged facts specifically supporting each element of the claims in the complaint; that is, she pled *prima facie* claims of discrimination that lower courts have found sufficient.[12] Not only did

---

[11] In the Guide, the terms "claim" and "count" are used synonymously; occasionally, we also use the term "cause of action."

[12] Lane did this even though, in *Swierkiewicz v. Sorema N.A.*, 534 U.S. 506, 512 (2002), the Supreme Court held that an ADEA plaintiff did not have to allege a *prima facie* claim of age discrimination in his complaint. According to the Court, Rule 8's "simplified notice pleading standard relies on liberal discovery rules and summary judgment motions to define disputed facts and issues and to dispose of unmeritorious claims." Although *Swierkiewicz* predated both *Iqbal* and *Twombly*, it has been favorably cited by the Court in more recent opinions. *See Johnson v. City of Shelby, Miss.*, 135 S. Ct. 346, 347 (2014); *Skinner v. Switzer*, 562 U.S. 521, 530 (2011). It was even cited in the *Twombly* opinion itself. 550 U.S. at 547. For further exploration of the "flexible plausibility" standard as applied in employment discrimination cases, see Charles A. Sullivan, *Plausibly Pleading Employment Discrimination*, 52 WM. & MARY L. REV. 1613 (2011).

Lane want all counts to survive a motion to dismiss, if possible that she wanted to deter such an attack and the needless time and cost that her client would incur in responding to it.

> **Tactical Tip** ✍
>
> **Alleging the Elements of a Cause of Action**
>
> When pleading a cause of action or "count," think about a table. In order to stand, a table must (usually) have all its legs. The "legs" of a count can be envisioned as the *elements* of the cause of action that you are pleading. To show the court that you have an adequately supported table, you should allege *all* the legs/elements. If your count omits a leg, the defendant will argue that the table must fall (i.e., that the cause of action should be dismissed for failing to state a claim).
>
> Most always, you can find court precedent explaining the elements that must be alleged to support a freestanding count. Provided that you have evidentiary support for each element, you should be able to allege a claim that deters or survives a motion to dismiss. A common cause leading to the dismissal of claims in a complaint is the lawyer's failure to adequately research and allege the requisite elements of a claim.

2. Preserving the Opportunity to Fully Litigate the Case with a Minimum of Procedural Cost

Lane knew that the scope of her pleadings would be important when she used other procedural rules later in the suit. Specifically, a more comprehensive complaint would facilitate her efforts to obtain the broadest *discovery* and the most comprehensive *relief* for the Olmans.

Rule 26(b)(1) permits parties to obtain discovery of any matter "relevant to any party's claim or defense." When such limiting language was added to Rule 26, the drafters stated that "the rule . . . signals to the court that it has authority to confine discovery to the claims and defenses asserted in the pleadings, and signals parties that they have no entitlement to discovery to develop new claims or defenses not already identified in the pleadings."[13] So Lane wanted a comprehensive complaint to support comprehensive discovery. For example, Lane made sure to allege that Full Moon's discriminatory treatment of the Olmans was part of a "pattern or practice" of discrimination affecting company-wide downsizing. This allegation would provide a pleading foundation for inquiring into the company's treatment of other

[13] Of course, this rule is a two-way street. To the extent that a plaintiff is concerned about broad discovery directed at it, it may have an incentive to plead with more restraint. For example, if Lane had pleaded that the Olmans suffered from "extreme emotional distress, pain and suffering" as a consequence of their termination, they might have made their mental condition and history fair game for discovery.

older workers, which Full Moon would likely contend had no relevance to the Olmans' individual claims.[14]

A more detailed complaint would also support more comprehensive relief for the Olmans. Rule 54(c) tells the court that "every . . . final judgment should grant the relief to which each party is entitled, even if the party has not demanded that relief in its pleadings." But a defendant can still object to the award of a remedy not alleged in the complaint by arguing that it was unaware during discovery or trial that the particular remedy was at issue. If lack of notice sufficiently prejudices the defendant's opportunity to argue the merits of the remedy, the remedy may be denied.[15] Consequently, Lane made a habit of specifically alleging every form of relief that her clients were entitled to and wished to obtain.

Finally, Lane knew that she might want to amend the complaint at a later date, possibly adding new claims. A complaint that contains only minimal detail can provide the defendant a basis for objecting to later amendment of the complaint. For example, if Lane sought to add a new claim after the statute of limitations governing the claim expired, she would need to show that the new claim "arose out of the conduct . . . set forth or attempted to be set forth in the original pleading" to circumvent the limitations bar.[16] Consequently, the more comprehensive the allegations in the original complaint, the better prepared Lane would be to argue that an amended claim "arose" out of those allegations.

In sum, a more detailed complaint would better enable Lane to fully investigate her clients' case and obtain the broadest relief for them. She did not want to discover later that a lack of detail in the complaint gave her opponents reason to claim "surprise" and so limit her clients' recovery.

3. Preserving a Client's Legal Rights

Under a doctrine called "claim preclusion" by federal courts, a plaintiff suing a defendant based on a specific transaction or occurrence must usually assert all legal claims arising out of that transaction or occurrence.[17] If a claim is neither included in the complaint nor introduced

---

[14] Similarly, the scope of a party's duty to provide "mandatory disclosure" of information under Rule 26(a) is determined by what is alleged in the pleadings. *See, e.g.*, Rule 26(a)(1)(A) (duty to disclose persons with discoverable information that party may use to support its "claims or defenses"). *See Albermarle Paper Co. v. Moody*, 422 U.S. 405, 424 (1975) (a party may not be "entitled" to a specific form of relief under Rule 54(c) if its conduct of litigation has prejudiced the opposing party).

[15] *See* Rule 15(c). For example, in *Marsh v. Coleman Co.*, 774 F. Supp. 608 (D. Kan. 1991), a plaintiff suing under the ADEA was prohibited from amending his complaint to add a fraud claim, even though his termination led to both the ADEA and the fraud claims. According to the court, the original complaint failed to give the defendant notice that fraud might be an issue in the case.

[16] Broader allegations might also help deter objections to evidence at trial. According to Rule 15(b), when a party presents trial evidence "not within the issues raised by the pleadings," an opponent may object if it believes that it will be prejudiced.

[17] *See Davis v. Dallas Area Rapid Transit*, 383 F.3d 309, 313 (5th Cir. 2004) (a party is barred from asserting a claim that, among other things, arises from the same transaction or "nucleus of operative fact" that was the subject of litigation in a prior suit).

later by amendment, the plaintiff is usually "precluded" from asserting that claim in a later suit. The litigation maxim that captures the concept of claim preclusion is "use it or lose it."

In the Olmans' complaint, Lane asserted all claims related to their termination that had factual and legal support. She did so even though it was possible that the Olmans might be fully compensated under a single claim in the complaint, and even though some claims might be weaker than others. Lane knew that if she did not assert all supportable claims, those omitted would likely be lost when the suit was over.

4. Pinning Down the Defendants

Every allegation in the complaint requires a specific response in the defendant's answer.[18] In this respect, the complaint serves an investigative function by requiring that a defendant admit or deny each alleged fact. Facts admitted by the defendant need not be investigated during discovery or proved at trial. Lane knew that the more specific the complaint's allegations, the less room a defendant has to avoid admitting matters that are not really in dispute. In other words, the complaint is a useful tool to narrow the scope of issues in dispute.

5. Telling a Good Story to the Court, the Defendants, and (Perhaps) the Public

The complaint is not evidence per se[19] and will seldom be seen by the jury. Nonetheless, the complaint can serve an important storytelling function.

To begin with, the complaint will often be read by the court and certainly will be studied by the defendants and their lawyers. The court's first impression of the merits of the suit will usually be derived from the complaint. That impression can influence how the court decides the array of motions typically filed before trial. At the very least, it can set a tone for the litigation. In this regard, Lane knew that she had a slight advantage under the pleading rules: the Olmans were permitted to narrate their version of the facts in the complaint, while Full Moon and Belcher were largely limited to responding to this narration in terse admissions or denials. *See* Rule 8(b).

So Lane wanted to use the complaint to preview her story of the Olmans' misfortunes to the court. Lane also knew that a strong complaint sends a message to the defendants. It shows that the plaintiffs' lawyer has competently investigated the law and facts before filing suit. The complaint would say something about the strength of the Olmans' case and about the quality of their lawyer. In some cases, a well-prepared complaint can be the catalyst for settling a suit.

---

[18] Rules 8(b), 10.

[19] There is one important qualification to this statement. Factual allegations made in pleadings are generally deemed to be "judicial admissions" that bind that party in litigation unless the pleading is amended or withdrawn. *See, e.g., In re Worldcom Inc. Securities Litigation,* 308 F. Supp. 2d 214, 232 (S.D.N.Y. 2004).

Finally, court files are usually open to inspection by the general public, including the press.[20] A lawyer should assume that what is said in a complaint will be a matter of public record. Consequently, a plaintiff may sometimes draft the complaint for an audience beyond the court and the plaintiff's adversaries.[21] And a lawyer should certainly not allege something in a complaint that she would not want the public to read.

6. Complying with a Lawyer's Ethical Obligations

As discussed earlier, Lane was required by both her professional code and Rule 11 to adequately investigate the facts and law before filing suit. The allegations in the complaint would reflect the results of her presuit investigation. Lane was required to sign the complaint, and her signature would certify her compliance with Rule 11. A well-pleaded complaint would signal that she had conducted the requisite investigation.[22]

Two ethical questions may arise when pleading a case whose facts are uncertain at the time of pleading. First, may a lawyer ethically allege a claim when concrete evidence to support it is not presently available but may become available through formal discovery? This question can be important when, in a case like the Olmans', the plaintiffs allege that the defendant is engaged in a company-wide practice of age discrimination but presently lack concrete evidence to support these allegations. Second, may a lawyer allege claims that are factually inconsistent, but where either of the two inconsistent allegations may later be proven true?

Rule 11(b)(3) is relevant to the first question. It permits a lawyer to allege matters that will "likely have evidentiary support after a reasonable opportunity for further investigation or discovery," provided that the complaint "specifically . . . identifie[s]" the matter requiring investigation. Examples of such exploratory pleading are found in paragraphs 36 and 56 of the complaint, where Lane alleges that Full Moon's age discrimination was "part of a pattern and practice of age discrimination affecting company-wide downsizing."

Regarding the second question, Rule 8(d)(3) permits multiple allegations "regardless of consistency," and the inconsistent allegations are not considered "admissions" by the plaintiff.[23] At the same time, a lawyer pleading inconsistent allegations must still consider ethical obligations under Rule 11.

---

[20] *See Nixon v. Warner Communications, Inc.*, 435 U.S. 589, 598 (1978) (recognizing a common law right to inspect and copy judicial records, subject to discretion of a supervising judge to prevent inspection for an "improper purpose").

[21] There are limitations on using the complaint for "public advocacy" purposes. For example, Rule 11(b)(1) requires that the complaint not be "presented for any improper purpose." In addition, there may be ethical concerns related to using the complaint for publicity. *See, e.g.*, Model Rule 8.4(d) (generally prohibiting conduct prejudicial to the administration of justice).

[22] Lane's obligations under Rule 11 would come into play whenever she "later advocate[d]" any matter alleged in the complaint. For example, if she later relied on the complaint in responding to a motion, she would again be certifying to the court that the complaint allegations had proper factual and legal support.

[23] *See Schott Motorcycle Supply, Inc. v. American Honda Motor Co., Inc.*, 976 F.2d 58, 61 (1st Cir. 1992).

Consider how these rules might apply in the question below.

Question 6.1

Count One of the complaint alleges that Otis was terminated because of *age discrimination*, while Count Two alleges that he was terminated in *retaliation* for his letter of protest to Full Moon.

1. Was Lane obligated under Rule 11(b)(3) to identify these allegations as matters that "likely will have evidentiary support after a reasonable opportunity for further investigation or discovery," since she obviously did not know when drafting the complaint exactly *why* Full Moon terminated Otis? Did she do this?

2. Assume that Fiona Olman recalls that Belcher sometimes made sexist remarks when he visited the Full Moon store. Assume also that Fiona was replaced by a male employee. Based on this information alone, can Lane allege that Fiona's termination was prompted by gender discrimination without violating Rule 11?

C. Specificity in Pleading

The only "special matters" in the Olmans' complaint *requiring* greater detail under Rule 9 were the fraud allegations in Count Five, and possibly some of the remedies that the Olmans sought.[24] It is worthwhile considering what, exactly, Rule 9 requires.

To begin with, not everything associated with a common law fraud claim needs to be pled with specificity. For example, Rule 9 states that allegations of the defendants' motive and intent in making allegedly fraudulent statements need only be "averred generally."

In alleging Otis's fraud count, Lane paid close attention to Eleventh Circuit precedent, which the trial court would use in assessing the sufficiency of her pleading. According to the Eleventh Circuit, a fraud count satisfies Rule 9(b) if it sets forth "(1) precisely what statements were made in what documents or oral representations or what omissions were made, and (2) the time and place of each such statement and the person responsible for making . . . same, and (3) the content of such statements and the manner in which they misled the plaintiff, and (4) what the defendants obtained as a consequence of the fraud."[25] Another way of stating a plaintiff's pleading burden is to consider the five W's: who, what, when, where, and why. If a fraud claim alleges (1) who

---

[24] Some courts have held, for example, that attorney's fees and damages for emotional distress are "special" damages. *See, e.g., National Liberty Corp. v. Wal-Mart Stores, Inc.*, 120 F.3d 913, 915 (8th Cir. 1997) (attorney's fees); *Smith v. DeBartoli*, 769 F.2d 451, 542-53 n.2 (7th Cir. 1985) (emotional distress).

[25] *Brooks v. Blue Cross and Blue Shield of Florida, Inc.*, 116 F.3d 1364, 1371 (11th Cir. 1997).

committed fraud, (2) the substance of the fraudulent comments, (3) the time when the fraudulent comments were made, (4) the place where the comments were made (e.g., in a writing or in a conversation), and (5) why the comments resulted in harm to the plaintiff, the claim will likely pass muster.

D. Filing and Serving the Complaint

With the complaint in final form, Lane filed it with the federal court along with a filing fee, and "commenced" the suit under Rule 3. Today, complaints and other pleadings are filed electronically in federal and most state courts.[26] The clerk accepts the complaint and fee, assigns the case a case number,[27] starts a file on the case, and randomly assigns the case to a U.S. District Court Judge.

What obligations did Full Moon and Belcher have after the complaint was filed? None. Although the filing of the complaint serves as the "commencement" of the action, filing alone does not require a response by the defendant. To trigger a defense obligation, the plaintiff must "serve" the defendant with the complaint, together with a summons, or get the defendant to agree to waive service.

Those of you who have already studied the materials in Chapter Two now appreciate the importance of the serving process and its relationship to personal jurisdiction. Those who have not studied these materials will later acquire such an appreciation. In either case, the following chapters assume that Lane has properly served process on the defendants.

"Some people say you can't put a price on a wife's twenty-seven years of loyalty and devotion. They're wrong."

---

[26] Certain other documents specified by the local rules of the various district courts are often required to be filed with the complaint. For example, federal courts require the filing of a "civil cover sheet" containing basic information about the case.

[27] Note that the Olmans' complaint has a blank space where the case number will be inserted after the case is filed and a number assigned. In many jurisdictions, the case number reveals information like the date of the complaint's filing, the judge to whom the case is assigned, and the nature of the case (e.g., civil or criminal), provided that one knows the codes used by the clerk of court.

Chapter Seven
The Opening Defense

Chapter Rule References: *5, 8, 9, 11, 12,* 13, 15, 41, 56

A. Full Moon Responds to the Complaint

Bart Tweedy was a seventh-year associate at the Atlanta law firm of Lord, Howe & Mercy, which served as outside counsel for Mizar and its subsidiaries like Full Moon. Tweedy had assumed the defense in *Olman* at the request of a senior partner of the firm, Morgan Ames. Ames was the partner in charge of Full Moon's account and was ostensibly lead counsel in *Olman*, but Tweedy knew that he would do almost all the work on the case prior to trial.[1]

After meeting with Ames, Tweedy immediately went to work developing a formal response to the Olmans' complaint. Defense lawyers are often at a disadvantage when called to represent clients who have been sued. They must respond quickly to a complaint on which the plaintiff's lawyers may have worked for some time.[2] Despite this disadvantage, defense lawyers have the same ethical obligation as plaintiff's counsel to adequately investigate the facts and relevant law before filing any document with the court.[3] And the defense's response to the complaint is ostensibly due within 21 days of the complaint's service. But Tweedy knew that Lane would agree to an extension of time under Rule 6(b). He also had the advantage of having

[1] To appear as counsel in the district court in which the Olmans filed their suit, Tweedy was required either to be a member of the court's bar or to obtain special permission from the court to appear in the suit. He sought such special permission by filing a motion requesting the right to appear *pro hac vice*. The court granted Tweedy's motion, and now he was authorized to, among other things, file motions or pleadings in response to the Olmans' complaint. As a condition of his *pro hac vice* admission, Tweedy had to associate with an attorney already admitted to practice before the court. Because Ames was a member of the court's bar, Tweedy satisfied the association requirement. He also had to comply with any of the district court's local rules, including its rules of professional responsibility.

[2] A defense lawyer faced with an impractical deadline has the option of requesting an extension of time from opposing counsel or the court. *See* Rule 6(b) (authorizing extensions of time for "good cause"). As a matter of professional courtesy, opposing counsel usually consents to such a request.

[3] *See* Rule 11(b).

represented Full Moon in the EEOC investigation, so he had already begun investigating the facts and the law.

At the outset of the EEOC investigation, Full Moon had offered Otis $100,000 to settle the charges (one year's salary for him). Tweedy thought this was a mistake and recommended against it. But Full Moon's president, Bertie Lurch, seemed concerned that the Olmans' charges could snowball. Already, a few other employees laid off during Full Moon's downsizing had filed charges of age discrimination with the EEOC. Tweedy suspected that Eleanor Lane was counseling some of these ex-employees.

Full Moon had offered nothing to settle Fiona Olman's complaint. The company had sensibly realized that any settlement offer to Fiona would signal its doubts about the enforceability of the liability releases that Fiona and many other former employees had signed. The generous settlement offer to Otis Olman was intended to placate Fiona as well, but it had not worked.

Tweedy felt fairly confident he could prove that Full Moon management in Atlanta had not acted with discriminatory motives. His conversations with executive decision makers convinced Tweedy that Full Moon's downsizing decisions were driven by corporate finances. Under prior management, Full Moon had been overpaying its store managers. A manager with Otis Olman's qualifications merited a salary of no more than $60,000-$75,000. Sid Shockley, for example, was now being paid a base salary of $70,000, with a bonus tied to annual sales.

The potential Achilles' heel for Full Moon's case was Bruce Belcher. During the EEOC investigation, Belcher had provided an affidavit supporting Full Moon's position that it had not discriminated against the Olmans. His affidavit stated that at the time he made recommendations for downsizing, he acted in good faith based on the company's financial goals dictated by management in Atlanta. And Belcher flatly denied Otis's assertions that he shared the ageist sentiments that Shockley had imprudently articulated.

But this was *before* Belcher left Full Moon. Belcher now worked for another company in Connecticut and would have separate defense counsel in the Olmans' suit. He had left the company under a cloud. For some time, Full Moon had suspicions about Belcher's expense accounts. Things came to a head when Belcher was arrested for soliciting a prostitute in Atlanta and Full Moon's accountants began scrutinizing invoices for room service and "bath supplies." Full Moon had severed its relationship with Belcher with as little acrimony as possible. But Belcher was unreliable, and he was the Olmans' best means of tying Full Moon to age discrimination. Atlanta management had considered the recommendations of regional managers like Belcher when making downsizing decisions. A jury might believe the Olmans' allegations that Belcher acted with ageist motives and, in turn, tainted management decisions in Atlanta. And he might have an incentive to recede from his earlier testimony supporting the company's defense if the Olmans agreed to dismiss him from the suit.

Shockley was also a problem. Shockley had openly professed to other employees that he was better suited than Otis to manage the Jacksonville store as it continued to expand into the youth-oriented, extreme sporting goods market. He also expressed his belief that Full Moon had already exhausted the market of older customers who identified with Otis. In response to Shockley's indiscreet remarks about older store managers and customers, Full Moon had even given him a written reprimand and required that he attend special "diversity training" in which he was counseled to speak more respectfully about older employees. But Shockley remained as store manager, and the Olmans were sure to interpret this as tacit support for a company culture disfavoring older employees.

Even assuming Tweedy could show that the decision to replace Otis as store manager was profit driven, he still faced significant hurdles defending against Otis's claim of retaliation. The company president, Bertie Lurch, had acted rashly in sending a termination letter to Otis on the heels of Otis's protest letter. Although Lurch may have believed that he had legitimate reasons for terminating Otis, the timing of his action looked suspicious. If a jury found that Lurch ultimately decided to fire Otis in retaliation for his complaint of age discrimination, the company would be liable.

Tweedy had identified several substantive defenses to the Olmans' suit. He would move to have *all* of Fiona's claims thrown out based on the release she signed. He would also move to dismiss Otis's fraud claim based on its patent legal insufficiency: How could Otis have "reasonably relied" on a promise of lifetime job security when his contract stated that his employment was for four years?

Tweedy had other statutory defenses under the ADEA. He thought he could show that Full Moon targeted higher-paid management during its downsizing, not older workers per se. Replacement of management for economic reasons would show Full Moon based its decisions on "reasonable factors other than age," which is a defense under the ADEA.[4] Tweedy also intended to show that Full Moon had "good cause" to terminate Otis, another defense under the ADEA.[5] A few current employees would testify that Otis had behaved poorly after receiving notice that he was being replaced by Shockley. This insubordination showed that Otis could no longer continue working for the Full Moon Sports Outdoor Center. Even worse, Shockley had told Tweedy about what appeared to be an act of theft by Otis. In spring 2022, Shockley saw Otis loading two costly fiberglass kayaks onto an SUV owned by Otis's son. Shockley could find no records indicating Otis's son had paid for the boats. The apparent theft of this, and possibly other store inventory, provided Full Moon good cause for terminating Otis.

Fortunately for Tweedy, he did not have to navigate litigation strategy through counsel for Full Moon's insurance company. Tweedy had reviewed Full Moon's commercial liability policy and found it excluded coverage for "intentional" wrongdoing by employees, which expressly encompassed violations of "employment discrimination laws." Full Moon's insurer had repudiated any obligation to indemnify or defend the company, and Tweedy concluded the insurer's response was well supported.

---

[4] Even if an employer's decision has an adverse impact on older employees, the decision is lawful if it is based on "reasonable factors other than age." *See* 29 U.S.C. § 623(f)(1).

[5] It is not unlawful to discharge an older employee "for good cause." *See* 29 U.S.C. § 623(f)(3).

Procedural rules provided Tweedy with two general options in responding to the complaint. First, Tweedy could file a "pre-answer motion" attacking some aspect of the complaint or the case. Second, he could respond to the complaint's allegations by filing an answer. We discuss both of these responses below.[6]

1. Pre-Answer Motions

If Tweedy chose to respond to the complaint by first filing an answer, he could include virtually all of Full Moon's defenses to the suit. His answer could include challenges to the court's power to hear the case, as well as challenges to the adequacy of the complaint's allegations.[7] But an answer merely *preserved* these defenses for later litigation. The court would normally not rule on them until Tweedy later filed a motion asking the court to rule.[8]

The Federal Rules provided Tweedy with a more aggressive option: he could assert some of Full Moon's strongest challenges in a pre-answer motion and request that the court rule on them early in the suit.[9] Over the years, Tweedy had developed a checklist of possible challenges to assert in a pre-answer motion, most of which are found in Rule 12. While several of

---

[6] Rule 7.1 also requires that private corporations like Full Moon file a "disclosure statement" that identifies, among other things, "any parent corporation." Full Moon was required to file this disclosure statement with its "first appearance, pleading, petition, motion, response, or other request addressed to the court." Rule 7.1(b)(1). By requiring Full Moon to disclose its parent corporation, Mizar, Inc., the rule enabled the judge to identify potential conflicts of interest, including any conflict the judge might have (e.g., if the judge was a shareholder of Mizar).

[7] Rule 12(b) states that "every defense to a claim for relief in any pleading must be asserted in the responsive pleading if one is required," but it goes on to say that the defenses enumerated in subsections (1) through (7) may be asserted by motion. On rare occasions an objection *must* be asserted before filing an answer. The best example is a Rule 12(e) motion for more definite statement. This motion "must be made before filing a responsive pleading" since the ground for seeking a more definite statement is that the complaint is so vague that the defendant "cannot reasonably prepare a response."

[8] A party that has preserved a Rule 12 defense by asserting it in the answer will typically file a motion at some point asking the court to rule on the defense. Rule 12(i) states that, on motion of a party, most Rule 12 defenses "must be heard and decided before trial unless the court orders a deferral until trial." Although it might seem more expeditious to assert Rule 12 defenses in a pre-answer motion, a party may want to defer action on the defense when, for example, it needs to obtain further information before asking the court to rule. If, say, a defendant suspects that the plaintiff's citizenship prevents the court from exercising subject matter jurisdiction, but needs to conduct discovery to verify its suspicion, the best tack is to include an objection to subject matter jurisdiction in the answer. Upon confirming its suspicion through discovery, the defendant can then file a motion asking the court to dismiss for lack of subject matter jurisdiction.

[9] In most federal courts, motions are not literally handed to the judge for a decision when filed. Instead, motions as well as supporting and opposing memoranda are typically reviewed by the judge's clerk. Most judicial clerks are recent law school graduates who are hired by individual judges to provide research and writing support. (Judicial clerks should be distinguished from "the clerk of court," an administrative officer involved with the administration of the court's business.) The clerk will read the parties' submissions, review necessary parts of the record, do legal research to independently assess the parties' characterizations of the law, and—usually—draft opinions for the judge. *See* Richard A. Posner, The Federal Courts: Challenge and Reform 143 (1996) (discussing the clerk's role as a "judicial ghostwriter"). This process takes time, and a motion may not be decided till long after its filing.

these challenges are also available to a plaintiff, they are most often used by a defending party. Tweedy's checklist of challenges included the following:

- *Power motions*: These are objections to the court's power to hear the case. They include challenges under Rule 12(b)(1)-(5) to the court's subject-matter jurisdiction, personal jurisdiction, venue, and service of process.[10]

- *Pleading motions*: These are challenges to the form or content of the complaint or other pleadings, and they include the motion to dismiss for failure to state a claim under Rule 12(b)(6); the motion for a more definite statement under Rule 12(e); and the motion to strike legally insufficient defenses or otherwise improper allegations (e.g., "impertinent" or "scandalous" statements) under Rule 12(f). In addition, Rule 9(b) sets forth heightened pleading requirements for certain matters; the failure to meet these requirements can serve as the basis for a pre-answer motion, as we will discuss later in this chapter.

- *Substantive motions*: In appropriate cases, one party may seek to have the claims or assertions of an opposing party summarily judged, based on the argument that indisputable evidence shows that the opponent's position lacks merit. This *summary judgment* motion is authorized by Rule 56 and can be sought by a defendant "at any time." *See* Rule 56(b). We will discuss summary judgment motions in much greater detail in Chapter Eleven. Suffice it to say for now that, if a defendant has incontrovertible evidence that the plaintiff's case, or part of it, must fail, the defendant may present this evidence to the court and avoid further litigation by obtaining summary judgment.

- *Miscellaneous motions*: There are other pre-answer motions not specifically addressed in the Federal Rules. For example, a defendant can seek to transfer the case to another federal court.[11] Or, in the right circumstances, the defendant might ask the trial judge to disqualify opposing counsel from handling the plaintiff's case, or even ask the trial judge to "recuse" herself from hearing the case.[12]

a. Power Motions

Detailed discussion of the "power" motions available to Tweedy requires background knowledge of the concepts of subject matter jurisdiction, personal jurisdiction, service of process,

---

[10] These power motions also included a challenge under Rules 12(b)(7) and 19 to the plaintiff's failure to join an indispensable party.

[11] *See, e.g.*, 28 U.S.C. § 1404 (authorizing a motion to transfer a case to another federal district court "for the convenience of parties and witnesses" and "in the interest of justice").

[12] For example, if the plaintiff's lawyer had previously represented the defendant in another matter, a motion to disqualify the lawyer might be proper. Similarly, if there were grounds for suspecting that the judge lacked impartiality (for example, the judge had a personal bias against the defendant), the defendant might ask the judge to recuse himself or herself. *See, e.g.*, 28 U.S.C. § 455(a) (a judge "shall disqualify himself in any proceeding in which his impartiality might reasonably be questioned").

and venue. These concepts are explored in Chapters Two through Five. For now, we focus on one important procedural aspect of power motions: many challenges to a court's power to hear a case can be *forfeited* early in litigation through a lawyer's inadvertence.

The Federal Rules establish numerous time periods for taking various procedural actions. Often a lawyer's failure to comply with these time limitations can be excused by the court for good reason.[13] But at other times, failure to comply with these limitations is fatal and results in the procedural waiver of a party's right to take action. Such waivers can even result in a party's loss of the right to assert an otherwise valid defense. Among the defenses that can be irrevocably waived by a lawyer's failure to act timely are objections to personal jurisdiction, venue, and service of process. *See* Federal Rule 12(g)(2) & 12(h)(1). To help you understand how a lawyer can inadvertently waive his or her client's right to make these objections, consider the following questions. Make sure that you carefully read Rule 12 when answering them.

Question 7.1

1. Assume that Tweedy files a Rule 12(b)(6) motion to dismiss Otis's fraud count on the ground that it fails to state a claim. He later discovers that service of process on his client was defective. Tweedy's Rule 12(b)(6) motion has not yet been ruled on by the court. Can Tweedy now file a second motion under Rule 12(b)(5) challenging service of process if he acts promptly?

2. Can Tweedy avoid the procedural waiver discussed above by simply asserting his objection to service of process later in Full Moon's *answer*? Why or why not?

b. Pleading Motions

The Olmans had alleged *prima facie* cases of age discrimination and retaliation, and Tweedy saw no plausible ground to attack the sufficiency of these allegations. Otis's fraud claim was a different matter.

Rule 9(b) states that when pleading fraud, "a party must state with particularity the circumstances constituting fraud." As discussed earlier,[14] Rule 9(b) alters the notice pleading standard set out in Rule 8(a). Tweedy carefully considered whether Otis's fraud claim satisfied Rule 9(b)'s pleading requirements and, if it did not, what he could do about it. Consider the question below.

---

[13] As we will see later in this chapter, if a defendant fails to file a timely answer to the complaint and default is entered, the court may set aside the default for "good cause."

[14] *See* Chapter Six.

Question 7.2

1. Review the earlier discussion in Chapter Six regarding the particularities required in a fraud allegation, and re-read Count Five of the complaint alleging fraud. Do the allegations in the fraud claim satisfy the special pleading requirements of Rule 9(b)?

2. If Tweedy concludes that Otis's fraud count is not pled with sufficient particularity, what Rule 12 motions can he file to assert his objection? (*Hint*: There are at least two available motions.) Which motion do you think preferable? Why? Can both options be used?

Tweedy ultimately declined to challenge the factual sufficiency of the fraud allegations. He chose instead to make what he considered to be a more decisive challenge to the fraud count. On its face, the count's allegations showed that Otis Olman was *legally precluded* from recovering for fraud. Whereas Otis might amend his complaint and cure any deficiency in the manner in which he had pleaded the fraud count, he could not amend to circumvent a basic flaw in his theory of recovery.[15]

The fraud count alleged that Otis was defrauded by Belcher's oral promise of a *lifetime* job, but it also alleged he had entered into a written employment contract limited to *four years*.[16] The legal precedent uncovered during Tweedy's research indicated that a victim of fraud has no claim if he has not "justifiably" relied on a promise. And when an allegedly fraudulent, oral promise contradicts the terms of a written contract—which Otis's own pleadings showed was the case with Belcher's promise of a lifetime job—reliance is unjustifiable as a matter of law. In short, Otis's complaint admitted that he could not satisfy one element of a fraud claim, justifiable reliance.

[15] Most jurisdictions give a party whose pleading is insufficient at least one chance to cure the defect by filing an amended pleading. This reflects the philosophy that cases should be decided on their merits, not as the result of technical pleading errors.

[16] *See* Chapter Six, complaint ¶ 20.

"No, Jimmy, I distinctly said you can *halve* your allowance if you mow the lawn. That's why we ask for things in writing."

Our earlier depiction of a legal claim as a table that relies on all its legs (i.e., elements of the claim) to stand helps illustrate the nature of Tweedy's challenge to Otis's fraud claim. A fraud claim is supported by four "legs" that include (1) a false representation, (2) which the promisor (Belcher, in this case) knew was false, (3) made to induce reliance by the promisee (Otis), and (4) on which the promisee had justifiably relied to his detriment. To prevail on a Rule 12(b)(6) motion, Tweedy only had to point out that *assuming* the allegations in Otis's fraud count were true, that count must fail as a matter of law, for it admitted that Otis didn't justifiably rely on Belcher's promise of lifetime employment. Somewhat ironically, Lane had actually alleged the fatal deficiency in Otis's fraud count by simultaneously pleading that he was promised a lifetime job and yet signed a contract obligating Full Moon to only four years of employment.

So Tweedy filed a motion under Rule 12(b)(6) seeking to dismiss Otis's fraud count for failure to state a claim. Below is an excerpted version of Tweedy's motion and supporting memorandum.[17] When you consider these filings, note that Tweedy does not argue facts outside those alleged in Otis's complaint, and he accepts as true the complaint's allegations. This is the hallmark of the motion to dismiss for failure to state a claim.

[17] Rule 7(b)(1)(B) requires that motions "state with particularity" the grounds supporting the motion. Most federal courts now require that the motion include supporting argument and legal authorities within it, and thus reject an older practice where the motion and supporting memorandum were two separate documents. *See, e.g.,* Local Rule 3.01(a) for the Middle District of Florida.

UNITED STATES DISTRICT COURT
FOR THE MIDDLE DISTRICT OF FLORIDA
JACKSONVILLE DIVISION

OTIS AND FIONA OLMAN,

Plaintiffs,

v. Case No. 8-23-CV-00637

FULL MOON SPORTS, INC.,
& BRUCE BELCHER

Defendants.

DEFENDANT'S MOTION TO DISMISS COUNT FIVE
FOR FAILURE TO STATE A CLAIM
AND SUPPORTING MEMORANDUM

Defendant Full Moon Sports, Inc., asks that this Court dismiss Count Five of plaintiff Otis Olman's complaint for failure to state a claim upon which relief can be granted. In Count Five, Olman alleges he was the victim of fraud when he justifiably relied on an oral promise of lifetime employment at the time he renewed his employment relationship with Full Moon. Yet Olman admits in his complaint that he signed a written contract with Full Moon in which he specifically agreed to a *four-year* term. Based on this admission, Olman's fraud count fails as a matter of Florida law. Florida courts consistently hold that a person alleging fraud cannot justifiably rely on an oral promise that is contradicted by the express terms of a contract he enters into. For this reason, the Court should dismiss Count Five of Olman's complaint under Rule 12(b)(6).

* * *

Count Five of Olman's complaint alleges he was defrauded when Full Moon's regional manager "promised Olman he could remain as manager of the Jacksonville store until he retired." Complaint ¶ 47. Olman also alleges he "reasonably relied" on this promise in renewing his employment with Full Moon and declining the opportunity to become partner in another business. *Id.* ¶ 50.

In order to state a claim for fraud, a plaintiff must allege (1) a false statement of material fact, (2) made by a person who knew or should have known the statement was false, (3) with the intent that the plaintiff rely on the false statement, and (4) on which the plaintiff justifiably or reasonably relies to his detriment. *See Taylor Woodrow Homes Florida, Inc. v. 4/46-A Corporation*, 850 So. Ed 536 (Fla. 5th DCA 2003). A long line of Florida decisions affirms that a party alleging fraud cannot "reasonably rely" on a promise that directly contradicts the term of a contract entered into after the alleged fraudulent statement is made. As one Florida court has observed, "a party may not recover in fraud for an alleged false statement when disclosure of the truth is subsequently revealed in a written agreement between the parties." *Taylor Woodrow, supra.* Likewise, in *Wilson v. Equitable Life Assurance Society of the United States* the court affirmed that "a party cannot maintain an action in fraud if the alleged misrepresentation is explicitly contradictory to a specific and unambiguous provision in a written contract." 622 So. 2d 25, 28 (Fla. 2d DCA 1993).

The federal district court's decision in *Eclipse Medical, Inc. v. American Hydro-Surgical Instruments, Inc.*, 262 F. Supp. 2d 1334 (S.D. Fla. 1999) is directly on point. In *Eclipse*, the plaintiffs alleged they were defrauded when the defendant "gave false assurances that [it] intended and agreed to a long-term relationship," but terminated their distributorship upon expiration of the written contract term. *Id.* at 1342. The court rejected the plaintiff's fraud claim as a matter of law because "the clear and unambiguous language of the Agreement itself specifically contradicts [the] alleged misstatements. . . ." As the court commented, "Florida courts have made clear that no action for fraud in the inducement will lie when the alleged fraud contradicts the subsequent written contract." *Id; see also Pettinelli v. Danzig*, 722 F.2d 706, 709-10 (11th Cir. 1984) (reliance was unjustified when alleged misrepresentations were contradicted by subsequent contract terms); *Barnes v. Burger King Corp.*, 932 F. Supp. 1420, 1428 (S.D. Fla. 1996) (reliance on promises contradicted by the terms of a franchise agreement was "unreasonable as a matter of law").

Therefore, Count Five of Olman's complaint fails to state a claim of fraud under Florida law because his complaint admits he unreasonably relied on a promise that was clearly and unambiguously contradicted by the employment contract he signed. Count Five of the complaint should be dismissed.

Respectfully submitted,

____

Harrison Ames, Esq.
Bart A. Tweedy, Esq.
Lord, Howe & Mercy, P.A.
Counsel for Full Moon Sports, Inc.
[Further detail omitted]

The undersigned certifies that this document was served on counsel of record via the Court's ECF System on March 21, 2023.[18]

____

Harrison Ames, Esq.

[18] Strictly speaking, Rule 5(d) requires no certificate of service when lawyers file documents using a court's electronic filing system. That system ensures that all party lawyers are sent electronic notice of such filings. But some lawyers continue to recite that service has been accomplished.

When Full Moon's attorneys file this document using the district court's electronic filing system, all attorneys who have appeared in the case will receive a Notice of Electronic Filing, with a link to the filed document (as well as any exhibits, if any). The Notice would look something like this:

> **U.S. DISTRICT COURT**
> **MIDDLE DISTRICT OF FLORIDA**
>
> **Notice of Electronic Filing**
>
> The following transaction was entered by Ames, Harrison on 3/21/2023 at 4:59 PM EST and filed on 3/21/2023.
>
> **Case Name:** Otis Olman, et al. v. Full Moon Sports, Inc., et al.
> **Case Number:** 8-23-CV-00637
> **Filer:** Full Moon Sports, Inc.
> **Document Number:** 3
>
> **Docket Text:**
> Defendant's Motion to Dismiss Count Five for Failure to State a Claim and Supporting Memorandum
>
> 8-23-CV-00637 Notice has been electronically mailed to:
>
> Eleanor Lane Elane@yahoo.com

Before we continue with a discussion of Full Moon's defensive motions, notice that the motion and memorandum filed by Tweedy contain none of the legalese too commonly found in court filings. The motion doesn't begin with the dreary formulation, "Now comes the Defendant by and through undersigned counsel and hereby alleges. . . ." The motion omits quotation and explication of the governing federal rule, Rule 12(b)(6), with which the federal judge is no doubt familiar.

The motion also states at the outset the relief Full Moon seeks and why it's entitled to that relief. According to legal-writing expert Bryan Garner,[19] lawyers fail to do this in some 99% of the legal filings he has reviewed[20]—an impression shared by your authors. One reason for this failure is that too many lawyers believe that they must draft memoranda and briefs that look like the documents they see other lawyers filing—the ones that put off telling the court the gist of the lawyer's position until the court has plowed through a lot of "boring word

---

[19] You might be interested to know that Bryan Garner headed the committee that revised and simplified the wording of the Federal Rules of Civil Procedure. If you think they're difficult to understand in their present form, you should have read them in past decades.

[20] *See* GARNER ON LANGUAGE AND WRITING xxxiv (ABA 2009).

gravel." Take a look at the Federal Rules and local rules governing the documents that you file. Nowhere will you find any requirement that you draft documents that look or read like those commonly found in court files. Nowhere.

So appreciate early in your legal study that much of what you read in the filings of other lawyers should be discarded. If you write simply and clearly and tell the busy judicial reader what you're asking for at the outset of your written advocacy, you'll please the court. As one judge has remarked, "Good writing is rewarded so automatically that you don't even think about it."[21]

c. Other Possible Motions

Tweedy considered two other possible pre-answer responses to the complaint. Full Moon had provided him a copy of Fiona's signed release, in which she waived all legal claims against the company in exchange for severance pay. Tweedy believed this document was irrefutable evidence defeating Fiona's claims of age discrimination.

Yet Tweedy could not assert this defense through a Rule 12(b)(6) motion. A motion under Rule 12(b)(6) is based on the assumption that the facts alleged in the complaint are true but legally insufficient. Tweedy wanted to interject a *new* fact never mentioned in the complaint—the release—which he believed provided an incontrovertible defense to Fiona Olman's claims. A motion to dismiss is not the proper tool to attack a claim when the movant intends to rely on facts not alleged in the complaint. To have Fiona's claims thrown out based on the release, Tweedy would have to use a Rule 56 motion for summary judgment.[22] This motion would allow Tweedy to introduce the release as evidence and seek to have Fiona's claims disposed of without further litigation. Later, we examine how Tweedy employed this procedural strategy.

---

[21] *Id.* at 62 (quoting Judge Murry Cohen of the Texas appellate courts).

[22] At the same time, Rule 12(d) permits a challenge to the complaint to be "treated as one for summary judgment under Rule 56" when matters outside the pleading are presented to the court.

Short of filing a motion for summary judgment, Tweedy considered another tack to induce Lane and Fiona to *voluntarily* dismiss Fiona's claims. When Lane filed the complaint, she certified under Rule 11(b) that she had made a "reasonable" inquiry into the facts underlying the Olmans' claims and those claims had evidentiary support. It appeared to Tweedy that Lane had either failed to make a reasonable inquiry or had been misinformed by her client. In any event, once Tweedy brought to Lane's attention the signed release, Lane could not persist with Fiona's claims without risking sanctions.[23] If Lane acknowledged her ethical duty to dismiss Fiona's legally unwarranted claims, Tweedy could achieve victory for his client with minimum cost.

Had Tweedy known Lane personally, he might have called Lane directly and advised her of the release. Among the lawyers Tweedy knew, it was considered good decorum to give one's adversary the opportunity to correct obvious mistakes. Judges also prefer to have lawyers fix obvious problems informally without involving the court, as is reflected in several procedural rules obliging lawyers to confer with opposing counsel before seeking relief from the court.[24] But Tweedy's prior dealings with Lane had been a bit contentious, and he decided to follow the formal procedures set out in Rule 11.

Question 7.3

Discuss the actions Tweedy must take if he wants to use Rule 11 to induce Lane to voluntarily dismiss Fiona's claims. Why can't Tweedy simply file a Rule 11 motion for sanctions with the court and bring Lane's mistake to the court's immediate attention?

2. Full Moon's Answer

A defendant's second general option for responding to the complaint is to file an answer. According to Rule 12(a), a defendant has 21 days after being served[25] with the summons and

---

[23] According to Rule 11(b), if Lane later "presented" or "advocated" Fiona's claims contained in the complaint, she would be certifying to the court that they had adequate evidentiary support. Unless Lane had some ground for invalidating the release, she could no longer advocate Fiona's claims in good faith.

[24] For example, Rule 37 governing sanctions for discovery misconduct often requires that a lawyer seeking sanctions certify that, before moving for court sanctions, the lawyer has conferred in good faith with opposing counsel in an effort to cure the problem without court action.

[25] According to Rule 5(a), most documents filed with the court—including pleadings and written motions—must be "served on every party." The service of documents, rather than their filing, is the act that typically triggers an opponent's responsive obligation. The service of pleadings, motions, and other documents on parties to the litigation, which is governed by Rule 5, should be distinguished from formal service of the initial complaint and summons, governed by Rule 4 and discussed in Chapter Two. In the federal courts, attorneys electronically file documents with the court using the CM/ECF system, which allows for automatic electronic service on all other parties to the case, in compliance with Rule 5. Attorneys are immediately notified of another party's new filing and provided with a link

complaint to serve a responsive answer.[26] As discussed earlier, this 21-day deadline can place defense counsel not already familiar with the case at quite a disadvantage because counsel is expected to research the law and the facts, and thus comply with his ethical obligations under Rule 11, before filing an answer. For this reason, many defendants don't in fact serve their answers within 21 days. One means of avoiding this deadline is to file a motion for extension of time under Rule 6(b). Most district courts require that the lawyer seeking an extension of time confer with opposing counsel before filing this motion. When the request for an extension is reasonable, standards of professionalism usually dictate that opposing counsel consent. Cooperation also makes good sense, given the likelihood that opposing counsel may herself need an extension at some point during the suit.

There is another way in which the 21-day deadline for serving an answer can be deferred. Consider the following question:

Question 7.4

1. According to Rule 12(a)(4), what effect does Full Moon's service of its motion under Rule 12(b)(6) have on the deadline for filing its answer? What is the new deadline for filing the answer?

2. Does the effect of filing a Rule 12 motion on the deadline for filing an answer suggest a tactical reason why a defendant might want to file *some* pre-answer motion? According to Rule 11(b), is it unethical to file a motion *solely* for the purpose of obtaining more time in which to serve the answer?

Although Tweedy's filing of a Rule 12(b)(6) motion extended the time he had to serve his answer, Tweedy decided he would file Full Moon's answer anyway. He had fully investigated the case and knew how he would respond to the complaint's allegations. In addition, he intended to assert a counterclaim against Otis in the answer that would put Otis on the defense, cast doubt on his credibility, and possibly improve Full Moon's litigation and settlement posture.[27]

---

to the document via an email automatically generated by the system. The Middle District of Florida's Administrative Procedures for Electronic Filing are found at: https://www.flmd.uscourts.gov/sites/flmd/files/documents/flmd-administrative-procedures-for-electronic-filing-4-1-2024-update.pdf (last visited July 23, 2024). Many state courts have adopted similar electronic filing and service systems.

[26] As explained in Chapter Two, the deadline for responding to a complaint is extended to 60, or even 90, days when the defendant agrees to waive service of process.

[27] Tweedy's decision was also influenced by other factors. First, he knew something about how Judge Sarah Goodenough, to whom the Olmans' case had been assigned, managed litigation. Goodenough usually required defendants to file an answer to the complaint despite a pending motion to dismiss. Second, Tweedy was pleased that the Olmans' case had been assigned to Judge Goodenough and he

Over time, Tweedy had developed a mental checklist for items to include in the answer. That checklist included the following:

- *Admit, deny, or DKI*: Under Rule 8(b), Full Moon was obliged to respond to each specific allegation in the Olmans' complaint. Full Moon could (1) admit the truth of an allegation, (2) deny the allegation, or (3) state that it did not have knowledge or information sufficient to determine the allegations's truth (summarized by the acronym "DKI," meaning "deny knowledge or information" sufficient to answer). Tweedy knew that it was important that Full Moon deny all allegations it believed were untrue. If Full Moon failed to deny an allegation, it would be deemed admitted.[28]

- *Affirmative defenses*: Rule 8(c) contained a nonexhaustive list of special defenses Full Moon needed to assert in its answer. These affirmative defenses are generally thought of as defenses that go beyond mere denial of liability allegations in the complaint. Affirmative defenses state grounds for denying the relief sought by a plaintiff regardless of whether the complaint's allegations are true. Full Moon was obliged to give the Olmans and the court notice in its answer that it intended to rely on these affirmative defenses. Although Full Moon might later seek to amend its answer to include affirmative defenses omitted from its original answer, Tweedy knew that courts might be more reluctant to permit later amendment of the answer to include them—especially when the facts underlying an affirmative defense were known at the time the original answer was filed.

- *Counterclaims and crossclaims*: Rule 13 authorizes a defending party to go on the offensive by asserting its own claims in a defensive pleading. Under Rule 13(a), Full Moon was *required* to assert counterclaims against the Olmans if these "compulsory" counterclaims arose from the occurrences alleged in the Olmans' complaint.[29] Under Rule 13(b), Full Moon was *permitted* to assert counterclaims not arising from the occurrences alleged in the Olmans' complaint. Rule 13(g) also permitted Full Moon to assert a crossclaim against its co-defendant Belcher, provided that the crossclaim arose from the occurrence alleged in the Olmans' complaint.[30]

---

wanted to ensure that she continued to preside over the case. According to Rule 41(a)(1)(A)(i), a plaintiff has the right to dismiss her case "before the opposing party serves either an answer or a motion for summary judgment. . . ." By filing Full Moon's answer, Tweedy could eliminate the risk that Lane might voluntarily dismiss the suit and attempt to obtain a different judge when she refiled. Although such attempts to "judge-shop" are not common, Tweedy had witnessed them in prior litigation.

[28] *See* Rule 8(b)(6). The exception is an allegation of the "amount of damages" claimed by the plaintiff, which does not require an explicit denial. Attorneys sometimes answer allegations with creative but unauthorized forms of responses, such as demanding "strict proof" of an allegation or answering that a document described in the allegation "speaks for itself." Such answers violate Rule 8(b), which authorizes only three possible responses: admit, deny, or DKI. *See Donnelly v. Frank Shirley Cadillac*, 2005 WL 2445902 (N.D. Ill. Sep. 29, 2005). Answering in a form that does not comply with Rule 8(b) is risky. The district court has discretion to treat such an answer as an admission of the allegation. *See id.*

[29] Rule 13(a) also states a few other grounds that will relieve a party from the duty of pleading what would otherwise be a compulsory counterclaim.

[30] *See* Chapter Ten (discussing joinder of counterclaims and crossclaims).

Tweedy had conducted a careful investigation of the Olmans' charges and was prepared to answer the complaint consistent with his obligations under Rule 11. Full Moon would deny all allegations of liability. In addition, Full Moon would assert a few affirmative defenses to liability, including that (1) Full Moon's downsizing decisions were based on "reasonable factors other than age" and (2) Fiona had executed a release absolving Full Moon of all liability.[31]

Question 7.5

Recall that Full Moon has filed a Rule 12(b)(6) motion seeking dismissal of Otis's fraud count. Assume, for the purposes of this question, that Full Moon had *not* filed this pre-answer motion. How, in its answer, would Full Moon assert the defense that the fraud count failed to allege a legally sufficient claim? Is this an affirmative defense that must be specifically pled in Full Moon's answer? Or can Full Moon assert this defense by simply denying allegations in the fraud count?

Finally, Tweedy intended to assert a counterclaim against Otis. He would base this claim on the tort of "conversion" and ask that Otis reimburse Full Moon for the cost of the two kayaks he had apparently "given" to his son, together with the cost of any other inventory Otis had taken. The counterclaim would also support Full Moon's affirmative defense that it had non-discriminatory "good cause" to terminate Otis and would lessen Otis's credibility in court.[32]

Tweedy decided not to assert a crossclaim against Belcher. Although Belcher might have a duty to indemnify Full Moon if the company was found liable for fraud, Tweedy did not want to make Belcher an adversary at this time. He could always amend Full Moon's answer to include a crossclaim at a later date, assuming the claim survived Full Moon's motion to dismiss. And because Full Moon's crossclaim for indemnification was not compulsory, the company could always file a separate suit seeking indemnification if it were found liable for Belcher's actions.

Below is the answer Tweedy filed on behalf of Full Moon. Note how the answer uses the various procedural responses discussed above.[33]

---

[31] Only the release is specifically identified in Rule 8(c) as an affirmative defense. But the list of affirmative defense in Rule 8(c) is not exhaustive. Tweedy decided to plead that Full Moon acted based on "reasonable factors other than age" because case law was still unsettled as to whether this constituted an affirmative defense. *See, e.g., Smith v. City of Jackson*, 544 U.S. 228 (2005).

[32] At first glance, one might think that a defendant that denies allegations in the complaint has a ready-made counterclaim for *libel*. But the prevailing rule in American law is that allegations in pleadings are "privileged" and cannot serve as the basis for a libel claim, so long as they are relevant to the subject matter of the suit. *See* 50 Am. Jur. 2d Libel & Slander § 285 (2016).

[33] Again, be reminded that the answer's format may differ from the format requirements of various local rules. At the same time, the wording and substance of the answer are compatible with all court rules we're aware of. Notice the relatively plain-spoken manner in which the answer responds to allegations in the complaint. The more formalistic phrasings often found in pleadings are not required and rarely serve any purpose.

IN THE UNITED STATES DISTRICT COURT
FOR THE MIDDLE DISTRICT OF FLORIDA
JACKSONVILLE DIVISION

OTIS AND FIONA OLMAN,

Plaintiffs,

v. Case No. 8-23-CV-00637

FULL MOON SPORTS, INC.,
& BRUCE BELCHER

Defendants

ANSWER AND COUNTERCLAIM
OF DEFENDANT FULL MOON SPORTS, INC.

Notice how the complaint's use of numbered allegations, as well as Full Moon's response to each allegation, made it easier to determine what issues are in controversy.

1. Admitted.

2. Defendant admits that it is incorporated in Delaware and that it has its principal place of business in Georgia. Defendant further admits that the Court has jurisdiction of Plaintiffs' ADEA claims. Defendant is without knowledge or information sufficient to admit or deny the remainder of Plaintiffs' jurisdictional allegations.

Rule 8(b)(5) permits a party lacking sufficient information to admit or deny an allegation to say so, and this is construed as a denial.

3. Defendant is without knowledge or information sufficient to admit or deny the allegations in paragraph 3.

Parties

4. Admitted.

5. Admitted.

6. Admitted.

7. Admitted.

General Allegations

8. Admitted.

9. Defendant admits Olman became store manager in 2011 but denies the Jacksonville store was a marginally profitable business.

Rule 8(b)(4) requires that a party exercise good faith in denying only those *parts* of an allegation that it can't admit.

10. Admitted.

11. Denied insofar as Plaintiffs imply Olman was responsible for the Jacksonville store's increased profitability.

12. Admitted.

13. Admitted.

14. Admitted.

15. Defendant is without knowledge or information sufficient to admit or deny the allegations in paragraph 15.

16. Admitted.

17. Defendant is without knowledge or information sufficient to admit or deny the allegations in paragraph 17.

18. Defendant is without knowledge or information sufficient to admit or deny the allegations in paragraph 18.

19. Denied.

20. Denied.

21. Admitted.

22. Admitted.

23. Defendant is without knowledge or information sufficient to admit or deny the allegations in paragraph 23, insofar as they are based on conversations between Belcher and Olman.

24. Defendant is without knowledge or information sufficient to admit or deny the allegations in paragraph 24, insofar as they are based on conversations between Belcher and Olman.

25. Defendant is without knowledge or information sufficient to admit or deny the allegations in paragraph 25, insofar as they are based on conversations between Belcher and Olman. Defendant admits Fiona Olman was terminated.

26. Defendant is without knowledge or information sufficient to admit or deny the allegations in paragraph 26, insofar as they are based on conversations between Belcher and Olman.

27. Denied.

28. Defendant admits that Olman wrote a letter to Full Moon's president and that Full Moon's president responded to the letter. Defendant admits that Full Moon terminated Olman. Defendant admits that Olman refused to sign a release. Defendant denies the remaining allegations of this paragraph to the extent they are inconsistent with the referenced documents.

29. Defendant is without knowledge or information sufficient to admit or deny the allegations in paragraph 29 insofar as they are based on conversations between Shockley and Olman. The remaining allegations are denied.

30. Defendant is without knowledge or information sufficient to admit or deny the allegations in paragraph 30.

COUNT ONE:

31. Defendant realleges its responses to paragraphs 8-30.

32. Defendant admits that Olman was 53 years of age when Defendant commenced its corporate downsizing. The remaining allegations are denied.

33. Defendant admits that Olman was replaced by a 32-year-old manager and later terminated. The remaining allegations are denied.

34. Denied.

35. Denied.

36. Denied.

37. Denied

COUNT TWO:

38. Defendant realleges its responses to paragraphs 8-30.

39. Defendant denies allegations that it violated the ADEA.

40. Denied.

41. Denied.

COUNT THREE:

42. Defendant realleges its responses to paragraphs 8-30.

43. Denied.

COUNT FOUR:

44. Defendant realleges its responses to paragraphs 8-30.

45. Denied.

COUNT FIVE:

46. Defendant realleges its responses to paragraphs 8-30.

47. Denied.

48. Denied.

49. Denied.

50. Denied.

51. Denied.

COUNT SIX:

52. Defendant realleges its responses to paragraphs 8-30.

53. Denied.

54. Denied.

55. Denied.

56. Denied.

57. Denied.

COUNT SEVEN:

58. Defendant realleges its responses to paragraphs 8-30.

59. Denied.

FIRST AFFIRMATIVE DEFENSE

60. Full Moon based all employment decisions affecting the plaintiffs on reasonable factors other than age.

SECOND AFFIRMATIVE DEFENSE

61. Fiona Olman previously executed a release waiving all claims of liability against defendant Full Moon Sports, Inc.

DEFENDANT'S COUNTERCLAIM FOR CONVERSION AGAINST OTIS OLMAN

62. The Court has supplemental jurisdiction of this counterclaim for conversion because it arises out the same occurrences alleged in Otis Olman's complaint, namely his termination by Full Moon and its reasons for his termination.

63. Early on the morning of March 6, 2022, prior to the opening of the Jacksonville store, Otis Olman was observed loading expensive kayaks and related equipment onto the vehicle of his son.

64. Subsequent review of store records indicates that neither Otis Olman nor his son paid the store for this merchandise, or otherwise made any record that this merchandise had been removed from store premises.

65. Based upon information and belief, Otis Olman has converted store merchandise on several occasions during the time he served as a store manager, including the occasion alleged in paragraphs 63-64.

Therefore, defendant Full Moon Sports, Inc. demands of Otis Olman compensatory damages, punitive damages, costs and attorneys' fees.

Respectfully submitted,

____

Harrison Ames, Esq.
Bart A. Tweedy, Esq.
Lord, Howe & Mercy, P.A.
Counsel for Full Moon Sports, Inc.
[Additional information omitted]

April 21, 2023

[Certificate of Service omitted]

Rule 8(a)(1) requires that all claims, including counterclaims, allege their jurisdictional foundation.

B. Belcher's Belated Response to the Suit

Even though Full Moon had terminated Belcher, for tactical reasons it offered to provide him legal counsel in response to the Olmans' suit. Belcher had somewhat rashly declined the offer.

After being served with the Olmans' summons and complaint in Connecticut (where Belcher now lived), he still neglected to hire a lawyer to respond to the complaint. Lane waited more than a month to receive some response from him. When she received no response, she asked the trial court to enter default against Belcher.

Question 7.6

1. According to Rule 55, what steps must a plaintiff take to have default entered against a nonresponsive defendant?
2. What is the consequence of entry of default?
3. What should a defendant do in response to entry of default if he intends to defend the suit? What must the defendant show the court to have entry of default set aside?
4. What is the difference between *default* and *default judgment*?
5. According to Rule 55, could Lane have asked the clerk of the court to enter default judgment against Belcher? Why or why not?

The clerk entered default against Belcher. When Belcher was notified that default had been entered, he immediately hired a lawyer in Jacksonville. Belcher's lawyer quickly contacted Lane and asked her consent to having the entry of default set aside.[34]

Lane knew that the trial court would inevitably grant Belcher's expeditious motion to set aside the entry of default, so she consented to the motion. Belcher's lawyer then filed an "Unopposed Motion to Set Aside Entry of Default," which was granted by the trial court. After Belcher's default was set aside, his lawyer filed a motion to dismiss the complaint based on the identical ground alleged in Full Moon's earlier motion to dismiss—that the complaint failed to state a claim for fraud.

[34] Local federal court rules typically provide that, prior to filing most motions with the court, counsel for the moving party confer with opposing counsel to see if she will consent to the relief sought in the motion. *See, e.g.*, Local Rule 3.01(g) for the Middle District of Florida. In a subsequently filed motion, the moving lawyer must certify she has complied with this requirement and state whether opposing counsel has consented.

Chapter Eight
Prelude to Discovery

Chapter Rule References: 7, 8, 11, 12, *16*, *26*, 54

A. Lane Responds to the Defendants

Eleanor Lane now had to make several decisions about what to do in light of the defendants' responses to the complaint. These responses included (1) the defendants' motions to dismiss Otis Olman's fraud claim; (2) Full Moon's demand that Lane voluntarily dismiss Fiona Olman's claims or be the subject of a sanctions motion; and (3) Full Moon's answer and counterclaim.

Lane had anticipated the defendants' motion to dismiss Otis's fraud claim. Her own research had uncovered the same case law cited by Full Moon in its motion, which seemed to say that Otis could not rely on an oral promise that contradicted the express provision of his employment contract. Yet Lane still believed she had a plausible argument that this precedent should not be followed in Otis's situation. After all, the Florida Supreme Court—the ultimate authority on Florida common law of fraud—had not specifically held that a fraud claim is precluded by conflicting contract language in a contract of employment.[1] Further, Lane believed the facts of Otis's situation supported an exception to the prevailing rule. Otis, a long-term employee, had been lied to by his regional manager and fraudulently induced to sign an employment contract. She had discovered several cases from other jurisdictions recognizing that, in appropriate circumstances, an employer should not be permitted to make false promises to an employee and then evade liability by relying on contract language.

Lane thought it likely that the trial court would grant the defendants' Rule 12(b)(6) motion, but she believed assertion of the fraud claim was both ethically and tactically sound. In fact, if she wished to preserve the option of appealing to a higher court and seeking to make new precedent, she had to assert the fraud claim.[2]

As for Bart Tweedy's Rule 11 demand that she voluntarily dismiss Fiona's claims because of the release she signed, Lane refused his request. Tweedy's demand had implied that Lane was either incompetent or unethical. But Tweedy had too readily assumed that the release was in fact enforceable.

---

[1] Note that the Florida case precedent regarding fraud is different from the hypothetical precedent you were asked to assume in Chapter One, question 1.1.

[2] A party is usually prohibited from raising an issue on appeal if it is not raised in the trial court. This rule is sometimes described as the "preservation-of-error" requirement, and it ensures that both opposing counsel and the trial court have an opportunity to respond to a suspected error. So Lane had to allege the fraud claim despite her conviction the effort would be futile in the trial court. Note that the necessity of raising and preserving a legal contention in trial court is why Rule 11(b)(2) permits a party to argue an issue foreclosed by existing precedent, so long as he can make "a nonfrivolous argument for extending, modifying, or reversing existing law or for establishing new law."

According to federal law, the release had to strictly comply with statutory requirements. One requirement is that an employee be "advised in writing to consult with an attorney prior to executing the agreement."[3] When Lane scrutinized her client's release, she noticed that it failed to specifically advise Fiona to consult "an attorney." Instead, it contained a vague admonition that Fiona consult with her "advisor" before signing. Based on U.S. Supreme Court precedent insisting that releases carefully comply with federal law, Lane believed she had a strong argument that the release was unenforceable.[4] She had explained this in her response to Tweedy's demand. Lane doubted he would now file a sanctions motion with the court, although he might later seek summary judgment based on the release.

The final decision for Lane was how to respond to Full Moon's answer. The answer contained several components, including (1) admissions and denials, (2) affirmative defenses, and (3) a counterclaim. Lane recognized that she had to consider the *distinct* procedural obligations pertaining to each component.

Question 8.1
Review Federal Rules 7(a) and 8(b)(6). What pleading, if any, must Lane serve in response to the three components of the answer? If she serves no response to Full Moon's answer, what are the consequences? Be specific.

Full Moon's counterclaim had the potential to ruin Otis's case. Otis had never mentioned the incident involving the kayaks, although Lane had questioned him closely about whether Full

---

[3] *See* 29 U.S.C. § 626(f)(4).

[4] *See Oubre v. Entergy Operations Inc.*, 522 U.S. 422, 427-28 (1998) (a release that fails to contain provisions required by federal law is unenforceable); *see also Moroni v. Penwest Pharmaceuticals Co.*, 2009 WL 3335504, at *9 (D.N.J. Oct. 13, 2009) (suggesting that, at a minimum, release language and the employer's oral advice must not leave to inference an employee's right to discuss the release with an attorney before signing it).

Moon might have legitimate reasons for his firing. But when Lane spoke with Otis about the theft allegations, he had an immediate and comforting response.

Otis explained that the kayaks in dispute had *not* belonged to Full Moon. It seems that the store had an annual "used equipment" sale at which customers could bring their sporting equipment to the store and offer it at a flea-market-like sale held in the store parking lot. When one customer brought in the two fiberglass kayaks in question to market at the sale, and Otis learned of the customer's asking price, Otis immediately called his son and told him he should consider buying them. His son contacted the owner and made an offer that was accepted before the day of the sale. Apparently, Shockley had misunderstood what was happening when he saw Otis loading these kayaks onto a vehicle. The kayaks never belonged to the store, and thus there was no "conversion" of Full Moon's merchandise. As for the remainder of Full Moon's allegation, stating that Otis had "converted store merchandise on several occasions," Otis assured Lane that discovery would prove this to be a baseless charge.

In fact, Otis was quite perturbed by Full Moon's allegation of bogus conversion allegations. As you have probably discovered in answering question 8.1, one of Lane's options was to simply deny Full Moon's allegations of conversion in the reply to Full Moon's counterclaim.[5] But Otis asked Lane to consider responding more vigorously to Full Moon's allegations. What were Lane's options other than simply denying Full Moon's allegations? Consider the following question.

Question 8.2

Assume that (1) Otis is particularly concerned that the allegations of theft against him might damage his reputation if they are reported by the news media and (2) in any event, he believes Full Moon should not "get away" with making such wild and frivolous charges in its pleading. How might Lane respond more aggressively to Full Moon's allegations? Which option would you recommend?

B. The Pleadings Are Closed . . . or Are They?

With Lane's serving of a reply to Full Moon's counterclaim, the pleadings were ostensibly closed. Rule 7(a) specifically limits the type and number of pleadings that litigants can file. These include:

- A complaint and an answer in response;
- A counterclaim and an answer in response;

[5] The reply to Full Moon's counterclaim would look in many respects like Full Moon's answer to the Olmans' complaint. Lane would need to admit, deny, or "DKI" each allegation. *See* Rule 8(b). In addition, she would need to plead any affirmative defense to the counterclaim available to her client. *See* Rule 8(c). Because Otis was a defending party with respect to Full Moon's counterclaim, he could employ all the options made available to defending parties, including the filing of Rule 12 motions. *See, e.g.*, Rule 12(b) (power motions), 12(e) (motion for more definite statement), and 12(f) (motion to strike).

- A crossclaim and an answer in response; and,

- A third-party complaint and an answer in response.

Rule 7(a) states that these are the "only" pleadings allowed unless the court orders a "reply to an answer." One way of understanding pleading under the Federal Rules is to focus on the principle that for every "offensive" pleading, there is a corresponding "defensive" pleading. In other words, pleadings form something of a matched set of bookends. According to this philosophy, when a party serves a pleading seeking affirmative relief, the defending party must respond to that pleading. But the pleadings should generally end at this point.

Although Rule 7(a) limits the types of pleadings that may be filed in a suit, Rule 15 adopts a liberal approach to the *amendment* of those pleadings. In the case of pretrial amendment, Rule 15(a) permits parties to amend their pleadings either (1) as a matter of right, or (2) by permission of one's adversary or the court.

A party's right to amend depends on whether that party has served an "offensive" pleading to which her adversary must respond (i.e., a complaint, a counterclaim, a crossclaim, or a third-party complaint) or instead has filed a "defensive" pleading to which there is no response. The basic rules governing the right to amend are these:

- When a party has served a purely defensive pleading—that is, her opponent will not be serving a response under Rule 7(a)—she has a right to amend it within "21 days after serving it." Rule 15(a)(1)(A).

- When a party has served an offensive pleading—and thus is expecting a response from her opponent under Rule 7(a)—she has the right to amend once, provided she amends (1) within 21 days after a responsive pleading is served on her; or (2) within 21 days after a motion under Rule 12(b), (e), or (f) is served. Rule 15(a)(1)(B). The right to amend is cut off 21 days after service of *either* a responsive pleading or a motion, "whichever is earlier." *Id.*

In light of Rule 15(a)'s provision for amendment by right, consider the following question:

Question 8.3

Recall that at this point in the suit, the Olmans have served a complaint on Full Moon; Full Moon has served an answer to the Olmans' complaint, which includes its own counterclaim; and Otis has served a reply to Full Moon's counterclaim. Does any party have the right to amend any of its pleadings at this point? What additional information, if any, do you need to answer this question?

Rule 15(a)(2) imposes no specific time limit on a party's request for permission to amend a pleading. It states instead that a party may amend a pleading "with the opposing party's written consent or the court's leave." The opportunity to amend with the court's permission "should [be] freely give[n] . . . when justice so requires." According to the Supreme Court, this means that an amendment should normally be permitted unless the party opposing it can show either that it will be unduly prejudiced or that the movant has acted in bad faith.[6] Rule 15(a) would suggest, then, that both the Olmans and Full Moon still had opportunities to amend their pleadings to change the claims or the parties, to allege new defenses, or to otherwise revise their allegations. Later in the Guide,[7] we will see how developments during discovery led the Olmans to consider amending their complaint. But as we will learn in the following discussion, the liberality of rules like Rule 15(a) is tempered by the trial court's power to impose its own plan and schedule for the conduct of litigation. We now consider this judicial power of case management.

C. Case Management

At this point in the Olmans' suit, pretrial procedures began to reflect a distinct approach to litigation found in the Federal Rules. This approach is best understood by contrasting it with the approach of state courts. In many state courts, lawyers are free to commence the discovery process soon after the case is filed. The lawyers are largely unsupervised by the court during the discovery process and may proceed according to their own plans and schedule. They also have considerable discretion in taking other pretrial action, including the filing of pretrial motions and the amending of pleadings. In many cases, this attorney freedom results in a pretrial process extending over years and a corresponding delay in the trial date.

Federal court practice is often different.[8] The Federal Rules require that a judge become involved in a suit at an early stage. A federal judge plays an active role in managing the pretrial process, and much of this process occurs within a framework established by the judge. For example, shortly after Lane filed suit, the case was randomly assigned to Judge Sarah Goodenough.[9] Judge Goodenough's first action was to order the parties to confer and develop a discovery plan under Rule 26(f). One important implication of the parties' Rule 26(f) conference was that all discovery, with one minor exception, was *prohibited* until the conference was conducted.[10] Judge Goodenough also scheduled a meeting in her chambers, at which the discovery plan and related matters would be discussed.

---

[6] *See Foman v. Davis,* 371 U.S. 178 (1962).

[7] *See* Chapter Ten.

[8] Both the judge and the parties can influence whether procedural rules operate as intended. Some judges are more lenient in supervising the pretrial process, and some lawyers succeed in bending the rules. Consequently, the text portrayal of the pretrial process reflects the behavior of our hypothetical judge and parties; it may not be an apt description of what occurs in some lawsuits before specific judges.

[9] The prevailing practice among district courts is to assign cases to judges randomly, often with the aid of computer software.

[10] *See* Rule 26(d)(1) ("A party may not seek discovery from any source before the parties have conferred as required by Rule 26(f)."). The exception is for "early" Rule 34 requests for production or inspection of documents or tangible things, including electronically stored information. *See* Rule 26(d)(2). These early document requests may be served prior to the Rule 26(f) conference and are treated as though they were served at the time of that conference. *See* Fed. R. Civ. P. 26(d)(2)(B). Allowing these early requests may permit the parties to identify and address potential issues with

As required by the judge's order and Rule 26(f), the lawyers for the parties in *Olman v. Full Moon* conferred with each other several weeks before their conference with the judge. Because they had experience litigating in federal court, they had a good idea of the type of discovery plan and schedule Judge Goodenough would be willing to approve. They knew that Judge Goodenough would probably approve any reasonable plan, but she would be extremely reluctant to change the plan once she confirmed it in an order.

The lawyers later met in the judge's chambers for a scheduling conference authorized by Rule 16(b). At this conference, Judge Goodenough was empowered to discuss a variety of matters, including deadlines for conducting discovery and filing motions. To begin the meeting, Judge Goodenough announced that she had reached a decision on the defendants' motion to dismiss Otis's fraud claim. She would grant the motion. This meant that Belcher was dismissed from the case, since the only claim asserted against him was a fraud claim. Although Belcher's lawyer was delighted by the judge's ruling, he silently wondered why he had been required to appear at a conference only to be told that his client was no longer a party.

Lane, on the other hand, now faced the prospect of litigating the case without addressing Otis's fraud claim. She still had some hope that, on appeal, she might persuade the federal circuit court to change precedent[11] and reinstate the claim. But the prospect of appealing *after* the trial and having Otis's fraud claim reinstated was not very attractive; essentially, she would

---

the document requests during the Rule 26(f) conference. *See* Fed. R. Civ. P. 26 Advisory Committee Notes (2015 amendment). Rule 26(d)(1) also allows other early discovery requests if authorized by stipulation or by court order.

[11] One option available to the Eleventh Circuit, to which Lane would appeal, was to certify a question to the Florida Supreme Court asking it to decide whether, under Florida law, Otis's employment contract precluded his reliance on the oral promise of lifetime employment made by Belcher. A federal court's ability to ask a state court to resolve an unsettled issue of state law is governed by the jurisdictional power granted to state courts by state law. If the state's jurisdictional law does not permit its courts to answer a question referred by a federal court, the federal court must decide the issue without direct assistance by state courts. For example, the Florida Constitution doesn't give the Florida Supreme Court jurisdictional authority to answer a certified question from a federal *district* court, which is why the trial court in *Olman v. Full Moon* couldn't seek guidance from the Florida Supreme Court. *See* Fla. Const. Art. V, sec. 3(b)(6).

have to try the case a second time. Lane would also lose whatever current settlement leverage the fraud claim had given her.

If Lane had been litigating the Olmans' case in state court, where *interlocutory* appeals are sometimes more liberally authorized, she might have had the option of appealing the judge's decision immediately. But according to the *final judgment* rule prevailing in federal court, she had very few options for immediately challenging the court's ruling. As with many other decisions that the court would make before and during trial, Lane would probably have to live with the court's ruling until the case ended and final judgment was entered.

A Note Concerning: Appeals

During the course of litigation and trial, the presiding judge will often make several rulings that can alter the outcome of the case. If the judge is mistaken, it might seem sensible to let the losing party immediately appeal the trial court's decision. By giving an appellate court the immediate opportunity to consider and correct the trial court's error, the judicial system may avoid the waste of a flawed trial and the need for a second one.

In federal court, a losing party is generally denied the opportunity to appeal a suspected error until the case is fully adjudicated. This limitation is called the "final judgment" rule and is codified in 28 U.S.C. § 1291 (federal appellate courts have "jurisdiction of appeals from all final decisions"). Although there are some exceptions to the final judgment rule, for the most part, the losing party cannot file an "interlocutory" appeal of the trial court's intermittent rulings while the suit is still being conducted. Instead, a party must litigate the case to final judgment and then assert all grounds for appeal collectively. One benefit of the final judgment rule is that litigation is not continually disrupted by piecemeal appeals. Another benefit is that the appellate court can consider an alleged error in the context of the outcome in trial court. For example, the outcome at trial may demonstrate that the alleged error was harmless and any appeal pointless. A final benefit is that the need for an appeal may become moot; if the party claiming error ultimately prevails at trial, the party will usually have no incentive to appeal.

One exception to the final judgment rule, potentially available to Lane, permits the trial court to enter a "final judgment" for part of the case. *See* Fed. R. Civ. P. 54(b). For example, she could ask the court to enter a *partial* judgment, essentially stating that its order on the fraud claim against Belcher, Full Moon, or both was "final." This action would satisfy the statutory requirement limiting appeal to final judgments and permit Lane to seek immediate review of the court's interpretation of the law of fraud. But trial courts are often reluctant to grant partial final judgments. Further, lawyers are often reluctant to seek such judgments since this requires that they simultaneously engage in a trial and an appellate proceeding.

After announcing her decision dismissing Otis's fraud claim, Judge Goodenough asked Lane and Tweedy whether they would consider participating in mediation and try to settle the remaining claims in the suit. Both lawyers agreed this was not a good idea at present because their clients had already attempted to settle the suit and probably were not in a position to alter their positions until more discovery was completed.

Judge Goodenough then questioned the lawyers about the witnesses they intended to depose, the documents they intended to inspect, and the time it might take to complete this discovery. She also asked them of their availability for trial in the coming year and similarly told them of her own availability.

After the conference ended, Judge Goodenough drafted a "scheduling order," which would be a template for the suit. According to Rule 16(b)(3), the scheduling order can set time limits for a variety of matters, including amending the pleadings, filing motions, conducting discovery, and conducting the trial. Rule 16(b)(4) specifically provides that the schedule developed by the court "may be modified only for good cause and with the judge's consent." In effect, this order *supersedes* several federal rules that otherwise give lawyers far greater flexibility in litigating a case.[12] Below are excerpts from Judge Goodenough's scheduling order.

[12] For example, Rule 15(a) does not state a time limit for seeking to amend pleadings by permission. Similarly, Rule 26(d) does not establish a fixed time period for conducting discovery. But scheduling orders routinely establish time limits for these activities. Later in Chapter 10, we explore the impact of such orders on lawyers' procedural options.

UNITED STATES DISTRICT COURT
FOR THE MIDDLE DISTRICT OF FLORIDA
JACKSONVILLE DIVISION

OTIS AND FIONA OLMAN,

Plaintiffs,

Case No. 8-23-CV-00637

v.

FULL MOON SPORTS, INC.,
& BRUCE BELCHER

Defendants

CASE MANAGEMENT AND SCHEDULING ORDER

1. **TRIAL:** This case is scheduled for jury trial in Jacksonville, Florida, during the week of November 6-10, 2023.

2. **PRETRIAL CONFERENCE:** A Pretrial Conference will be held Thursday, October 26, 2023 at 2:00 p.m. before the Honorable Matthew Malarkey, United States Magistrate Judge, in the United States Courthouse, Courtroom 3414. Parties are directed to meet the pretrial disclosure requirements and deadlines in Fed. R. Civ. P. 26(a)(3) and to adhere to all requirements in Local Rule 3.02 concerning final pretrial procedures. The parties shall file a Joint Pretrial Statement no later than three (3) days before the date of the Pretrial Conference. Failure to do so may result in the imposition of sanctions. The Pretrial Conference shall be attended by lead trial counsel who are vested with full authority to make agreements touching on all matters pertaining to the trial.

3. **MOTIONS TO AMEND:** Motions to Amend any pleading or to continue the pretrial conference or trial are distinctly disfavored after entry of the Case Management and Scheduling Order.

4. **DISCOVERY CUTOFF:** All discovery is to be completed by the parties on or before August 31, 2023.

5. **DISPOSITIVE MOTIONS CUTOFF:** Dispositive motions shall be filed on or before September 29, 2023.

* * * *

DONE and ORDERED at Jacksonville, Florida, this 25th day of April, 2023.

[Judge's signature omitted.]

Chapter Nine
The Discovery Process

Chapter Rule References: 1, 8, *26*, 29, *30*, 31, *32*, *33*, *34*, 35, 36, *37*, *45*

A. Preparing for Discovery

Both Eleanor Lane and Bart Tweedy knew that, with the pleadings and Rule 16(b) conference behind them, they were able to begin the single largest pretrial stage in federal court litigation: discovery. The parties would now use the discovery tools available under the Federal Rules to assemble the information necessary to establish their claims or defenses. Without good use of discovery, they knew the chances of success in litigation would be greatly diminished. They also knew that the discovery process was an important ingredient in any settlement discussions that might later occur, as the parties would be better able to assess the strengths and weaknesses of their positions in light of information obtained in discovery.

Lane and Tweedy also knew they could take advantage of means to gather information not addressed in the Federal Rules. They could search the internet for relevant information, file Freedom of Information Act[1] requests with the federal government (or use the state equivalents), or even hire a private investigator. In this case, for example, Full Moon and its parent corporation, Mizar, were publicly traded companies, and Lane could obtain certain documents the companies were required to file periodically with the U.S. Securities and Exchange Commission. In employment discrimination cases, former employees of a defendant employer can also be an important source of informal discovery. Attorneys seeking information from former employees must take care not to run afoul of certain ethical restrictions on communications with unrepresented parties.[2] We will focus our discussion in this chapter on the formal discovery tools available under the Rules, but you should not forget about other important means of obtaining valuable information.

---

[1] 5 U.S.C. § 552.

[2] ABA Model Rule 4.3 governs attorney communications with unrepresented parties and provides, among other things, that when dealing "with a person who is not represented by counsel, a lawyer shall not state or imply that the lawyer is disinterested." Further, ABA Model Rule 4.4 prohibits attorneys from using "methods of obtaining evidence" that violate the legal rights of a third party (here, the *employer's* legal rights). Rule 4.4 could be implicated if an attorney seeks information from a former employee that would be protected by attorney-client privilege, by a contractual nondisclosure agreement, or by trade secret protections. Attorney contact with *current* employees of the defendant may, depending on your jurisdiction and the particular circumstances of the employee in question, run afoul of Model Rule 4.2, which prohibits an attorney from communicating about the subject matter of her representation "with a person the lawyer knows to be represented by another lawyer in the matter, unless the lawyer has the consent of the other lawyer or is authorized to do so by law or a court order." For a detailed examination of these subjects, see James L. Burt & Jeremy L. Cook, *Ethical Considerations Concerning Contacts by Counsel or Investigators with Present and Former Employees of an Opposing Party*, 28 St. Mary's L.J. 963 (2007).

The formal information-gathering process under the Federal Rules essentially proceeds on two tracks. One track focuses on experts, while the other focuses on factual information. We will return to expert discovery/disclosure later in this chapter. For now, we focus on factual discovery.

The Federal Rules establish a two-phase process for obtaining factual information. First, the parties are required to exchange certain information, principally concerning matters they may use to establish their claims or defenses,[3] without waiting for a request from the opposing party. This process is one of required *disclosure*. Thereafter, the parties may use various methods provided under the Rules for obtaining information from parties and nonparties alike.[4] This latter process is called *discovery*.

Before Lane and Tweedy could engage in either disclosure or discovery, they needed to comply with Rule 26(f)'s mandate to prepare a "discovery plan." As we have already seen in Chapter Eight, they prepared this plan in preparation for their initial meeting with Judge Goodenough. Among other things, the lawyers discussed possible changes in their required disclosures, changes in limits on the use of discovery devices imposed by the Rules, the content and timing of discovery, and concerns relating to the preservation, discovery, and production of electronically stored information (commonly referred to as "ESI"). Ultimately, the lawyers agreed to abide by disclosure requirements and discovery restrictions stated in the Rules. They also agreed on a discovery completion date that was memorialized in Judge Goodenough's Case Management and Scheduling Order.

Tactical Tip ✍

Party Autonomy in Discovery

Among other things, Rule 26(f) requires that parties confer about changes in disclosure obligations and discovery limitations. This requirement highlights an often underestimated feature of the Federal Rules discovery regime: the rules governing disclosure and discovery are largely default rules. Rule 29 allows the parties to modify "procedures governing or limiting discovery," although modifications that would "interfere with the time set for completing discovery, for hearing a motion, or for trial" require court approval. Absent party modification, the Rules govern. You should not lose sight of the ability to craft discovery rules suited to your case.

Lane and Tweedy knew that planning for discovery required that they fully consider all aspects of the case. They needed to consider what the law required each side to prove at trial, what evidence they currently had (good or bad), and what additional evidence they needed. Thus, the elements of the claims and defenses asserted in the pleadings became important yet again.

[3] *See* Rule 26(a)(1).

[4] *See* Rule 26(d).

Before we explore the disclosure and discovery process itself, you should try your hand at a bit of planning.

Task 9.1

Planning for Discovery

Put yourself in Lane's position. If you represented Otis Olman on his retaliation and age discrimination claims:

- What information would you want to obtain?
- Why would you want to obtain it?
- From whom would you seek it?

Now put yourself in Tweedy's shoes. If you represented Full Moon as a defendant on the retaliation and age discrimination claims:

- What information would you want to obtain?
- Why would you want to obtain it?
- From whom would you seek it?

As they headed into the disclosure and discovery process, Lane and Tweedy reminded themselves that discovery was a means, not an end. Lawyers can sometimes lose perspective when conducting discovery and thus generate needless conflict with opposing counsel. The lawyers' ultimate goal is to achieve their clients' purposes in litigation, not to notch victories in discovery controversies. Rule 1 emphasizes this point. Litigants, their attorneys, and the court itself have an obligation to employ the Rules so as to achieve "just, speedy, and inexpensive" resolution of disputes.

B. The Parties Make Their Required Disclosures

Rule 26(a)(1) generally requires a party to make certain disclosures without awaiting a request from the other party.[5] The Rule sets forth four categories of information that a party is required to disclose. Rather than memorizing these categories, Lane had developed the sound habit of returning to the Rules to confirm her obligations.

[5] Exceptions are recognized in Rule 26(a)(1)(B) (listing categories of proceedings exempt from required disclosure obligations) and Rule 26(a)(1)(A) (allowing required disclosures to be avoided by a stipulation or order of the court).

Tactical Tip ✍

Read the Rules

Closely read the Federal Rules each time you use them. Few lawyers have the capacity or inclination to memorize all the details found in the Rules. It is more important to (1) generally know what Rule addresses the topic at hand, and (2) read the Rule *each time* it is used. If you follow this advice, you will seldom make mistakes when using a Rule.

When drafting the Olmans' disclosures, Lane needed to review both her offensive and defensive theories of the case. First, to identify which documents and witnesses she needed to disclose, Lane had to determine which of these she might "use to support [her clients'] claims or defenses."[6] When Lane was unsure whether she might use a given witness or document, she tended to err on the side of disclosure. She reasoned that this information would likely be discovered by Full Moon anyway, and if she did not disclose it, she might be precluded from using the material later at trial.[7]

A second reason Lane needed to review the Olmans' case closely was to develop a more precise figure of the damages her clients would demand. While the complaint made a general "demand for the relief sought" by the Olmans,[8] Lane needed to be far more specific in her required disclosure statement.[9]

Estimating damages can be particularly difficult in the early stages of a lawsuit, but Lane knew she could supplement her disclosures later.[10]

Before reviewing Lane's disclosures, consider the following hypothetical disclosure issues based on the Olmans' suit:

---

[6] *See* Rule 26(a)(1)(A)(i), (ii).

[7] *See* Rule 37(c)(1) (stating that a party who fails to provide required disclosures "is not allowed to use that information or witness" unless the failure "was substantially justified or is harmless").

[8] *See* Rule 8(a)(3).

[9] *See* Rule 26(a)(1)(A)(iii) (requiring disclosure of "a computation of each category of damages claimed by the disclosing party").

[10] *See* Rule 26(e)(1).

Question 9.1

1. Assume that Lane had spoken with a former employee at the Jacksonville store. This employee told Lane that she never heard any ageist comments directed against Otis or Fiona. Why would Lane *not* have to disclose the identity of this former employee to Full Moon?

2. Assume that, in Question 1, Full Moon later asks Otis in an interrogatory to "identify any person known to you who has knowledge concerning whether any ageist comments were made about either Otis or Fiona Olman at the Jacksonville store?" Would Lane have to identify the former employee? Why?

3. Now assume that Lane was in possession of a tape recording of a meeting in which Bertie Lurch, Full Moon's president, said that he was going to get rid of Otis because he was "too old to handle the job." According to Rule 26(a)(1)(A), what factor determines whether Lane must disclose the recording? What risk does Lane run if she chooses *not* to disclose?

4. Assume that, after making her required disclosures, Lane discovers a memorandum from Lurch she believes she may use to support Otis's claim of discrimination. What obligation, if any, does Lane have to disclose this memorandum? What risk does she run if she takes no action? Consider Rules 26(e) and 37(c)(1) in answering these questions.

Excerpts from the disclosure statement Lane served after reviewing her case file and consulting with Otis and Fiona are given below.

IN THE UNITED STATES DISTRICT COURT
FOR THE MIDDLE DISTRICT OF FLORIDA
JACKSONVILLE DIVISION

OTIS AND FIONA OLMAN,

Plaintiffs,

v. Case No. 8-23-CV-00637

FULL MOON SPORTS, INC.
& BRUCE BELCHER,

Defendants.

REQUIRED DISCLOSURE STATEMENT
OF PLAINTIFFS OTIS AND FIONA OLMAN

Plaintiffs Otis and Fiona Olman (collectively "Plaintiffs") hereby submit their Required Disclosure Statement concerning their claims and the counterclaim asserted by defendant Full Moon Sports, Inc. ("Defendant").

I. Disclosures Under Rule 26(a)(1)(A)(i)

Lane could use Rule 26(a)(1)(A) as a checklist to determine the information that she needed to include in this section of the disclosure statement.

Plaintiffs identify the following individuals who are likely to have discoverable information that Plaintiffs may use to support their claims or defenses:

1. Otis Olman, 105 Boxwood Lane, Jacksonville, Florida, 32210, phone: (904) 555-3607. Mr. Olman has information concerning Defendant's unlawful termination of him, including but not limited to the ageist attitude of the company and its representatives and the damages he suffered as a result of that attitude. He also has information concerning the lawfulness of his actions that form the basis for Defendant's counterclaim.

*****

While the Olmans weren't required to identify Ornstein in their complaint, they now had to if they intended to call him as a supporting witness at trial.

4. Rex Ornstein, 2702 Skimmer Point Way, Atlanta, Georgia, 30303, phone: (404) 555-1110. Mr. Ornstein had information regarding the ageist attitudes of Defendant's employees in Atlanta, Georgia, including its officers and other senior management.

*****

II. Disclosures Under Rule 26(a)(1)(A)(ii)

Plaintiffs identify the following documents that are in their possession, custody or control that they may use to support their claims or defenses:

1. Plaintiff Otis Olman's employment evaluations for the period of time he served as manager of the Jacksonville store.

*****

2. Pay stubs and other related records showing the Plaintiffs' lost pay resulting from Defendant's unlawful activities.

*****

III. Disclosures Under Rule 26(a)(1)(A)(iii)

Plaintiffs provide the following computation of the categories of damages claimed in the Complaint. In addition, Plaintiffs agree to make available for inspection and copying documents and any other evidentiary material, not privileged or otherwise protected from disclosure, on which their computation is based.

As requested in his Complaint in this action, Plaintiff Otis Olman seeks to recover (1) damages of back pay and future pay; (2) double back pay; (3) other compensatory damages; (4) prejudgment interest; (5) costs; and (6) attorneys' fees in this action. Each category of damages is discussed separately below:

Note that the disclosure rule requires more specific explanation of the plaintiff's damages than is required in the complaint.

1. Damages of Back Pay and Future Pay: Mr. Olman seeks to recover damages in the form of lost income from back pay and future pay. Mr. Olman will request that these amounts be determined based on a salary of $100,000 per year, increased by the cost of living, from the time of his wrongful termination through and including the year in which he will turn seventy-two, when he had planned to retire.

*****

5. Attorneys' Fees: Mr. Olman will seek to recover the fees reasonably incurred by his attorney in prosecuting and defending this case.

*****

IV. Disclosures Under Rule 26(a)(1)(A)(iv)

Plaintiffs state that no insurance agreement provides coverage for the matters set forth in Defendant's counterclaim.

Plaintiffs reserve the right to supplement this disclosure statement pursuant to the Federal Rules of Civil Procedure.

OTIS OLMAN
FIONA OLMAN
By their attorney,

____

Eleanor Lane
Lane & Quincy, P.A.
Trial Counsel for Plaintiffs
[Address, etc. omitted]

Lane's signature constituted her certification under Rule 26(g) concerning the legal foundation for her disclosures and her good faith in making them.

Note that discovery disclosures, requests, and responses are generally not filed with the court, but only served on the parties to the litigation. Because the electronic filing system is not used, Eleanor is providing a Certificate of Service to establish proof of service of these initial disclosures on the other parties.

Certificate of Service

The undersigned certifies that this document was served on counsel of record listed below via electronic mail on _______, 2023 at 4:59 p.m. EST:

Harrison Ames, Esq.
Lord, Howe & Mercy, P.A.
Hames@LHMlaw.com

Bart A. Tweedy, Esq.
Lord, Howe & Mercy, P.A.
BTweedy@LHMlaw.com

Now consider the following hypothetical questions concerning Full Moon's obligation to disclose:

Question 9.2

Assume that Full Moon intends to argue at trial that its decisions to replace Otis and some 35 other store managers in the southeast region were motivated by (1) the managers' excessive salaries and (2) their stores' relatively weak sales records. To support these claims, Full Moon has a substantial body of documents and electronic files showing manager salaries and store sales during the time of the company's downsizing. Under Rule 26(a)(1)(A)(ii), must Full Moon disclose this voluminous information? If so, in what manner must it be disclosed?

After completing their Required Disclosure Statements, the Olmans and Full Moon had to serve them on all parties.[11] But as with all discovery documents, they were precluded from filing the statements with the court.[12]

C. Discovery Devices: Uses and Disputes

1. General Considerations

a. Relevance, Proportionality, and Privilege

Lane and Tweedy knew that the parameters of discovery were set by Rule 26(b)(1). They could discover without court permission any matter that was (1) "relevant to any party's claim or defense," (2) "proportional to the needs of the case," and (3) "nonprivileged."[13] We will examine each requirement in turn here.

The first thing to notice is that relevance is defined by reference to the claims or defenses that the parties have set out in their *pleadings*. Allegations in the complaint, answer, and any other pleading essentially set the stage on which discovery will take place. This interconnection between pleading and discovery conveys a simple lesson. At the pleading stage, one must be looking forward to discovery; and at discovery, one must look back to the pleadings.

The second requirement is that the requested discovery be "proportional" to the needs of the case. Rule 26(b)(1) directs that proportionality should be determined by considering:

- The importance of the issues at stake;
- The amount in controversy;
- The parties' relative access to relevant information;
- The parties' resources;
- The importance of discovery in resolving the issues; and
- The burden or expense of the requested discovery, relative to its likely benefit.

Many of these considerations are self-explanatory, but some are worth a bit more exploration here. First, the Advisory Committee Notes clarify that "monetary stakes are only one factor" in the analysis.[14] Sometimes litigation has important "philosophical, social, or institutional"

---

[11] *See* Rule 5(a)(1)(C).

[12] *See* Rule 5(d)(1). The rule's general prohibition on filing extends to deposition transcripts, interrogatories and answers, document requests and responses, and requests for admissions and responses until these documents are "used in the proceeding or the court orders filing." *Id.* The most common ways in which discovery papers may be "used in the proceeding" are as part of a motion to compel further discovery responses, discussed later in this chapter, or as exhibits supporting or opposing motions for summary judgment. *See infra* Chapter 7.

[13] Rule 26(b)(1).

[14] *See* Fed. R. Civ. P. 26 Advisory Committee Notes (2015 amendment).

value despite its limited monetary value.[15] Second, in a case like the Olmans', the parties' relative access to relevant information may favor allowing more searching discovery requests by plaintiffs. The reason is that in most employment discrimination cases, much of the critical information on which the case may turn is in the hands of the employer. This situation is sometimes called an "information asymmetry."[16] Think about it. After the Olmans were terminated, which party was most likely to have discoverable documents or electronic files potentially relevant to their discrimination claims or Full Moon's defenses? Probably Full Moon.

At the outset of the discovery process, neither party can be expected to have a complete picture of all the proportionality factors. A plaintiff requesting certain electronic files may not fully understand the difficulty or burden to the defendant in producing them. Likewise, the defendant asked to produce such files may not have a full understanding of the potential importance of those files in resolving issues that the plaintiff seeks to raise in the litigation.[17] Through their ongoing communications, and acting in accordance with the spirit of Rule 1, the attorneys should be able to resolve many proportionality disputes on their own, without the intervention of the court.

The third requirement for discovery is that the information sought be "nonprivileged." While relevance is concerned more with the content of the matter sought to be discovered, privilege focuses on the *source* from which the information is sought. For example, a commonly asserted privilege is that between attorney and client. A party seeking discovery is normally not permitted to ask a lawyer what her client told her. That does not mean, however, that the underlying *information* possessed by the client is privileged. The client may be asked to convey information she possesses, provided it is relevant. But any communication with her lawyer per se is protected from discovery.[18] Society has made a determination that the attorney-client relationship is one worthy of enhanced protection.

Next, we briefly note some of the other privileges that have traditionally been recognized in American law.

---

[15] *See id.* The Advisory Committee Notes specifically suggest that litigation challenging "employment practices" may carry importance beyond the dollar amount in controversy. *Id.*

[16] *See* Fed. R. Civ. P. 26 Advisory Committee Notes (2015 amendment) ("Some cases involve what often is called 'information asymmetry.' One party—often an individual plaintiff—may have very little discoverable information. The other party may have vast amounts of information.").

[17] *See* Fed. R. Civ. P. 26 Advisory Committee Notes (2015 amendment).

[18] To illustrate, Full Moon could properly ask Otis Olman how early he complained to Full Moon's representatives about age discrimination. But Full Moon could not ask Lane to disclose what *Otis conveyed to her* during the course of a privileged conversation about his complaints. The information is relevant and discoverable from Otis, but it cannot be accessed by asking Lane to breach a privilege.

A Note Concerning: Common Privileges

In litigation, a "privilege" is a right to prevent the disclosure of information even if it is relevant. The concept of privilege reflects the belief that some values are more important than resolving the dispute at hand by full disclosure of relevant information. For example, we protect information communicated between a lawyer and her client not because there is something about the *information* that makes disclosure inappropriate. Rather, we protect the information because we value the *relationship* and want to encourage clients to confide in lawyers and want lawyers to provide full advice to clients. Because of their effect on the litigation process, privileges tend to be narrowly construed.

There are numerous privileges. Although there are common-law privileges, most privileges are created through legislation. According to Federal Rule of Evidence 501, federal courts apply a federal common law of privileges to claims based on federal law, but apply state-law privileges to claims based on state law.

You will learn much more about privileges in your evidence class. In the meantime, here are some of the more common privileges you may encounter in your career (in addition to the attorney-client privilege already discussed):

- *The marital privilege:* This privilege generally prevents one spouse from giving testimony against the other.
- *The Fifth Amendment privilege against self-incrimination:* The Fifth Amendment to the U.S. Constitution allows a person to decline to provide testimony that might lead to or support criminal charges against him.
- *The doctor-patient privilege:* This privilege precludes a doctor from testifying concerning communications that she has had with a patient.
- *The religious advisor-penitent privilege:* This privilege protects communications between priests, ministers, rabbis, mullahs, and other religious figures and their congregants.

Rule 26(b)(3) creates a unique restriction on the scope of discovery that is specifically related to the trial process. This restriction—which is not technically a privilege—extends to "trial preparation" or "work product" and is intended to protect from disclosure "documents and tangible things . . . prepared in anticipation of litigation or for trial." While the work-product protection encompasses materials developed by a party's lawyer, it is not limited to the lawyer's work product. Rather, it encompasses materials prepared in anticipation of litigation "by or for" a "party or its representative (including the . . . party's attorney, consultant, surety, indemnitor, insurer, or agent)." The key question to ask in determining whether material is protected work product is: Was it prepared in anticipation of litigation or for trial? In other words, the *purpose* for which material was prepared is critical. The Advisory Committee Notes to Rule 26 make this clear. Those notes emphasize that material "assembled in the ordinary course of business, or pursuant to public requirements unrelated to litigation, or for other nonlitigation purposes" are not protected.

If material qualifies as work product, it is generally immune from discovery unless the party seeking it can show that he "has substantial need for the materials to prepare its case" *and* "cannot, without undue hardship, obtain their substantial equivalent by other means." The burden of overcoming a valid claim of work product is heavy. What is more, Rule 26(b)(3) provides a heightened level of immunity to that part of work product containing "mental impressions, conclusions, opinions, or legal theories of a party's attorney or other representative concerning the litigation." As a consequence, even if a party makes the compelling case that he should be permitted to discover work product, any parts of that product containing a lawyer's recorded thoughts will be redacted prior to disclosure.

As with privileges, work-product protection generally cannot be used to conceal relevant information. Thus, a party may object to disclosing a document or report that was prepared in anticipation of litigation but cannot refuse to answer questions that seek information contained in the work product. For example, a party might authorize its agent to prepare a special accident report and feel secure that the report will be protected work product. But information obtained while preparing the report (e.g., the names of eyewitnesses, observations at the accident site) will be discoverable through mechanisms like depositions and interrogatories.

The work-product protection is intended to permit parties to prepare for litigation without fear that their preparation materials will be revealed to adversaries. A good lawyer, appreciating the value of work product protection, will often take steps to ensure that he or she is in a strong position to argue that material is "work product" when discovery commences. For example, the lawyer may advise his or her client that all materials generated pertaining to a lawsuit (or potential lawsuit) contain an introductory legend with words like, "Attorney Work Product—Prepared at the Direction of an Attorney in Anticipation and Preparation of Litigation." If an adversary later seeks this material, the party will be well positioned to argue that it purposefully developed it "in anticipation of litigation or for trial."[19]

Later in this chapter, we will see how Full Moon's claim that material sought by Lane was work product evolved into a discovery controversy.

b. Tools of Discovery

Lane and Tweedy knew that so long as they sought relevant, proportional, nonprivileged information, they could choose from a wide array of tools. The following table summarizes those tools and some of the limitations on their use:

[19] Such notations are commonly used in practice to signal protection under the work-product doctrine or the attorney-client privilege. Of course, they are not dispositive of the question of whether the document is actually protected from discovery.

A Guide to Gathering Information under the Rules

Method	Rule Terminology	Rule(s)	Court Permission Required?	Available against Nonparties?
Requiring a person to produce documents, data, or things	"Production of documents and things . . ."	34, 35, and 45	No	Yes (via R.45)
Obtaining entry to land or property	"Entry upon land for inspection and other purposes"	34 and 45	No	Yes (via R.45)
Requiring written answers to questions under oath	"Interrogatory"	33	No	No
Requiring submission to exam by a health professional	"Physical and mental examination"	35	Yes	No
Requiring answers to questions orally under oath	"Deposition upon oral examination"	30 and 45	No	Yes (via R.45)
Requiring a party to admit whether something is true	"Requests for admission"	36	No	No

So how were Lane and Tweedy to figure out how to use this array of tools in a coordinated way? An interesting feature of the discovery rules is that they simultaneously provide considerable detail about how each tool is to be used and say little about how these tools are to be used together. There is, for example, no required chronological order for submitting written questions to parties (interrogatories) and questioning the party orally (by deposition). In the end, the choice of the order in which to use discovery tools is based on the needs of the individual case and the experience and preferences of the lawyers.

The professional experience of Lane and Tweedy had led them to similar conclusions regarding the relative value of discovery devices. They each saw depositions as the crown jewels of discovery. They devoted the greatest preparation to depositions and expected that depositions would yield much of the information important at summary judgment and trial. Therefore, they usually waited until later in the discovery period, after first acquiring information through other discovery tools, to take depositions.[20]

[20] This approach was not invariable, as each case is unique. For example, Lane had at times taken the deposition of a corporate decision maker in discrimination cases early on to lock that person into a single version of events.

Lane and Tweedy would use "paper discovery" devices early in the process, including document requests and interrogatories. This information might be valuable in its own right, and it would also prepare them for depositions. They would, however, typically save one form of paper discovery to the end of the process: requests for admission. These requests were designed to take matters out of contention at trial. To use this tool most effectively, Lane and Tweedy would seek admissions after assembling information obtained through other forms of discovery.[21]

One final consideration is important before we turn to the parties' use of the various discovery devices. Both Lane and Tweedy knew they needed to consider the prospect of discovery from two perspectives. First, they would consider their opportunity to *seek* discovery to build their own clients' case. Second, they would consider their responsibility to *provide* discovery to assist their opponents in building their case.

There are several reasons for viewing discovery from an opponent's perspective. First, sound litigation practice requires that a lawyer know the weak points of a client's case and the discovery product that will be used to expose these weak points. By thinking about weaknesses early on, a lawyer is often able to anticipate and address problems in her client's case. In addition, by considering the discovery an opponent may seek, a lawyer can engage in some preparatory work, such as collecting material on her own schedule instead of one dictated by her opponent.

Yet another reason for defensive consideration of discovery material is that clients and lawyers are under a duty to *preserve* discoverable material once litigation is filed or there is a reasonable prospect of litigation about a given issue.[22] If harmful evidence is lost or destroyed, clients and lawyers may pay a steep price for this "spoliation" of evidence.[23] For example, if a court determines that a party has not done enough to preserve relevant evidence, it can sanction that

---

[21] In appropriate cases, it is also possible to compel a party to undergo a mental or physical examination as part of the discovery process. *See* Rule 35. Unlike the great majority of other discovery devices, a party needs court permission to obtain this type of discovery. *Id.* In certain ADEA cases, mental or physical examinations may be allowed because the plaintiff has, in the words of Rule 35(a), placed his "mental or physical condition . . . in controversy." A plaintiff may also place his or her mental condition in controversy, for example, by claiming damages for emotional distress. *See, e.g., Cauley v. Ingram Micro, Inc.*, 216 F.R.D. 241, 243 (W.D.N.Y. 2003) (claim of severe emotional distress in employment discrimination case sufficient to place the plaintiff's emotional condition in controversy under Rule 35). In practice, parties who have placed their mental or physical condition in controversy know that their opponents are entitled to have them examined. Consequently, most mental and physical examinations will be conducted by agreement of the parties rather than by court order.

[22] *See, e.g., Silvestri v. General Motors Corp.*, 271 F.3d 583, 591 (4th Cir. 2001) ("The duty to preserve evidence arises not only during litigation but also extends to that period before the litigation when a party reasonably should know that the evidence may be relevant to anticipated litigation."); *Fujitsu Ltd. v. Federal Express Corp.*, 247 F.3d 423, 436 (2d Cir. 2001) ("The obligation to preserve evidence arises when the party has notice that the evidence is relevant to litigation or when a party should have known that the evidence may be relevant to future litigation."); *Zubulake v. UBS Warburg LLC*, 2004 U.S. Dist. LEXIS 13574 at *31-*43 (S.D.N.Y. Jul. 20, 2004) (discussing counsel's duties to ensure compliance with duty to preserve relevant evidence).

[23] *See, e.g., West v. Goodyear Tire & Rubber Co.*, 167 F.3d 776, 779 (2d Cir. 1999).

party by, among other things, awarding costs to an opponent, or worse, informing the jury of the destruction of evidence and allowing the jurors to draw adverse inferences against the responsible party. Thus, in some circumstances, a jury might be allowed to infer that lost or destroyed evidence was extremely harmful to the party responsible for preserving it.[24] As you can imagine, such an instruction is often fatal to a party's case.

The preservation of electronically stored information poses unique and challenging problems. The circumstances of electronic storage can vary widely. For example, parties may have electronic files within their custody or control stored on a personal computer hard drive, a smartphone, a flash drive, a local server, a remote server, a third-party cloud storage service, or backup tapes or discs. The potential cost of "aggressive preservation efforts"[25] could be substantial, and possibly disproportionate to the stakes of the litigation.

Recognizing this, the 2015 amendments to Rule 37(e) limited the availability of certain types of curative orders for failure to preserve electronically stored information.[26] First, the amended Rule 37(e) emphasizes that parties need only take *reasonable* steps to preserve electronically stored information. Unreasonably aggressive preservation efforts are not required. Where a party fails to take reasonable steps, and where the lost information cannot be "restored or replaced through additional discovery," then the court must determine if there has been prejudice to the other party. Only upon a finding of such prejudice may the court "order measures no greater than necessary to cure the prejudice."[27]

The most severe curative orders, however, are reserved for only those cases where the court finds "that the party acted with the *intent* to deprive another party of the information's use

---

[24] The standards for permitting adverse inference jury instructions for spoliation of materials other than electronically stored information vary by jurisdiction. For example, the Second Circuit has permitted adverse inference instructions for conduct that is merely negligent. *Residential Funding Corp. v. DeGeorge Fin. Corp.*, 306 F.3d 99, 108 (2d Cir. 2002); *William Coale v. Metro-North R.R. Co.*, 2016 WL 1441790, at *4, n.7 (D. Conn. Apr. 11, 2016). The Eleventh Circuit permits an adverse inference for failure to preserve evidence only where "the absence of that evidence is predicated on bad faith." *Mann v. Taser Intern., Inc.*, 588 F.3d 1291, 1310 (11th Cir. 2009) (quoting *Bashir v. Amtrak*, 119 F.3d 929, 931 (11th Cir. 1997)).

[25] *See* Fed. R. Civ. P. 37, Advisory Committee Notes (2015 amendment).

[26] Fed. R. Civ. P. 37(e). Amended Rule 37(e) does not alter prior case law providing sanctions for spoliation of evidence other than electronically stored information. *See Living Color Enterprises, Inc. v. New Era Aquaculture*, 2016 WL 1105297, at *4, n.2 (S.D. Fla. Mar. 22, 2016 ("Newly amended Rule 37(e) specifically relates solely to ESI and not to non-ESI such as tangible documents or evidence. One question that will surely arise in the future is whether there are now two standards for spoliation depending on whether the allegedly spoliated item constitutes ESI or non-ESI."); *U.S. v. Safeco Ins. Co. of Am.*, 2016 WL 901608, at *7, n.3 (D. Idaho Mar. 9, 2016); *William Coale v. Metro-North R.R. Co.*, 2016 WL 1441790, at *4, n.7 (D. Conn. Apr. 11, 2016). For a comprehensive discussion of counsel's common law obligations concerning document preservation, including ESI, prior to the 2015 amendments, *see Zubulake v. UBS Warburg LLC*, 2004 U.S. Dist LEXIS 13574 (S.D.N.Y. Jul. 20, 2004).

[27] Rule 37(e)(1). The possible array of curative orders is extensive, and the selection of an appropriate order is left to the discretion of the court. Such orders could include, for example, the exclusion of a particular item of evidence to offset the prejudice. *See* Fed. R. Civ. P. 37 Advisory Committee Notes (2015 amendment).

in the litigation."[28] Only upon a finding of such intent may the court presume, or instruct the jury that it may presume, that the lost information was unfavorable to the party.[29] Likewise, the finding of intent is also required before the court may dismiss the action or enter a default judgment against the party for losing the electronically stored information.[30]

The risk of spoliation particularly concerned Tweedy. His client was a large corporation with numerous employees at various locations. The opportunities for inadvertent destruction of either hard copy or electronically stored documents were quite high. Fortunately, Full Moon had taken proper steps to preserve documents from spoliation. As soon as it became clear that the Olmans might sue, Full Moon's general counsel (its in-house lawyer) issued a "litigation hold" to all employees. This litigation hold described the nature of the suit the company faced, specifically identified the types of documents and electronically stored information that needed to be preserved, and explicitly directed that those documents and files be retained.

When Tweedy became involved in the case, he reconfirmed the litigation hold. In addition, he personally met with management-level personnel in Full Moon's business divisions to reiterate the importance of the litigation hold. Tweedy's most difficult task was ensuring that Full Moon did not inadvertently destroy any electronically stored documents such as email. He educated himself about how Full Moon stored electronic material and then issued appropriate directions for preserving this material while litigation was pending.[31] Tweedy's efforts at document preservation took time, but he knew that the time was well spent, given the potential consequences Full Moon would face if the job were not done right.

2. Initial Paper Discovery

a. Lane Begins the Discovery Process[32]

Lane determined that she would start the discovery process by seeking documents from Full Moon and certain nonparties. She would also send interrogatories to Full Moon. Lane would then use the information she obtained to identify the individuals she wanted to depose and begin preparing to take these depositions.

Lane began with documents. Her ability to require the production of documents was an exceptionally important asset. She knew from experience that documents often contain important information unavailable elsewhere. She also knew that, at least initially, the relative burden of document production was greater for Full Moon than the Olmans. Lane's clients had

---

[28] Rule 37(e)(2) (emphasis added).

[29] Rule 37(e)(2)(A)-(B).

[30] Rule 37(e)(2)(C).

[31] For a comprehensive treatment of counsels' obligation to preserve electronically stored information, see Jay E. Grenig & William C. Gleisner III, eDiscovery & Digital Evidence (West 2023).

[32] Full Moon will be engaging in discovery simultaneously with the Olmans. Although we will consider some of Full Moon's discovery requests in this chapter, we will primarily focus on the Olmans' discovery efforts and Full Moon's responses.

few documents relevant to their claims. Full Moon, on the other hand, likely had thousands of potentially relevant documents. Thus, documentary discovery was an inexpensive way for Lane to obtain quite valuable information. She knew, however, that the burden involved in document discovery would soon shift to her when she began the time-consuming task of reviewing the documents Full Moon produced.

Before we consider Lane's use of document discovery, think about what documents you would seek to discover if you served as counsel for the parties in *Olman v. Full Moon*.

Task 9.2

Put yourself in *Lane's* position:

1. What documents, described either specifically or by category, would you want to obtain through discovery? Why would you want these documents? Consider not only paper documents, but also electronically stored information.

2. From whom would you seek these documents?

3. What specific discovery mechanism would you use to obtain these documents from the persons and entities you identified?

Now put yourself in *Tweedy's* position:

1. What documents, described either specifically or by category, would you want to obtain through discovery? Why would you want these documents? Again, consider any electronically stored information.

2. From whom would you seek these documents?

3. What specific discovery mechanism would you use to obtain these documents from the persons and entities you identified?

Lane first focused on obtaining documents from Full Moon. She knew that Rule 34 allowed her to serve a request for production of documents or other tangible items on any party.[33] Before she began drafting the document request, she reminded herself of some of the important features of the Federal Rules governing her request. First, she knew there were no specific limits on the number of document requests she could make, unlike limits restricting the number of interrogatories she might ask. Second, she needed to ensure that her document

[33] In an appropriate case, Rule 34 would also authorize a party to enter another party's property for the purpose of conducting an inspection. *See* Rule 34(a)(2). That provision of the Rule was not likely to be of use in the Olmans' case.

requests complied with Rule 26(b)(1)'s parameters concerning relevance, proportionality, and privilege.

Finally, Lane knew that, although discovery papers are not subject to the requirements of Rule 11,[34] her signature on the document requests constituted a certification similar to that made under Rule 11. According to Rule 26(g), Lane would be certifying that her requests were (1) "consistent with [the discovery rules] and warranted by existing law or by a nonfrivolous argument for extending, modifying, or reversing existing law, or for establishing new law";[35] (2) "not interposed for any improper purpose, such as to harass, cause unnecessary delay, or needlessly increase the cost of litigation";[36] and (3) "neither unreasonable nor unduly burdensome or expensive, considering the needs of the case, prior discovery in the case, the amount in controversy, and the importance of the issues at stake in the action."[37] Lane took these certifications seriously and thus paid close attention when identifying the documents she requested from Full Moon.[38]

Here is an excerpted version of the document requests Lane served on Tweedy:

[34] *See* Rule 11(d) (Rule 11 "does not apply to disclosures and discovery requests, responses, objections, and motions under Rules 26 through 37.").

[35] Rule 26(g)(1)(B)(i).

[36] Rule 26(g)(1)(B)(i).

[37] Rule 26(g)(1)(B)(iii).

[38] These three certifications apply to all discovery requests, responses, and objections, as well as to initial disclosures. See Rule 26(g)(1).

IN THE UNITED STATES DISTRICT COURT
FOR THE MIDDLE DISTRICT OF FLORIDA
JACKSONVILLE DIVISION

OTIS AND FIONA OLMAN,

Plaintiffs,

v. Case No. 8-23-CV-00637

FULL MOON SPORTS, INC.,
& BRUCE BELCHER,

Defendants.

PLAINTIFF'S FIRST REQUEST FOR PRODUCTION OF DOCUMENTS

As authorized by Federal Rule of Civil Procedure 34, Plaintiffs hereby request that Defendant produce for inspection and copying the documents described below.

Definitions

Unless otherwise indicated, the following definitions shall apply to all the requests set forth below.

1. The term "concerning" means relating to, referring to, describing, evidencing, or constituting.

2. The term "Defendant" means Full Moon Sports, Inc. and any of its officers, agents, employees, or representatives.

3. The term "Jacksonville Store" means the Full Moon Outdoor Center, a retail sporting goods store located in Jacksonville, Florida, and owned by Defendant.

* * * *

Document Requests

1. The personnel files for Otis Olman and Fiona Olman.

2. The personnel or employee handbook(s) or manual(s) in effect at the Defendant for the period during which either Otis Olman or Fiona Olman were employed by Defendant.

* * * *

6. All documents concerning any investigation performed by Defendant or at its request concerning allegations that any employee, including either Plaintiff in this action, was terminated, demoted, transferred, denied a promotion, or otherwise harmed as a result of such employee's age.

7. All documents concerning or supporting Defendant's allegation in its Answer and Counterclaim that Plaintiff Otis Olman converted Defendant's property.

* * * *

15. All communications, including but not limited to email or other electronic communications, concerning the reduction in force at the Jacksonville store.

16. All documents concerning reductions in force for the period from 2022 to the present at any of the Defendant's retail locations, corporate headquarters, or any other location at which the Defendant conducts its business that indicate the ages of those employees terminated, transferred, or demoted as well as the ages of those persons who replaced such persons in the positions they held prior to the reduction in force.

* * * *

OTIS OLMAN
FIONA OLMAN
By their attorney,

____

Eleanor Lane
Lane & Quincy, P.A.
Trial Counsel for Plaintiffs
[Address etc. omitted]

[certificate of service omitted]

Lane sought information about other employees. Which rule supports this request?

Lane sought discovery of documents "concerning or supporting" Full Moon's defenses and counterclaim. Does this request go beyond what Full Moon is required to mandatorily disclose under Rule 26(a)(1)?

Lane also wanted to obtain documents from nonparties. She would use one of the most powerful discovery tools authorized by the Federal Rules. Rule 45 grants lawyers the authority to compel nonparties to produce documents or appear for a deposition without prior court authorization.[39] Lane knew that it was important that she exercise this power wisely. Consider the following comment:

> **Tactical Tip** ✍
>
> **Subpoenaing Nonparties**
>
> Simply having the power to compel a nonparty to take a certain action does not mean that a lawyer should automatically use that power. It may be the case that a nonparty will be willing to cooperate without a subpoena or that he will be more cooperative if warned ahead of time that a subpoena is on its way. Of course, there will be many situations in which a lawyer knows she should use the subpoena power surely or swiftly. For example, a lawyer may already know a nonparty will be uncooperative, or a lawyer may suspect that evidence will be lost or destroyed if it is not requested formally without advance warning. Still, these concerns should not blind a lawyer to the possibility that you might get more using honey than vinegar.

There were several nonparties who might provide Lane useful documents or deposition testimony. Key among them was Bruce Belcher. Recall that Belcher had been dismissed from the case and was no longer subject to discovery under rules governing parties. Further, he no longer worked for Full Moon and now lived in Connecticut. Absent his agreement to come to Florida, Lane would need to seek discovery from Belcher within 100 miles of where he resides or works in Connecticut.[40]

Under the Federal Rules, Lane did not need to initiate any special judicial proceeding in Connecticut to obtain discovery from Belcher. This was so even though the Olmans' case was pending in federal court in Florida. Nor did Lane need to associate herself with a lawyer admitted to practice law in Connecticut. Under Rule 45, an attorney may use the subpoena power to compel production of documents and/or testimony at a deposition, so long as the attorney is admitted to the bar of the federal district court in which the action is *pending*.[41] Thus, because Lane was admitted to the bar of the Middle District of Florida, where the Olmans' suit was pending, she could issue a subpoena directed to Belcher compelling him to produce documents and appear at a deposition in Connecticut.[42]

---

[39] *See* Rule 45(a)(3).

[40] *See* Rule 45(c)(1)-(2).

[41] *See* Rule 45(a)(3).

[42] You can view a Rule 45 subpoena through the web page for the federal judiciary. *See* https://www.uscourts.gov/forms/notice-lawsuit-summons-subpoena/subpoena-testify-deposition-civil-action (last visited July 24, 2024). Note that under Rule 45(d)(3)(A)(ii), a person who is subpoenaed may move to

"GREETINGS: YOU ARE HEREBY SUBPOENAED TO APPEAR..."

The final form of paper discovery Lane prepared was a set of interrogatories directed to Full Moon. Lane did not consider interrogatories to be a particularly useful discovery tool. Interrogatories are written questions that a party may ask another party,[43] which must be answered in writing under oath.[44] But in practice, the answers to interrogatories are most often drafted by a party's lawyer and only reviewed for factual accuracy by the party. The result is that interrogatory answers tend not to be that helpful.

Still, Lane knew that interrogatories had some value for obtaining specific information from Full Moon. For example, she could ask for a summary of information contained within Full Moon's business files. Rule 33 requires that a party answering interrogatories provide information *available* to it, like that contained in an electronic database. Similarly, if Full Moon had an officer or employee with knowledge of a matter addressed by an interrogatory, it would have to consult with that person and incorporate his knowledge into its answers. Consequently, Lane would think carefully about how to use the 25 interrogatories permitted her under Rule 33.

---

quash the subpoena if it requires him to travel more than the geographic restrictions specified under Rule 45(c).

[43] Interrogatories cannot be served on a nonparty (like Belcher). *See* Rule 33(a)(1) ("a party may serve on any other party . . . written interrogatories").

[44] Some unscrupulous lawyers submit excessive interrogatories to cause an adversary to spend unnecessary time and incur unwarranted costs. Using interrogatories for either of these purposes is obviously unethical. *See, e.g.*, Rule 26(g)(1)(B)(ii) (A party serving any discovery request certifies that the request is "not interposed for any improper purpose, such as to harass, cause unnecessary delay, or needlessly increase the cost of litigation."); Model Rule of Professional Conduct 3.4(d) ("A lawyer shall not: . . . (d) in pretrial procedure, make a frivolous discovery request.").

Task 9.3

1. Recall that the Olmans allege Full Moon engaged in a "pattern and practice of age discrimination affecting company-wide downsizing." *See* Complaint ¶ 36. What interrogatories might Lane frame to obtain information to support this allegation?

2. Recall that Full Moon has asserted a counterclaim against Otis in which it alleges he "converted store merchandise on several occasions during the time he served as store manager." *See* Answer ¶¶ 62-65. What interrogatories might Lane frame to obtain information to refute this allegation?

Below are brief excerpts from the interrogatories Lane served on Tweedy:

IN THE UNITED STATES DISTRICT COURT
FOR THE MIDDLE DISTRICT OF FLORIDA
JACKSONVILLE DIVISION

OTIS AND FIONA OLMAN,

Plaintiffs,

v. Case No. 8-23-CV-00637

FULL MOON SPORTS, INC.
& BRUCE BELCHER,

Defendants.

PLAINTIFFS' FIRST SET OF INTERROGATORIES TO DEFENDANT

As authorized by Federal Rule of Civil Procedure 33, Plaintiffs hereby request that Defendant, though its officers or agents, answer the following interrogatories under oath.

According to Rule 33(b)(1), who must answer the interrogatories on behalf of Full Moon?

Definitions

[Definitions omitted]

Interrogatories

1. Identify the person or persons who made the determination to promote Mr. Sid Shockley to manager of the Jacksonville store.

2. Identify the manager or managers of Full Moon's information systems, information management or computer department (or other similar department or organizational structure) for the period from January 2022 to the present.

What further discovery will Lane seek after receiving Full Moon's response to these interrogatories?

* * * *

8. State the age of all managers of all Full Moon retail stores as of January 2022 and January 2023.

* * * *

15. Identify all facts that support your contention that Otis Olman converted Full Moon's property as Full Moon has alleged in its counterclaim in this action.

* * * *

22. Does Full Moon contend that Otis Olman was unqualified to continue serving as manager of the Jacksonville store at the time of his replacement? If your answer is yes, identify all facts that support this contention.

While Rule 33(a)(1) permits a party to submit such "contention interrogatories," the court can defer the obligation to respond if a party needs to conduct more discovery before responding.

* * * *

OTIS OLMAN
FIONA OLMAN
By their attorney,

____

Eleanor Lane
Lane & Quincy, P.A.
Trial Counsel for Plaintiffs
[Address etc. omitted]

[certificate of service omitted]

b. Full Moon Responds

When Tweedy received the Olmans' document requests and interrogatories, he immediately sent them to his client. Tweedy asked his contact at Full Moon, the associate in-house counsel Judy Kaufman, to begin the process of locating and collecting the documents requested by the Olmans. He instructed Kaufman to read the requests broadly when making this initial collection. Tweedy knew that he—along with several younger associates—could always remove documents from those initially collected by Full Moon. It would be much more difficult for him to recognize that something was missing and then ask Full Moon to find it. When he and his associates reviewed the documents initially assembled by Kaufman, they would have two principal considerations in mind. First, were the documents actually responsive to the requests? Second, was there a proper basis to withhold a document even if it was responsive? One common basis for withholding documents is privilege, a topic to which we will return shortly.

Tweedy also instructed Kaufman to keep good notes about how the company went about locating and assembling responsive documents. In particular, he wanted a record of who actually looked for documents, what instructions the searchers were given, and where they looked. Tweedy emphasized to Kaufman that this included a detailed record of the search for electronically stored information, including which computers or servers were searched, what search terms or rules were used, who conducted the searches, and how the files were organized.[45] He knew that such records could be quite useful should Lane claim that Full Moon had not conducted a diligent search. This information would also allow Tweedy to monitor what Full Moon was doing to assemble the documents.

Tweedy also sent the interrogatories to the client. He asked for specific information he could use to draft responses. Although a representative of Full Moon would have to sign the responses,[46] Tweedy would actually draft them. When he completed his draft, he would send it to Full Moon for a careful review to ensure that what he said was accurate.

---

[45] Any issues relating to complications or excessive burdens of searching for and producing electronically stored information should have been raised at the parties' Rule 26(f) conference.

[46] *See* Rule 33(b)(5) ("The person who makes the answers must sign them. . . .").

As with the document requests, Tweedy reviewed the interrogatories to determine whether he could object to any of them. Tweedy kept a list of common discovery objections. These include requests that (1) seek privileged information; (2) seek work-product materials prepared in anticipation of litigation or trial; (3) seek irrelevant material; (4) are overbroad; (5) are vague or ambiguous; (6) are unduly burdensome; (7) will cause undue expense; (8) will cause undue annoyance or embarrassment; and/or (9) are otherwise not proportional to the needs of the case. Tweedy used this list to verify he had not missed a viable objection. At the same time, he knew that Full Moon's responses to discovery requests, as well as its objections, required his signature certifying that the company's positions were advanced in good faith and were based on solid legal grounds.[47] Tweedy knew that drafting the responses to the document requests required extra care and specificity. Rule 34(b)(2)(B) required him to state that each requested item would be produced as requested, or else "state with specificity the grounds for objecting to the request, including the reasons." A conclusory objection that the request was overbroad would not be sufficient. Also, if Tweedy decided to object to a document request, he was required to affirmatively "state whether any responsive materials are being withheld on the basis of that objection."[48]

As the deadline for serving Full Moon's discovery responses neared,[49] Tweedy was ready to finalize its formal responses. He had younger lawyers and paralegals at his firm prepare the documents for production. Tweedy would never actually give original documents to opposing counsel. Rather, he normally used one of two options. First, he might make the documents available to Lane for her review, after which she could ask that certain documents be copied. Alternatively, if there were relatively few documents to be produced, Tweedy would offer to have his firm make copies (at a reasonable rate) and send them to Lane. In the Olmans' case, Tweedy and Lane had previously agreed that he would make the responsive documents available to Lane for her review.[50]

Below are excerpts from Full Moon's responses to the Olmans' document requests and interrogatories.

---

[47] *See* Rule 26(g)(1) (specifying certifications).

[48] *See* Rule 34(b)(2)(C).

[49] According to Rule 34(b)(2)(A), Tweedy had 30 days to serve his responses after receiving them. But parties often exercise their discretion under Rule 29 and agree to a longer period in which to respond.

[50] Rule 34(b)(2)(B) reflects these options, permitting a responding party to state that it will produce copies rather than permit inspection. Tweedy also had another choice about how to produce documents and electronically stored information to Lane. He could either provide documents specifically organized in response to each of her requests or he could produce the documents as they were "kept in the usual course of business." Rule 34(b)(2)(E)(i). Regarding electronically stored information, Tweedy was required to produce it in the form in which it was ordinarily maintained or in a "reasonably usable form." Rule 34(b)(2)(E)(ii). Whatever choices he made regarding the organization and form of documents, Tweedy would place sequential identification numbers on each page so they could be traced to Full Moon's production (and provide a useful means of referring to the documents in, for example, later depositions). These identification numbers are often physically affixed to documents before copying for hard copies and electronically affixed to documents produced in electronic form. In the sample responses that follow in the text, we have omitted these identification numbers.

IN THE UNITED STATES DISTRICT COURT
FOR THE MIDDLE DISTRICT OF FLORIDA
JACKSONVILLE DIVISION

OTIS AND FIONA OLMAN,

Plaintiffs,

v. Case No. 8-23-CV-00637

FULL MOON SPORTS, INC.,
& BRUCE BELCHER,

Defendants.

DEFENDANT'S RESPONSES AND OBJECTIONS TO PLAINTIFF'S FIRST REQUEST FOR PRODUCTION OF DOCUMENTS

As authorized by Federal Rule of Civil Procedure 34, Defendant Full Moon Sports, Inc. ("Defendant") hereby responds to Plaintiffs' First Request for Production of Documents as follows:

General Objections

Lawyers often begin with general objections applicable to several requests.

The following General Objections are applicable to, and incorporated by reference into, each of Defendant's responses to the specific document requests.

1. Defendant objects to the Document Request to the extent it demands production of any document protected from disclosure by the attorney-client privilege, the work-product doctrine, or any other applicable privilege. To the extent any privileged document is produced by defendant, its production is inadvertent and does not constitute a waiver of any privilege.

2. Defendant objects to the Document Request to the extent it demands production of information concerning employment actions taken regarding any employee other than Otis Olman and Fiona Olman. Such records are irrelevant and confidential.

* * * *

Specific Responses and Objections

Full Moon's use of a request/response format is not required by the Rules. As with most format used in drafting discovery documents, parties are free to devise their own manner of presentation.

Request #1

The personnel files for Otis Olman and Fiona Olman.

Response #1

Subject to the General Objections, Defendant states that it will produce all documents in its possession, custody, or control responsive to this Request.

Did Full Moon respond properly in agreeing to produce only those documents in its "possession, custody, or control"? Consider Rule 34(a)(1).

Request #2

The personnel or employee handbook(s) or manual(s) in effect at the Defendant for the period during which either Otis Olman or Fiona Olman were employed by Defendant.

Response #2

Subject to the General Objections, Defendant states that it will produce all documents in its possession, custody, or control responsive to this Request.

*****

Request #6

All documents concerning any investigation performed by Defendant or at its request concerning allegations that any employee, including either Plaintiff in this action, was terminated, demoted, transferred, denied a promotion, or otherwise harmed as a result of such employee's age.

Response #6

Defendant objects to Request #6 on the ground that it calls for the production of documents protected from disclosure by the attorney-client privilege or the work-product doctrine. Defendant further objects to this request on the ground that it is overbroad and calls for the production of irrelevant material to the extent it seeks the production of information concerning persons other than plaintiffs Otis Olman and Fiona Olman. Based on these objections, Defendant declines to produce documents responsive to this Request.

Request #7

All documents concerning or supporting Defendant's allegation in its Answer and Counterclaim that Plaintiff Otis Olman converted Defendant's property.

Response #7

Defendant objects to Request #7 on the ground that it is vague and calls for the production of documents protected from disclosure by the attorney-client privilege and/or the work-product doctrine. Subject to and without waiving these or any objections, Defendant states that it will produce all nonprivileged documents in its possession, custody, or control that are responsive to this Request. Defendant states that documents otherwise responsive to this Request are being withheld on the basis of the attorney-client privilege and/or the work-product doctrine, and that all such withheld documents are reflected on the accompanying privilege log.

Rule 34(b)(2) requires that a party respond to each "item or category," and selectively object to portions deemed objectionable.

****

Request #15

All communications, including but not limited to email or other electronic communications, concerning the reduction in force at the Jacksonville store.

Response #15

Defendant objects to Request #15 as being overbroad. Further, Defendant objects to this Request specifically with respect to the production of "email and other electronic communications" on the ground that compliance with the request would be financially burdensome and not proportional to the needs of the case. Defendant states that documents otherwise responsive to this Request are being withheld on the basis of the foregoing objections. Without waiving and subject to these objections, Defendant will produce nonprivileged documents in its possession, custody, or control that are responsive to this request with the exception of "email and other electronic communications." With respect to "email and other electronic communications," Defendant will make available for plaintiffs' inspection and copying all responsive documents that are readily available without undue burden. Defendant states that it is withholding, pursuant to the foregoing objections, nonprivileged "email and other electronic communications" maintained in such a manner as would make retrieval unduly expensive or would impose a burden disproportionate to the needs of the case.

Are Full Moon's objections supported by Rule 26 (b)(1) & (b)(2)(B)? Is its offer to make available only some of the emails and electronic information requested supported by Rule 34 (b)(2)?

Request #16

All documents concerning reductions in force for the period from 2022 to the present at any of the Defendant's retail locations, corporate headquarters, or any other location at which the Defendant conducts its business that indicate the ages of those employees terminated, transferred, or demoted as well as the ages of those persons who replaced such persons in the positions they held prior to the reduction in force.

Response #16

Defendant objects to Request #16 on the ground that it is overbroad and thus calls for the production of documents that are irrelevant to the claims or defenses of the parties and would impose a burden disproportionate to the needs of the case. In addition, Defendant objects to this request on the ground that it calls for the production of confidential and private information concerning nonparties. Defendant states that nonprivileged documents otherwise responsive to this Request are being withheld on the basis of the foregoing objections.

[Signature block and certificate of service omitted]

IN THE UNITED STATES DISTRICT COURT
FOR THE MIDDLE DISTRICT OF FLORIDA
JACKSONVILLE DIVISION

OTIS AND FIONA OLMAN,

Plaintiffs,

v. Case No. 8-23-CV-00637

FULL MOON SPORTS, INC.
& BRUCE BELCHER,

Defendants.

DEFENDANT'S ANSWERS AND OBJECTIONS TO PLAINTIFF'S FIRST SET OF INTERROGATORIES

As authorized by Federal Rule of Civil Procedure 33, Defendant Full Moon Sports, Inc. hereby responds to Plaintiff's First Set of Interrogatories as follows:

General Objections

[omitted]

Answers and Specific Objections

Interrogatory #1

Identify the person or persons who made the determination to promote Mr. Sid Shockley to manager of the Jacksonville store.

Response #1

Subject to the General Objections, Full Moon states that the ultimate decision to promote Mr. Shockley was made by Full Moon's Reorganization Committee.

Interrogatory #2

Identify the manager or managers of Full Moon's information systems, information management, or computer department (or other similar department or organizational structure) for the period from January 2022 to the present.

Response #2

Subject to and incorporating the General Objections, Full Moon states that Mr. Noah Stephen held the position of Vice President of Information Management at Full Moon during the specified period.

* * * *

Interrogatory #8

State the age of all managers of all Full Moon retail stores as of January 2022 and January 2023.

Response #8

Full Moon objects to Interrogatory #8 on the grounds that it is overbroad and calls for information that is not relevant to the claim or defense of any party. Accordingly, Full Moon declines to answer.

* * * *

Interrogatory #15

Identify all facts that support your contention that Otis Olman converted Full Moon's property as Full Moon has alleged in its counterclaim in this action.

Response #15

Full Moon objects to Interrogatory #15 as being premature. Further responding, Full Moon states that it will respond to Interrogatory #15 after it has had an opportunity to engage in discovery as contemplated by the Case Management Order in this case.

* * * *

Interrogatory #22

Does Full Moon contend that Otis Olman was unqualified to continue serving as manager of the Jacksonville store at the time of his replacement? If your answer is yes, identify all facts that support this contention.

Response #22

Yes, Full Moon contends that Plaintiff Otis Olman was unqualified to continue serving as manager of the Jacksonville store at the time of his replacement. Full Moon objects to Interrogatory #22 as being premature to the extent it calls for an identification of "all facts that support this contention." Full Moon states that it will respond to Interrogatory #22 after it has had an opportunity to engage in discovery as contemplated by the Case Management order in this case.

* * * *

As to Objections,
Full Moon Sports, Inc.
By its attorneys

____

Harrison Ames, Esq.
Bart A. Tweedy, Esq.
Counsel for Full Moon Sports, Inc.

[Address, phone number, etc. omitted]
As to Answers:

____

Bertie Lurch
President, Full Moon Sports, Inc.

Before me personally appeared Bertie Lurch, who swore under the penalties of perjury that the foregoing answers were true and accurate based on a review of the books and records of Full Moon Sports, Inc.

____

Thomas Alva
Notary Public, my commission expires: 12/10/2024

[Certificate of Service omitted]

After completing the responses to both the document requests and interrogatories, Tweedy served them on Lane. He was pleased to have completed the work, but he knew that the Rules required him to supplement these responses should additional responsive information come to light, or if anything contained in the responses later turned out to be "incomplete or incorrect."[51]

c. Lane Reacts

Lane immediately reviewed Full Moon's responses to her interrogatories and document requests. As expected, she was unsatisfied with several of the responses. Of course, not all of the responses were deficient. Full Moon had provided substantive responses to many of her interrogatories. In addition, Full Moon had agreed to make available what appeared to be a substantial number of documents. Lane now intended to contact Tweedy to set a mutually convenient time to review those documents and to discuss her disagreement with some of his other responses.

[51] *See* Rule 26(e)(1)(A).

Lane saw three areas in which Full Moon had been unresponsive to her document requests. First, Tweedy had refused to produce documents or answer interrogatories concerning Full Moon's action regarding workers other than the Olmans.[52] Lane knew that such information could be critical to her case. She would try to convince Tweedy to disclose this information voluntarily rather than requiring that she seek a court order compelling disclosure.

Second, Full Moon had withheld a document specifically addressing age-related issues that was prepared in connection with its reduction in force.[53] Lane knew about the existence of this document because Rule 26(b)(5)(A) required Tweedy to identify the document even though Full Moon claimed that it was privileged and could be withheld from production. Tweedy had complied with this Rule by preparing a "privilege log," which was intended to "enable other parties to assess the applicability of the privilege."[54] The log disclosed existence of a report dated February 15, 2023, prepared by Samantha Brown, a member of Full Moon's Human Relations Department and entitled "The Personnel Impact of Full Moon's 2022 Reduction in Force." The report had been sent to the Full Moon president, Lurch, and a copy of the report had been distributed to Full Moon's general counsel. Lane would try to obtain that report, which might contain evidence damaging to Full Moon's position.

Finally, Tweedy had indicated that Full Moon was willing to produce email relevant to the claims in the case, except that it would not produce email that was stored in a manner that would make retrieval unduly expensive or impose a burden disproportionate to the needs of the case.[55] The issue of electronically stored information had been raised during the parties' Rule 26(f) conference and included in the discovery plan, as required by Rule 26(f)(2) and (3). At the time, however, neither Lane nor Tweedy envisioned that the volume of electronically stored documents would be particularly large or difficult to retrieve, relative to most federal litigation. Tweedy's objection, however, suggested that the responsive emails were either more voluminous or more difficult to retrieve than they had first anticipated. Lane suspected that Full Moon's primary concern resulted from the way in which the email was stored on its computers and the cost and effort involved in retrieving it. Because Lane needed access to these communications, she would negotiate with Tweedy some way to reduce these costs.

Lane raised each of the problems she had identified during a phone conference with Tweedy. Lane and Tweedy were able to resolve two of their three disputes. First, Lane and Tweedy resolved the issue of email production by compromising. They agreed that she would

---

[52] *See, e.g.,* Full Moon's Responses to Document Requests Nos. 6 and 15 and Full Moon's response to Interrogatory No. 8.

[53] *See* Full Moon's Response to Document Request No. 6.

[54] *See* Rule 26(b)(5)(A) ("When a party withholds information otherwise discoverable by claiming that the information is privileged or subject to protection as trial-preparation material, the party must (i) expressly make the claim; and (ii) describe the nature of the documents, communications, or tangible things not produced or disclosed—and do so in a manner that, without revealing information itself privileged or protected, will enable other parties to assess the claim.").

[55] *See* Full Moon Response to Document Request No. 15. In most cases, the responding party bears the cost of responding to nonobjectionable discovery requests. *See, e.g., Oppenheimer Fund, Inc. v. Sanders,* 437 U.S. 340, 358 (1978) ("under [the discovery] rules, the presumption is that the responding party must bear the expense of complying with discovery requests").

narrow her request by limiting the emails produced to a briefer time period and to particular individuals or departments. They also agreed, after consulting with their clients, that the Olmans would pay a small portion of the cost of retrieval and production of the emails. Both lawyers knew that the issue of cost shifting in electronic discovery is filled with uncertainty. Each decided it was better to craft a compromise solution than risk having an unfavorable solution imposed by the court.

Lane and Tweedy also compromised concerning discovery of the impact of Full Moon's reduction in force on workers other than the Olmans. To a considerable extent, the lawyers' disagreement reflected differing views of the law regarding the relevance of such information to age discrimination claims. As Lane stressed to Tweedy, courts uniformly recognize that statistics showing a disparity in the ages of employees terminated in a corporate downsizing constitute circumstantial evidence of an ADEA violation. As Tweedy argued in response, Lane's request went too far. She had requested companywide information for all store employees. Case law, however, generally requires that requests for statistical information target an appropriate group, considering factors such as job title and responsibility, as well as location (both geographically and within the structure of the company).[56]

Lane and Tweedy eventually agreed that Full Moon would produce records showing the ages of those persons in the position of store or department manager, both before and after the company's reduction in force. Finally, after much resistance, Full Moon agreed to provide the data for all its stores, including the information requested in the interrogatories. Tweedy concluded it was highly likely a court would order Full Moon to produce this data if Lane filed a motion to compel.

Tactical Tip ✍

Courts and Discovery Disputes

Some of the willingness of Lane and Tweedy to compromise was driven by a litigation reality—many judges dislike resolving discovery disputes, which can bring out the worst in lawyers. An experienced lawyer will present a discovery dispute to the court only when it is truly important to the client. Judges appreciate this approach and, over the long term, come to trust a lawyer who is discriminating in seeking the court's involvement.

One issue remained. Despite their best efforts, Lane and Tweedy were unable to resolve their dispute concerning production of the report "The Personnel Impact of Full Moon's 2022 Reduction in Force." Tweedy was insistent that the document was protected from disclosure either by the attorney-client privilege or the work-product doctrine. Lane was equally insistent that the document was fully discoverable. Lane was able to convince Tweedy to withdraw his

[56] *See, e.g., Balderston v. Fairbanks Morse Division of Coltec Industries*, 328 F.3d 309, 319-20 (7th Cir. 2003).

objection based on the attorney-client privilege,[57] but he did not budge on the work-product objection. At the end of their conference, Lane informed Tweedy that she would file a motion to compel seeking the production of this document. Tweedy good-naturedly responded that he would "see her in court," if they had the opportunity to argue the motion at a hearing.[58]

Before we discuss Lane's action to compel discovery of the report, consider the following hypothetical questions to assess your understanding of the procedural aspects of a motion to compel.

Question 9.3

1. What steps should Lane take to properly present her motion to compel to the court? Be sure to cite specific provisions of Rule 37.

2. Assume that, although Tweedy makes several plausible, good-faith arguments that the personnel report is a protected work product, the court ultimately rules in Lane's favor. What sanctions, if any, can the court award under Rule 37? Is the court required to impose a sanction? Does Rule 26(g) provide the court with an alternative authority to sanction Full Moon in this situation? Why or why not?

3. Assume, for the purposes of this question, only that Full Moon simply failed to respond to the Olmans' request for production of the personnel report. What action should Lane take under Rule 37 to compel compliance with her request? What sanctions can the court order against Full Moon?

4. Assume that instead of seeking the personnel report from Full Moon, Lane issued a subpoena under Rule 45 directing Belcher to produce the personnel report. (He had apparently retained a copy when he left the company.) Recall that Belcher is no longer a party to the suit and currently resides in Connecticut. Belcher fails to respond to Lane's subpoena. What action can Lane take to compel compliance with her subpoena? In which court must Lane proceed to compel production of the report from Belcher?

---

[57] Tweedy was wise to abandon the attorney-client privilege objection. That privilege protects (1) communications, (2) between lawyers (including certain of their agents) and clients, (3) made in confidence and remaining private, (4) for the purpose of obtaining legal advice. *See* Edna Selan Epstein, The Attorney-Client Privilege and the Work-Product Doctrine at 64-66 (American Bar Assn. 2007). Ms. Brown, author of the report, was not a lawyer and neither was Mr. Lurch, to whom it was presented. It is true that a copy of the report was sent to Full Moon's general counsel, but simply "copying" a lawyer is not enough. *See id.* at 68 ("Clients and their attorneys often assume, erroneously, that merely conveying something to an attorney will cloak the underlying facts from compelled disclosure. It will not.").

[58] Practice varies by court and by judge as to whether oral argument is held on motions, especially those related to discovery.

Motion Commotion by Charles Fincher

MOTION TO COMPEL

d. The Discovery Dispute Is Resolved

After consulting with Tweedy, Lane turned to drafting her motion to compel. Tweedy had originally asserted two bases for Full Moon's refusal to turn over its personnel report: attorney-client privilege and work-product protection. All that remained now was Full Moon's work-product objection.

Under Rule 26(b)(3), work product, now referred to as "trial preparation materials," consists of "documents and tangible things" that are protected from disclosure because they were "prepared in anticipation of litigation or for trial by or for another party or its representative." It seemed to Lane to be a close call whether the personnel report met the requirements of "trial preparation material."

Consider the following questions concerning work product.

Question 9.4

1. Assume that Samantha Brown, the author of the personnel report, is not an attorney. She was asked by President Lurch to prepare the report immediately after Lurch received Otis's letter complaining of age discrimination. He made this request on his own initiative because "I wanted to see what was going on." Lurch is not a lawyer and did not speak with Full Moon's general counsel before he ordered the report. In light of these limited facts, what argument might Tweedy make to support his assertion that the personnel report is protected "trial preparation material"? What argument might Lane make to rebut this claim? How should the court rule?

2. Assume for the moment that the report is, in fact, trial preparation material as defined by Rule 26(b)(3). Would there be any way that Lane might still be entitled to it? Please explain.

3. In document request No. 7, Lane sought "All documents concerning or supporting Defendant's allegation in its Answer and Counterclaim that Plaintiff Otis Olman converted Defendant's property." Tweedy responded that, with respect to some of the documents encompassed within this request, Lane sought material protected by the "work-product doctrine." What might be the basis for Tweedy's objection?

Lane prepared her motion and supporting memorandum with the understanding that the dispute would almost certainly be resolved by U.S. Magistrate Judge Matthew Malarkey.[59] Magistrate judges serve as a form of judicial adjunct to the district court. Unlike district judges, who are appointed by the President, confirmed by the U.S. Senate, and serve for life, magistrate judges are appointed to eight-year terms by the district judges in each federal district.[60] In civil matters, magistrate judges may decide nondispositive pretrial matters, such as discovery disputes, if such motions are referred to them by a district judge.[61] A magistrate judge's decision on nondispositive motions may be reversed by the district judge on appeal, but only if the decision is clearly erroneous.[62]

District judges may also refer dispositive motions, such as motions to dismiss or motions for summary judgment, to a magistrate judge. The magistrate judge will then make a "report

---

[59] In the Middle District of Florida, each case is randomly assigned to both a district judge and a magistrate judge. *See* Local Rule 1.03(a). Other federal districts use different methods to assign magistrate judges to cases.

[60] *See* 28 U.S.C. § 631.

[61] *See* 28 U.S.C. § 636(b)(1)(A).

[62] *See* 28 U.S.C. § 636(b)(1)(A). The clearly erroneous standard of review is highly deferential. In other words, the magistrate judge's decision is highly likely to be upheld under this standard.

and recommendation" to the district judge.[63] If there is an appeal from such a report and recommendation, the district judge decides the matter *de novo* (i.e., without giving any deference to the magistrate's recommendation).[64] Finally, parties may consent to having a magistrate judge conduct all proceedings in a case, including trial.[65] In this case, Full Moon and the Olmans had not consented to such an action.

Judge Goodenough referred Lane's motion to compel to Magistrate Judge Malarkey for resolution. When Tweedy received Lane's motion papers, he prepared an opposition. He also asked that Lane be sanctioned for making the motion.[66] The matter was now ready to be decided.

As was common practice in the Middle District of Florida, Judge Malarkey did not hold a hearing on the motion. Instead, he issued his decision "on the papers." Lane and Tweedy received his brief decision through the court's electronic filing system. Judge Malarkey denied Lane's motion to compel Full Moon to disclose its personnel report. He ruled that it was a close question whether Full Moon had a strong enough basis to fear litigation when Lurch ordered the report prepared.[67] This "fear" was critical under the Rules because the document could be considered trial preparation material only if it were "prepared in anticipation of litigation."[68] Judge Malarkey ultimately concluded that "anticipation of litigation" was the primary motivating factor in the report's preparation, but he believed that Lane's motion had

[63] *See* 28 U.S.C. § 636(b)(1)(B).

[64] *See* 28 U.S.C. § 636(b)(1).

[65] *See* 28 U.S.C. § 636(c).

[66] Such a request was common, but probably unnecessary. Rule 37 makes sanctions mandatory unless the court makes certain findings. *See, e.g.*, Rule 37(a)(5)(B) (mandating the payment of expenses and fees unless the court finds the motion was "substantially justified or other circumstances make an award of expenses unjust").

[67] *See* Epstein, The Attorney-Client Privilege and the Work Product Doctrine 871-74 (discussing the work-product status of documents that could be characterized as "routine investigatory documents"). A document that is prepared as part of the normal course of business simply does not meet Rule 26(b)(3)'s requirement that the trial preparation materials be prepared "in anticipation of litigation."

[68] *See* Rule 26(b)(3).

been "substantially justified." Accordingly, while he denied the motion to compel, he also denied Tweedy's request for sanctions because it would be "unjust."[69]

3. Depositions

a. Lane Prepares for Depositions

Now that Lane had reviewed the documentary discovery and answers to interrogatories, she felt ready to begin taking depositions. In a deposition, the lawyers are allowed to question a deponent under oath. All the questions and answers are recorded for later use at trial or in connection with a summary judgment motion.[70] A party's lawyer typically deposes witnesses whose testimony will likely be used by an *adversary*. For one thing, witnesses favorable to a party will usually provide information to that party without being subject to formal discovery. Further, because deposition testimony is frequently used to challenge (impeach) the witness's later in-court testimony, the witness is likely to be deposed by opposing counsel. The task of a lawyer whose supporting witnesses have been summoned for deposition by an adversary is to prepare and assist those witnesses so they avoid giving harmful testimony. Such preparation and assistance are limited, of course, by a lawyer's obligation to refrain from suborning false testimony.

Lane knew that depositions can be very important in resolving litigation.[71] In a deposition, she could assess how a witness would appear to the jury, explore the meaning of documents, and delve into areas of the case not covered by documents. What's more, she was able to get information unfiltered by a lawyer, unlike the answers to interrogatories.

The principal downside of depositions is expense. The party taking the deposition must spend the time necessary to review relevant materials and prepare good questions. The person being deposed—particularly if represented by counsel—will try to anticipate likely questions and prepare the best responses. Then, all the parties will need to be present for the deposition itself.[72] Add to these factors the cost of the court reporter's time and the transcript, and you can see what an investment in time and resources a single deposition can be. Thus, lawyers and parties need to balance the utility of the deposition against its costs.

---

[69] *See* Rule 37(a)(5)(B).

[70] The most common form of deposition is the "deposition upon oral examination" governed by Rule 30. There is also a seldom used "deposition by written questions" governed by Rule 31. In a deposition by written questions, one lawyer gives a list of questions to a court reporter. The court reporter then reads the questions to the witness and also records the answers given. The device is not all that useful, principally because it does not allow for follow-up to the answers actually given. Several other Rules also concern depositions, including Rule 28, which specifies before whom a deposition may be taken, and Rule 32, which addresses the use of depositions in court proceedings.

[71] *See, e.g.*, Andrew J. Ruzicho et al., Litigating Age Discrimination Cases at § 7:14 (2015) ("Depositions have taken on additional importance under the ADEA due to the propensity of courts to grant summary judgment.").

[72] Under the Federal Rules, a single "deposition day" is limited to seven hours. *See* Rule 30(d)(1).

The first order of business was for Lane to determine whom to depose. Apart from cost considerations, she would have to make her selections carefully. The Federal Rules limited the number of depositions she could take without leave of court or party stipulation to 10.[73] One of the people whom Lane clearly wanted to depose was Belcher. Because Belcher was no longer a party to the suit, Lane had a bit more work to compel his attendance. Had Belcher still been a party, Lane could have simply sent him a "notice of deposition" compelling his attendance. This notice was a one-page document stating the date, time, and place where the deposition was to be taken. Lane was required to serve the notice on all other parties and make sure that she had given each of them a "reasonable" amount of time to prepare for the deposition.[74] However, Belcher was not a party, so in addition to sending the required notice of deposition, Lane would need to serve a subpoena to compel him to appear.[75] Lane prepared the subpoena, which required Belcher to appear for a deposition in Connecticut.

Lane also wanted to depose Kay Bailey, the chairperson of Full Moon's corporate board of directors. Lane believed that Bailey had information relevant to the Olmans' claim that Full Moon had discriminated against its older workers. From all she could gather, Full Moon had a corporate plan to reduce its number of older workers. Who better to discuss and/or know about these plans than the leader of the board of directors? An incidental benefit of taking Bailey's deposition was to underscore the seriousness of the Olmans' lawsuit. Lane prepared and served the appropriate paperwork, although she expected that Tweedy might fight it. Time would tell.

Finally,[76] Lane wanted to take the deposition of Full Moon itself, something the Federal Rules allowed under Rule 30(b)(6).[77] This procedural device relieved her of the obligation of guessing which corporate official might have the information she sought. She would identify what matters she wanted to explore in the deposition, and Full Moon would choose its own spokesperson. This deposition device, however, did not preclude her from taking the depositions of specific individuals in the corporation.[78] So, for example, Lane could still depose Bertie Lurch, Full Moon's president.

---

[73] *See* Rule 30(a)(2)(A)(i).

[74] *See* Rule 30(b)(1) ("A party who wants to depose a person by oral questions must give reasonable written notice to every other party. The notice must state the time and place of the deposition and, if known, the deponent's name and address."). In most jurisdictions, a lawyer noticing a deposition will contact other lawyers (and perhaps the intended deponent) to arrive at a mutually convenient time for taking the deposition. Otherwise, a seriously inconvenienced lawyer will seek a protective order from the court requiring a rescheduling of the deposition. *See* Rule 26(c) (stating grounds for protective orders). The notice of deposition is a single-page document that sets out the date, time, and place of the deposition. It must be served on all parties.

[75] *See generally* Rule 45.

[76] Lane had many other potential deponents. We limit the text discussion to just a few.

[77] *See* Rule 30(b)(6) ("In its notice or subpoena, a party may name as the deponent a public or private corporation, a partnership, an association, a governmental agency, or other entity and must describe with reasonable particularity the matters for examination.").

[78] *See* Rule 30(b)(6) ("This paragraph (6) does not preclude a deposition by any other procedure allowed by these rules.").

When Full Moon received the Rule 30(b)(6) deposition notice, it was required to "designate one or more officers, directors, or managing agents, or . . . other persons who consent to testify on its behalf" to be deposed regarding each matter about which Lane requested testimony.[79] Tweedy knew that he was obligated to prepare any person designated pursuant to Rule 30(b)(6) so the person was able to "testify about information known or reasonably available to [Full Moon]."[80] The Rule further requires that before or promptly after the notice of 30(b)(6) deposition has been served, the parties must "confer in good faith" about the matters identified for examination.

A Note Concerning: **Corporate Testimony**

The large majority of litigants in private, civil suits in federal court are business entities like corporations. There are several useful distinctions that can be drawn when seeking deposition testimony from persons employed by a corporate litigant.

First, "apex" officials in the corporation, including *officers, directors, and managing agents,* are equated with the corporation and can be deposed by simply noticing the corporation that you intend to depose the apex person in her "official" capacity. (The discovery rules don't expressly state this, but that is their accepted meaning. *See, e.g., Folwell v. Hernandez,* 210 F.R.D. 169, 172 (M.D.N.C. 2002).) Consequently, Lane could simply notice the deposition of board member Kay Bailey. As discussed later, however, attempts to depose apex persons can generate dispute during discovery.

Second, as Lane did with Full Moon, you can notify a corporation through a notice or a subpoena of the matters that you wish to explore on deposition and permit it to designate its spokesperson. Rule 30(b)(6) states that the corporation may designate an apex person to testify for it ("officers, directors, or managing agents") or may designate "other persons who consent to testify on its behalf."

Third, you can subpoena current or former corporate personnel who are not apex persons. While the Rules presume that apex persons speak for the corporation and can be noticed to testify without a subpoena, other persons are not equated with the corporation and may require a subpoena.

The classification of corporate personnel is important for determining how their testimony can be used at trial. According to Rule 32(a)(3), the testimony of an apex person or any other person who consents to testify for the corporation under Rule 30(b)(6) can be used by an opponent "for any purpose." Consequently, the testimony of these persons poses a risk for corporate litigants, and the corporation's lawyer will take pains to prepare these persons properly for deposition.

---

[79] *See* Rule 30(b)(6).

[80] *See* Rule 30(b)(6).

b. A Discovery Controversy

Lane and Tweedy had conferred and worked out a schedule for proposed depositions, but they were unable to resolve one issue. Recall that Lane sought to depose Kay Bailey, chairperson of Full Moon's board of directors and an apex official. While Tweedy recognized that Bailey's deposition could be noticed under Rule 30, he still objected that she failed to satisfy one of the key requirements of Rule 26(b)(1)—Bailey had no information "relevant" to the issues in contention. Tweedy also wondered whether Lane might be deposing Bailey as a not so subtle means of harassment.

As required under the Rules, Lane and Tweedy discussed Tweedy's reservations about Bailey's deposition.[81] Tweedy referred Lane to several cases in which courts have precluded the depositions of apex corporate officials when the officials lack unique personal knowledge of matters in dispute.[82] For her part, Lane stressed that the decisions leading to her clients' termination were corporate ones, reflecting at some level Full Moon's corporate culture. As she asked Tweedy: Who better to speak about that corporate culture than the chairperson of the board of directors? Moreover, Lane reminded Tweedy that the Rules gave her a great deal of leeway in using the various discovery tools. Tweedy responded by making two points. First, he underscored for Lane that Bailey had never heard of the Olmans, had never been to Jacksonville, and knew about the facts of the case only through conversations with counsel. Second, Tweedy told Lane that, in his experience, notices of deposition to apex officials such as Bailey were nothing more than a harassment device.

Despite their best efforts, Lane and Tweedy were unable to resolve their disagreement. This time, it was Tweedy's turn to seek the court's help. To prevent Bailey's deposition, Tweedy turned to Rule 26(c), which allows the court to enter a "protective order" to prevent or limit discovery "for good cause . . . to protect a party or person from annoyance, embarrassment, oppression, or undue burden or expense."[83] There was already a protective order in place in the case, but it was of a far different nature. Early on, Tweedy had proposed and Lane had stipulated to a protective order, later entered by the court, that mandated certain procedures by which Full Moon would produce relevant documents that it claimed were confidential and proprietary business information.[84]

The situation here was quite different because the parties were not in agreement. Tweedy began the formal process of resolving their dispute by preparing, serving on Lane, and filing

---

[81] *See* Rule 26(c) (requiring that, before seeking the court's intervention to prevent discovery through a protective order, the objecting party confer in good faith with the other party in an effort to resolve the dispute).

[82] *See, e.g., Evans v. Allstate Insurance Co.*, 216 F.R.D. 515 (N.D. Okla. 2003); *Folwell v. Hernandez*, 210 F.R.D. 169 (M.D.N.C. 2002); *Baine v. General Motors Corp.*, 141 F.R.D. 332 (M.D. Ala. 1991).

[83] Rule 26(c); *see also* Rule 26(b)(2)(C) (conferring similar authority on the court as a means to limit discovery).

[84] *See* Rule 26(c)(1)(G) (providing specific authorization for the court to enter a protective order specifying "that a trade secret or other confidential research, development, or commercial information not be revealed or be revealed only in a specified way").

with the court a motion, memorandum of law, and certain supporting papers such as Ms. Bailey's affidavit attesting that she had no personal knowledge of the matters at issue in the complaint. Tweedy once again sought sanctions based on Lane's refusal to withdraw the deposition notice.[85] He believed that Lane not only was wrong about the law allowing Bailey's deposition, but she had no good-faith basis for her argument. Lane responded to the motion with her own memorandum of law opposing the entry of a protective order.

Motion Commotion by Charles Fincher

MOTION FOR PROTECTIVE ORDERS

As with Lane's earlier motion to compel, Judge Goodenough referred Full Moon's motion for a protective order to Magistrate Judge Malarkey for resolution. After reviewing the parties' submissions, Magistrate Judge Malarkey issued a brief written order in which he granted the motion. However, he gave Lane the opportunity to seek permission later to depose Bailey should she uncover information suggesting that Bailey did, in fact, have firsthand knowledge of relevant matters. Judge Malarkey also awarded sanctions against Lane and the Olmans, requiring them to reimburse Full Moon for its costs, including a reasonable attorneys' fee, incurred in connection with the motion for a protective order.[86] Unlike the situation involving the motion to compel, Magistrate Judge Malarkey did not find Lane's position here to be "substantially justified."[87]

[85] *See* Rules 26(c)(3) and 37(a)(5) (concerning award of sanctions in connection with motion for a protective order).

[86] *See* Rule 26(c)(3) (directing that the provisions of Rule 37(a)(5) concerning the award of expenses apply to motions for a protective order).

[87] *See* Rule 37(a)(5) (directing that the court "must" impose the shifting of costs as a sanction if a motion is granted unless the court finds that the conduct of the party opposing the motion was "substantially justified" or that cost-shifting would be "unjust"). The Olmans did not appeal Magistrate Judge Malarkey's decision to Judge Goodenough. Lane advised them that, in her experience, Judge Goodenough did not look favorably on such appeals of discovery orders. In this case, the Olmans' legal position was weak. Lane determined that it would be better to save her "judicial capital" for later in the case.

c. Preparing Witnesses

Tweedy received Lane's notices and subpoenas and began preparing for the depositions. Lane had subpoenaed Shockley, and Tweedy knew that he would have his hands full getting him ready for deposition. He also knew how important this preparation would be.

The lawyer representing a deponent has his principal work to do before the day of the deposition. The lawyer needs to put himself in the shoes of opposing counsel. What questions will she ask? What documents will she use? What style of questioning will she use? To the extent possible, the lawyer preparing a witness wants to ensure that the witness is not surprised by any document or line of questioning. The lawyer also wants to prepare the witness for the experience of a deposition.

A deposition is a deceptively informal proceeding. It usually takes place in a law office or a hotel conference room. Although a witness is typically nervous at the beginning, after a while the court reporter blends into the background, and the questioning seems more and more like a conversation. It was Tweedy's job to make sure that his witnesses were not lulled into a sense of false security at their depositions. They needed to be reminded they should remain on their guard for the entire time.

Tweedy also knew it was important to caution his witnesses against the common tendency to say more than is needed to answer a question. He had been amazed in his career how many witnesses actually believe that if they just explain everything, the other party will see things their way! Tweedy worked with his witnesses so they understood their job was to answer only the question asked. Of course, he began and ended his preparation sessions with the most important rules he wanted deponents to remember—always tell the truth and don't guess.

d. Taking a Deposition

The skills involved in taking effective depositions are usually introduced to law students in a pretrial practice course and later developed through experience. In the following discussion, we offer a very brief introduction to the subject of taking depositions by focusing on one of Lane's key deponents, Shockley. We begin by offering some practical advice gleaned from experience, which we hope gives you a sense of the personal dynamics involved in a deposition and how the rules of civil procedure come to life in practice. We then offer an illustrative excerpt from Shockley's deposition, which demonstrates how lawyers can respond when deposition questions provoke controversy.

Shockley's deposition took place on August 5, 2023 at Lane's offices in Jacksonville. Present at the deposition were Lane, Tweedy, Shockley, and a court reporter. Lane had considered having Otis attend the deposition, but she eventually concluded that it was best not to create a situation in which there could be a "scene." Below are excerpts from the transcript of that deposition:

****

Ms. Lane: Mr. Shockley, have you ever referred to Otis Olman as the "old man"?

Mr. Shockley: Oh sure, several times. That's what we always called the commander of the ship when I was in the Navy. He . . . Otis was store commander and you know. . . .

Ms. Lane: Did you call Mr. Olman old man to his face?

Mr. Shockley: I can't say for sure, probably not right in his face.

Ms. Lane: Did you believe Mr. Olman would be displeased by your calling him the old man?

Mr. Shockley: Well I don't know, maybe if I said it in front of customers.

Ms. Lane: Did you ever refer to Mr. Olman as the old man in front of customers?

Mr. Shockley: Not that I recall.

Ms. Lane: Did you ever refer to Mr. Olman as the old man when speaking with Bruce Belcher?

Mr. Shockley: I might have. Bruce was cool and you could say things to him.

Ms. Lane: You mean saying things like you could do a better job running the store?

Mr. Shockley: Yeah.

Ms. Lane: Did you ask Mr. Belcher to give you the job as store manager?

Mr. Shockley: Not exactly. Actually I think he was the one who asked me if I wanted to manage the store. One day, he said that Atlanta was going to be making some changes in stores . . . in store managers and maybe I could manage the Jax store.

Ms. Lane: When was it you spoke with Mr. Belcher about becoming store manager?

Mr. Shockley: It seems like it was month or so before the decision was made. When Atlanta first starting talking about making changes. I'm not sure about the date and all.

Ms. Lane: Did you ever tell Mr. Belcher Otis was too old to be running the store?

Mr. Shockley: No, I never said that. I mean, he wasn't that knowledgeable of extreme sport lines and that's where the store was heading. He was into kayaks and scuba, some camping. He didn't relate to board sports at all.

Ms. Lane: Would you say that extreme sports appeal to younger customers?

Mr. Shockley: For sure. Not too many 40-year-old men like falling onto the sidewalk off a skateboard.

Ms. Lane: Do you believe a younger man like yourself . . . by the way Mr. Shockley, how old are you?

Mr. Shockley: Just turned 32.

Ms. Lane: Well, do you believe a relatively younger man like yourself can do a better job marketing extreme sporting goods?

Mr. Shockley: I don't mean . . . it's not that there's any specific age for selling extreme lines. But if you don't relate to the customers and know the equipment from the point of view of a user you have a harder time selling or even knowing what to stock. Otis had that problem.

Ms. Lane: You mean Otis was better suited for an older customer, boomers for example.

Mr. Shockley: That's right. Otis could sell to a niche customer . . . don't get me wrong. These people have money to spend and are important to the store. They don't have any problem throwing down $1,500 for a kayak or $400 for a GPS.

Ms. Lane: You are referring now to older customers?

Mr. Shockley: Yeah, more middle-aged people. Boomers.

Ms. Lane: Did Mr. Belcher share your views?

Can you speculate as to why Tweedy objected to this question? Did Tweedy have to object?

Mr. Tweedy: Objection.

Mr. Shockley: Well, I can't speak for Bruce. But I know he was concerned with getting sales figures up and thought extreme lines had more potential over the long run.

Ms. Lane: Did Mr. Belcher indicate whether he thought you were better able to appeal to younger customers?

Mr. Shockley: I'm not clear on what you're asking.

Ms. Lane: Never mind. Mr. Shockley, would you consider Mr. Belcher to be your friend?

Mr. Shockley: Certainly.

Ms. Lane: Have you ever socialized with him outside the store?

Mr. Shockley: Yes.

Ms. Lane: Have you ever observed Mr. Belcher dating a store employee?

Mr. Tweedy: I object, Ms. Lane. That is totally irrelevant to any issue in this case.

Ms. Lane: Well, as you know Mr. Tweedy, that's an objection you can make at trial if you think it's that important.

Mr. Tweedy: I hope you don't intend to carry this further.

Ms. Lane: Well, actually I do. Mr. Shockley, to your knowledge, has Mr. Belcher ever had a romantic relationship with a store employee?

Mr. Tweedy: Again, I object. Our question calls for irrelevant, private, and prejudicial testimony.

Ms. Lane: Mr. Tweedy, for the record, are you instructing Mr. Shockley not to answer my question?

Mr. Shockley: Do I have to?

According to Rule 30(c)(2), could Tweedy have ordered Shockley not to answer the question?

Mr. Tweedy: For the record, I am not instructing Mr. Shockley to do anything. I am simply making a proper objection to your irrelevant line of questioning.

Ms. Lane: Mr. Shockley, did you discuss your testimony at an earlier meeting with Mr. Tweedy?

According to Rule 30(c)(2), were Tweedy's objection and instruction to Shockley proper?

Mr. Tweedy: I do object to that question and direct Mr. Shockley not to answer it. You know Mr. Shockley's discussion with me is protected by the attorney-client privilege.

Ms. Lane: Well, Mr. Shockley, I'm interested to hear whether Mr. Tweedy prepared you to testify today. Now let's get back to my earlier question. Do you know whether Mr. Belcher ever had a romantic relationship with a store employee?

Mr. Tweedy: Objection.

Ms. Lane: The witness may answer.

Mr. Shockley: Bruce may have dated an employee a few years ago.

Ms. Lane: Do you remember her name?

Mr. Shockley: Wanda Welcome. She worked as a cashier around 2020-21.

Ms. Lane: Is she still employed with Full Moon?

Mr. Shockley: No.

Ms. Lane: Do you know why she is no longer employed with Full Moon?

Mr. Shockley: No.

Ms. Lane: How old would you guess Ms. Welcome was when she worked at the Jacksonville store?

Mr. Tweedy: Objection.

Mr. Shockley: I can't say definitely. But I know she had recently graduated from Fletcher High in Jacksonville Beach.

*****

Shockley's deposition occurred outside the presence of a judge. This meant that Tweedy's objections to Lane's questioning could not be resolved during the course of the deposition. To facilitate the uninterrupted taking of depositions, Rule 32(b) permits lawyers to defer most common evidentiary objections till the objectionable testimony is used later at a hearing or at trial. In addition, Rule 30(c)(2) prohibits a lawyer from instructing a witness not to answer a question except where "necessary to preserve a privilege, to enforce a limitation ordered by the court, or to present a motion under Rule 30(d)(3)." The motion authorized in Rule 30(d)(3) permits a lawyer to suspend a deposition and seek court protection when the deposition is being conducted "in bad faith or in a manner that unreasonably annoys, embarrasses, or oppresses the deponent or party."

In light of these Rules, consider the questions below.

Question 9.5

1. When Lane asked Shockley whether Belcher had ever been romantically involved with a store employee, Tweedy objected that the question called for an answer that was "irrelevant, private, and prejudicial." Could he have deferred making this objection till Lane used the testimony later in court? Could he have properly instructed Shockley not to answer the question?

2. Why do you think Tweedy felt the need to object to inquiries into Belcher's romantic relationship with a store employee? What relevance might these questions have to the Olmans' suit?

3. Recall that when Lane asked Shockley whether he had discussed his testimony earlier with Tweedy, Tweedy objected and directed Shockley not to answer the question. Was this proper? If she had persisted with this line of questioning, what could Tweedy have done other than directing Shockley to remain silent?

After the deposition, the court reporter transcribed what had been said. The transcript was then forwarded to the deponent and, for a fee, counsel in the case. In most cases, deponents will request an opportunity to read the transcript and make any changes in their testimony. The Rules allow for the submission of such an "errata sheet" within 30 days of the deponent's being notified that the transcript is available.[88] Tweedy had requested an opportunity for Shockley to read and sign his deposition. Given the importance of Shockley's testimony, Tweedy would work closely with him when the time came for the review.

4. The Second Wave of Paper Discovery: Admissions[89]

A final form of paper discovery Lane and Tweedy needed to consider was the Rule 36 request for admissions. The response to a request for an admission may have greater consequence than the response to other forms of discovery. In particular, if a party actually admits the matter addressed in a request, it is no longer in dispute. Both the judge deciding a motion for summary judgment and the jury deliberating its verdict have to accept the admission as true. In comparison, an answer to an interrogatory or a deposition question constitutes evidence the decision maker may consider, but it is not usually conclusive.[90]

Despite the potential impact of requests for admissions, Lane and Tweedy knew Rule 36 was really most useful for two purposes: (1) to establish the authenticity of documents, and (2) to establish relatively uncontroversial matters or background information for trial (e.g., the number of employees working for Full Moon on a certain date). While requests for admission could help narrow the issues in dispute, neither Lane nor Tweedy had found them particularly valuable to establish the more controversial points in litigation; it is usually not difficult for an opposing lawyer to find "reasonable ground" for refusing to admit a matter.[91] So, they each drafted and served limited requests for admissions and responded in kind to the requests that they received.

---

[88] *See* Rule 30(e) ("On request by the deponent or a party before the deposition is completed, the deponent must be allowed 30 days after being notified by the [court reporter] that the transcript or recording is available in which: (A) to review the transcript or recording; and (B) if there are changes in form or substance, to sign a statement listing the changes and the reasons for making them."). The Rules place no limitation on what can be changed in an errata sheet. There are, however, powerful practical limitations on this ability. An opponent can use the uncorrected original answer to impeach, or undermine, later testimony at trial. Thus, it is possible to use the errata sheet to change a "no" to a "yes," but it will not often happen.

[89] We are treating requests for admissions as the "second wave" of paper discovery. It is also possible for a party to serve second, or even third, document requests or sets of interrogatories, assuming that such additional requests are not barred by court order or by any limitations in the Rules (such as the limit on the number of interrogatories) or are not otherwise unduly burdensome or disproportionate. Neither the Olmans nor Full Moon made such additional requests in this case.

[90] *See* Rule 36(b) ("A matter admitted under this rule is conclusively established unless the court, on motion, permits the admission to be withdrawn or amended.").

[91] Rule 37(c)(2) insulates a party from sanctions for refusing to admit a matter later proved at trial when, among other things, the party had "reasonable ground" to believe it would prevail on the disputed matter or other "good reason for the failure to admit."

D. Expert Discovery

As they were assembling the factual information needed to try their cases, Lane and Tweedy proceeded along the second, parallel discovery path concerning experts. You will learn much more about experts in your Evidence class. For now, you should know that in civil litigation, an "expert" is someone who has "knowledge, skill, experience, training or education" such that he or she is able to assist the finder of fact (i.e., the judge or the jury) understand some concept beyond his or her normal everyday experience.[92] Experts are in some sense hired guns. A lawyer will retain an expert to advise him or her about technical issues in the case, and perhaps to testify at trial. It is often said that you can find an expert to testify about almost anything,[93] even though this may be an exaggeration, and certainly is contrary to the intent of the Rules of Evidence, to keep "junk science" and the like out of the courtroom.

Lane understood the importance of experts generally, particularly in employment discrimination litigation.[94] Early on, she retained Dr. Lily Meloy, a faculty member in the statistics department at a major university. She wanted Dr. Meloy to analyze Full Moon's employment statistics and determine (1) whether there was a significant disparity between employees terminated who were protected under the ADEA versus those who were not and (2) whether any such disparity could be explained by controlling for other, lawful factors. Lane knew that such information, supported by expert testimony, was an important source of proof in ADEA cases.[95]

The Federal Discovery Rules recognize the pivotal importance of experts. As with factual discovery, the Federal Rules create a regime under which expert discovery proceeds in two phases. First, the parties must exchange certain information concerning any expert witness the party "may use at trial," as well as that expert's written report, if one is required by Rule 26(a)(2)(B).[96] The timing for the exchange of these disclosures and written reports is usually set by the court based on the parties' recommendations.[97] The second phase of expert discovery

---

[92] *See* Fed. R. Evid. 702. *See also* BLACK'S LAW DICTIONARY (10th Edition 2014) (defining "expert evidence" as "evidence about a scientific, technical, professional, or other specialized issue given by a person qualified to testify because of familiarity with the subject or special training in the field").

[93] *See, e.g.*, Jack B. Weinstein, *Improving Expert Testimony*, 20 U. RICH. L. REV. 473, 482 (1986) ("[A]n expert can be found to testify to the truth of almost any factual theory, no matter how frivolous.").

[94] Of course, a lawyer should not retain an expert without consulting with her client and considering the needs of the particular case. For example, a given case might not warrant an expert due to the amount of money at issue. Similarly, there might not be issues that truly require an expert. Once again, the key lesson is to take each of your cases on their own terms and act appropriately.

[95] *See, e.g., Benson v. Tocco, Inc.*, 113 F.3d 1203, 1208-09 (11th Cir. 1997) (discussing importance of expert testimony in ADEA cases); *see also Culley v. Trak Microwave Corp.*, 117 F. Supp. 2d 1317, 1319-21 (M.D. Fla. 2000) (recognizing the importance of statistical evidence in ADEA cases but rejecting such evidence in the particular case due to fatal errors in the plaintiff's expert witness testimony).

[96] *See* Rule 26(a)(2).

[97] *See* Rule 26(a)(2)(D). If the parties do not agree on a time for disclosure, the default under the Rules requires that the disclosure essentially be made at least 90 days before trial.

occurs after the Rule 26(a)(2) disclosures have been made. In this phase, the parties are allowed to take the deposition of any person "identified as an expert whose opinions may be presented at trial."[98] The Rule contemplates that this deposition will take place only after the expert's written report is provided.

Question 9.6

1. What information would Lane need to disclose about Dr. Meloy, and in what form would these disclosures have to be made? Be specific about the Rule governing her disclosure.

2. Assume that in addition to Dr. Meloy, Lane retained and consulted Dr. Harold Smeltzly, another statistician, about Full Moon's employment data. After reviewing the data, Dr. Smeltzly concludes that they show no statistically significant correlation between employees' ADEA-protected status and Full Moon's reduction in force. Lane ultimately decides that she will not call Dr. Smeltzly as a witness at trial.

   a. What information must Lane disclose about Dr. Smeltzly and his conclusions?

   b. Assume that Tweedy learns that Lane has consulted with Dr. Smeltzly. Will Tweedy be permitted to depose the doctor?

After receiving Dr. Meloy's report, Tweedy studied it closely. He also shared it with his own, nontestifying expert (sometimes called a "consulting expert") statistician to get her input. Whenever cost allowed, Tweedy retained two experts on important subjects. One expert would be designated to testify at trial. The other expert would be Tweedy's sounding board. He could freely discuss all his thoughts and conjectures with this second expert, and he could receive an informal evaluation of the opinions of his own testifying expert.

But Tweedy's discussions with his testifying expert would need to be more carefully structured. Some of those communications would be discoverable by his opponent. Recent amendments to the Federal Rules have added significant protections against discovery for communications between counsel and a testifying expert, but they did so against a historical backdrop of case law that permitted broad discovery of such communications and nonfinal drafts of expert reports.[99] Of course, this led to inefficient and undesirable restrictions on the expert's preparation and communications between counsel and the expert.

---

[98] *See* Rule 26(b)(4)(A).

[99] Rule 26(b)(4) Advisory Committee Notes (2010 amendments). For a discussion of the breadth of discovery courts had allowed prior to the 2010 amendments, see *Amster v. River Capital International Group, LLC*, 2002 U.S. Dist. LEXIS 13669 at *5-*6 (S.D.N.Y. July 26, 2002) (generally discussing the requirement under the predecessor to Rule 26(b)(4)(C) that a testifying expert must disclose the "facts

The current Rule 26(b)(4) protects from discovery (under the work-product rules discussed above) any nonfinal drafts of written expert reports and any communications between counsel and a testifying expert, except for three categories of unprotected communications. Those three categories include communications that (1) relate to the expert's compensation; (2) identify the "facts or data" that counsel provided to the expert and that the expert "considered in forming the opinions to be expressed"; and (3) identify "assumptions" conveyed by counsel to the expert that the expert "relied on in forming the opinions to be expressed." These new Rules gave Tweedy the freedom to discuss the written report of Olman's economic expert, Dr. Stevens, with Tweedy's own testifying expert, but Tweedy nonetheless remained conscious of the limitations of the work-product protection when communicating with his testifying expert.

Now Tweedy needed to decide what to do with the Olmans' expert, Dr. Meloy.[100] Following his usual practice, Tweedy decided to take a brief deposition of Meloy. Accordingly, he served the appropriate notice and prepared to take the deposition.

* * * *

Having completed discovery, Lane and Tweedy now turned in earnest to resolving the parties' dispute. While they ruled nothing out, given the negotiations to date, it did not appear likely that the Olmans and Full Moon would settle the lawsuit. Thus, the lawyers prepared to present their cases, first at summary judgment and then later at trial. We cover these litigation stages in Chapters Eleven and Twelve. But before doing so, we will consider how the lawsuit was initially structured and how, even now, it could be restructured to reflect developments in the case. These matters concern the joinder of claims and the joinder of parties, which we address in Chapter Ten.

---

or data" upon which she bases her opinion, and noting that this requirement has been held to include producing attorney client privileged or work product information disclosed to an expert).

[100] A lawyer needs to be careful that she does not give too much away in an expert deposition. A common tendency among lawyers is to charge into an expert deposition and aggressively question the expert about every error and deficiency in his or her report. There may be some cases where this is a good strategy, as when a lawyer believes this approach will foster serious settlement discussions. In most cases, however, this approach will actually be welcomed by opposing counsel. As soon as the deposition is concluded, opposing counsel will begin work correcting the errors and deficiencies brought to his or her attention. Imagine how much more effective it would be to raise these errors during the expert's trial testimony. As a result, many lawyers use the expert deposition for two rather limited purposes: (1) to clarify any ambiguities in the expert's report and (2) to get a firsthand look at the expert and assess how he or she will come across to the jury or judge.

Chapter Ten
Joinder and Amendment

Rule References: 4, 7, 11, *13*, *14*, *15*, *16*, *18*, *19*, *20*, *23*, *24*, 26

A. Structuring Litigation

From the outset, Eleanor Lane had been alert to the possibility of amending the complaint to change the claims, and possibly the parties as well. A lawyer seldom has exhaustive knowledge of the facts when she files her initial pleadings. And so long as the initial allegations have some "evidentiary support" under Rule 11, a lawyer can plead based on imperfect information. As a consequence, the initial complaint represents a lawyer's tentative judgment about which claims and parties to include. That judgment may change as more is learned about the case, and it may be necessary to amend the initial pleadings. Federal Rule 15(a) accommodates this need by endorsing a policy of "liberal" amendment.[1]

In this chapter, we examine two issues: (1) how the rules of joinder permitted the parties in *Olman* to structure their initial pleadings and (2) how these rules, used in conjunction with Rule 15, permitted the parties to amend that structure. We begin by examining joinder rules that permitted the Olmans to include the claims and parties found in their initial complaint. We then consider how joinder rules permitted Full Moon to add its own claims to the suit. Next, we follow Lane as she contemplates amending the complaint later in the suit, and we consider the procedural, strategic, and ethical issues she must address.

Joinder can be one of the more challenging topics addressed in Civil Procedure. To help you understand joinder issues in *Olman v. Full Moon*, we proceed step-by-step through the process of constructing the case pleadings. As each claim is added to the pleadings, we both *diagram* the claim and ask that you consider how its assertion is supported by a *particular* rule of civil procedure.[2]

1. Otis's Claims against Full Moon and Belcher[3]

We begin with the lead plaintiff, Otis Olman. The heart of Otis's case was his charge that Full Moon discriminated and retaliated against him in violation of age discrimination statutes. For many reasons, Otis wanted to assert all these related claims against Full Moon in one complaint. These reasons included litigating in the most efficient manner possible, presenting the

---

[1] *See Foman v. Davis*, 371 U.S. 178 (1962).

[2] We recommend that you develop the habit of diagramming the structure of cases you study in Civil Procedure. This habit will prove invaluable as you try to understand joinder rules and apply them to more complex cases. Diagramming is also valuable when, for example, you need to assess whether a court has subject matter jurisdiction over claims in a suit.

[3] We suggest you refresh your memory of the claims and parties identified in the initial complaint, which is found in Chapter Six.

strongest case against Full Moon, obtaining the widest variety of remedies, and ensuring that no claims were forfeited by failing to plead them.[4]

Consider the structure of Otis's claims against Full Moon:[5]

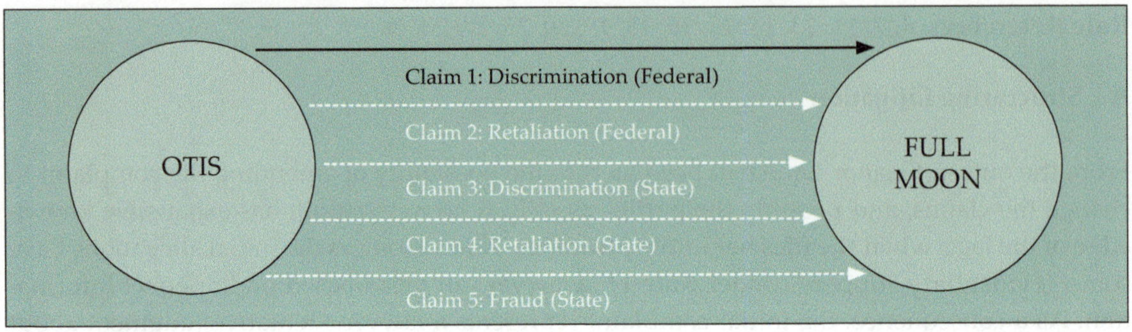

Now consider how Rule 18 authorized Otis's joinder of these claims against Full Moon.

Question 10.1

According to Rule 18, was there *any* limitation on Otis's right to join his five claims against Full Moon?[6] Does Rule 18 require that Otis's claims be factually related? Does Rule 18 require that they be based on the same law? And does Rule 18 require that Otis allege all his claims?[6]

[4] This last point refers to the doctrine of claim preclusion, or res judicata. In federal court, this doctrine generally requires that all factually related claims be pled in a single suit; otherwise, they are forfeited.

[5] Note that, as an additional claim is added to the pleadings, that claim is described using white font and a white arrow. In parentheses, we first state the nature of the claim (e.g., "discrimination") and then state the source of applicable law (e.g., "federal").

[6] Those of you who have studied jurisdiction will be aware that Otis had to satisfy other requirements before asserting his various claims in the suit. First, he had to verify that the federal court had *subject matter jurisdiction* over each claim. Subject matter jurisdiction is discussed in Chapter Three. Second, he had to verify that the court had *personal jurisdiction* over both defendants with regard to all claims. Personal jurisdiction, discussed in Chapter Two, was not a problem.

Recall that, in Count Five of the complaint, Otis also asserted a claim for fraud against Bruce Belcher.[7] But Rule 18 addresses the joinder of claims, not parties. Consequently, Otis had to identify a joinder rule authorizing the addition of another *defendant* in order to assert a claim against Belcher. The pertinent rule is Rule 20. After using Rule 20 to join Belcher as co-defendant to the fraud claim, the case might be diagrammed as follows:

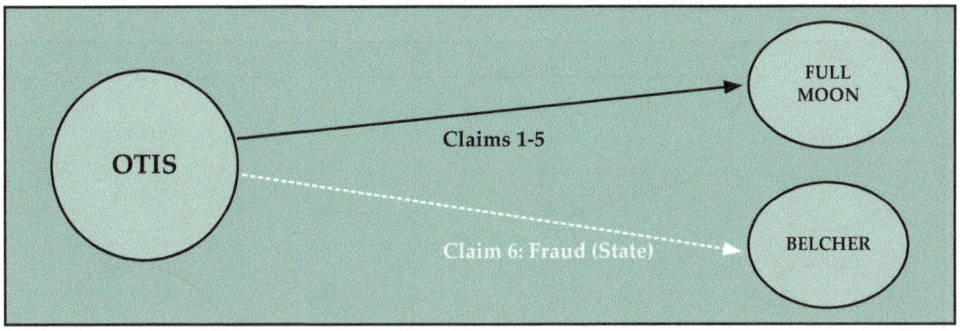

Notice that Rule 20, governing joinder of parties, is more restrictive than Rule 18, governing joinder of claims by a single party. Rule 20 authorizes the "permissive joinder" of additional defendants when a plaintiff seeks relief against the additional defendant (1) "arising out of the same transaction, occurrence, or series of transactions or occurrences" that is the subject of a claim against a codefendant; and (2) there is "any question of law or fact" common to both defendants. Consider the following question related to the joinder of Belcher:

Question 10.2

According to Rule 20, why was Otis permitted to join Belcher as co-defendant? Specifically, what is the "common transaction or occurrence" that underlies Otis's fraud claim against Belcher and an existing claim against Full Moon? Does it matter that the fraud claim against Belcher does *not* appear to arise out of the same occurrence underlying Otis's discrimination and retaliation claims (claims 1-4) against Full Moon?

[7] Although we have diagrammed the fraud claim against Belcher as a sixth claim, note that it is combined into a single "count" (Count Five) in the complaint. The diagrams distinguish each substantive legal claim because this is required when applying the rules of joinder.

2. Fiona's Claims against Full Moon

Now that you understand how Otis was permitted to join all his claims against Full Moon and Belcher in one complaint, consider the claims of co-plaintiff Fiona Olman. Fiona, you recall, wanted to assert her own claims for age discrimination under both federal and state law. After adding Fiona's claims, the structure of the case now looked like this:[8]

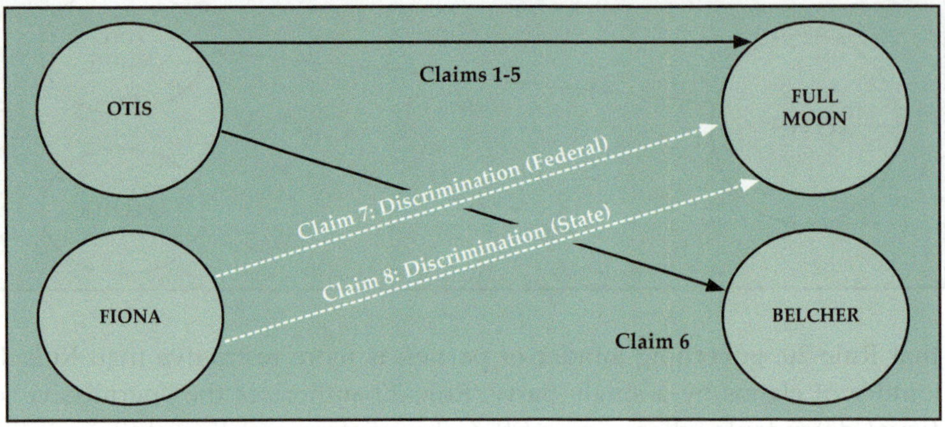

Now consider how Rules 18 and 20 permitted Fiona to join these claims in the complaint.

Consider the following questions concerning the Olmans' use of Rule 20 to join as plaintiffs and to join Full Moon and Belcher as co-defendants:

Question 10.3

1. According to Rule 20, why was Fiona permitted to join Otis as co-plaintiff? Specifically, what is the "common transaction or occurrence" that underlies their claims? What is the "question of law or fact" common to the claims asserted by Fiona and Otis? Can you think of any argument Full Moon might make that the Olmans' joinder as plaintiffs does *not* satisfy Rule 20?
2. Once Fiona properly joined as co-plaintiff with Otis, did Rule 18 impose any limitation on her assertion of *additional* claims against Full Moon?

3. Full Moon's Counterclaim against Otis

Once a party has been placed on the defensive by having a claim asserted against it, that party is permitted to go on the counteroffensive. Rule 13 authorizes the assertion of counterclaims against an "opposing party" and classifies these counterclaims as either compulsory (Rule 13(a)) or permissive (Rule 13(b)). Unlike Rules 18 and 20, Rule 13(a) sometimes compels a party to assert a claim.

[8] Again, we have numbered and diagrammed the parties' "claims" rather than the actual "counts" in the complaint. Claims 7 and 8 in the diagram appear as Counts Six and Seven in the complaint.

The Olmans' suit following Full Moon's assertion of its counterclaim might look like this:

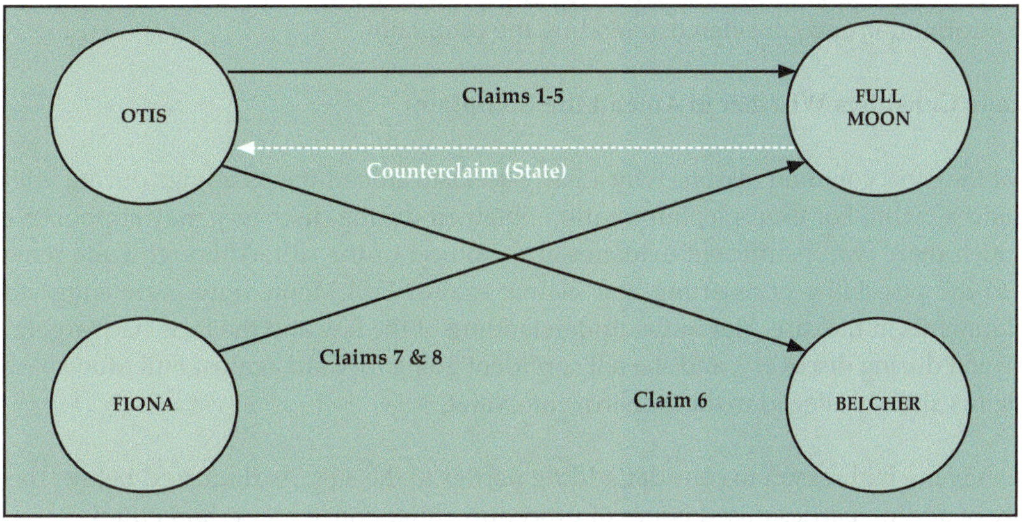

Now consider the following questions concerning the assertion of a counterclaim:

Question 10.4

1. Review Rules 13(a) and 13(b). Was Full Moon's counterclaim against Otis a compulsory or permissive counterclaim? Why?

2. According to Rule 13, how does a party go about asserting a counterclaim (i.e., in what pleading is it included)? According to Rule 7(a), must the opposing party respond to a counterclaim? How?

Finally, you may recall that Full Moon considered asserting a crossclaim against co-defendant Belcher to seek indemnification if it were required to pay for Belcher's fraudulent acts. Rule 13(g) permits the assertion of crossclaims against "co-parties" arising out of the same transaction or occurrence that underlies an existing claim or counterclaim. Consider the following question concerning Full Moon's potential crossclaim against Belcher:

Question 10.5

1. Is a crossclaim for indemnification authorized by Rule 13(g)? Why will a crossclaim for indemnification inevitably satisfy the requirement that it arise out of the same transaction or occurrence underlying an existing claim?

2. According to Rule 13(g), how does a party go about asserting a crossclaim (i.e., in what pleading is it included)? According to Rule 7(a), must the opposing party respond to a crossclaim? How?

As you can see, the structure of the parties' initial pleadings was authorized by a handful of joinder rules. Next, let's examine what happened when, as the suit progressed, Lane obtained more information and considered amending the complaint.

B. Lane Considers Whether to Amend the Complaint

One of the most common reasons why a party seeks to amend the pleadings during litigation is to add a claim. For example, information obtained during discovery may support a claim for which there was insufficient evidence at the outset of the suit. Although Lane remained alert to the possibility of asserting new claims against Full Moon, none were suggested by developments in the case. Her initial understanding of the law and the facts had largely been confirmed during discovery, and she felt confident going forward against Full Moon based on the claims already alleged in the Olmans' complaint.

But Lane now had reason to consider adding parties to the suit. As discussed below, the possibility of adding parties raised issues of procedure, litigation strategy, and ethics.

1. Joining a New Defendant

Based on deposition testimony obtained during discovery, Lane believed she had grounds for adding Sid Shockley as a new *defendant*. Shockley, you will recall, had replaced Otis as manager of the Jacksonville store. Deposition testimony confirmed that Shockley had continually disparaged Otis in the months leading up to Otis's replacement as manager. These disparaging comments may have contributed to Full Moon's decision to replace Otis, even though they were largely unsubstantiated. Evidence of Shockley's conduct would be useful at trial to rebut Full Moon's claim that it had "good cause" to replace Otis. But Lane believed Shockley's conduct might justify adding him as a co-defendant.

Lane thought that Shockley had maliciously poisoned Otis's relationship with Full Moon. Legal research suggested that Shockley's behavior might constitute "tortious interference with a business relationship." To establish this tort, she would need to prove four elements:

1. The existence of a business relationship between Otis and Full Moon;

2. Shockley's knowledge of that relationship;

3. Shockley's intentional and unjustified interference with the relationship; and

4. Resulting damage to Otis.[9]

Lane thought she had evidentiary support for each of these elements.

[9] *See, e.g., KMS Restaurant Corp. v. Wendy's Intern., Inc.,* 361 F.3d 1321, 1325 (11th Cir. 2004).

Now consider the procedural issues Lane had to address if she wanted to join Shockley as co-defendant.

Question 10.6

1. Recall that all the required pleadings in the Olmans' case were served months ago. If Lane now seeks to add Shockley as a defendant in her complaint, what procedural steps must she take? Make sure that you consider Lane's obligations under both Rules 4 and 15.

2. Does Lane's attempt to add Shockley satisfy the requirements of Rule 20 governing joinder of defendants? Make sure that you consider the likely arguments of both Lane and Tweedy.

In addition to considering whether procedural rules permitted joinder of Shockley, Lane had to decide whether joinder made strategic sense.[10] The principal value in joining Shockley as co-defendant was to improve Otis's chances of recovering damages. If Shockley tortiously interfered with Otis's business relationship with Full Moon, he would be liable for the resulting damages.

On reflection, Lane didn't believe the possibility of obtaining damages from Shockley provided a compelling strategic reason to join him to the suit. First, the damages from Shockley's conduct essentially overlapped with those already recoverable from Full Moon. Second, Full Moon might seek to mitigate its own liability by *shifting* blame to Shockley. If Full Moon succeeded in shifting the blame, Lane was unsure that Shockley had sufficient assets to satisfy Otis's judgment. All things considered, she was not convinced that the potential recovery of damages from Shockley outweighed the risks and additional procedural costs of joining him.[11] It was probably better to call Shockley as a witness at trial and let the jury impose liability on the sole defendant, Full Moon. After Lane conferred with the Olmans and shared her judgment, they agreed to leave Shockley out of the suit.

2. Joining an Additional Plaintiff

Lane next considered the possibility of adding a new *plaintiff* to the suit. Several months after agreeing to represent the Olmans, she also agreed to represent Ruby Dubidoux, a former manager of a Full Moon store in Savannah, Georgia. Dubidoux, like Otis, was over 40 years old

[10] She would also need to consider whether there was subject matter jurisdiction over the claims she sought to add. If you have already addressed subject matter jurisdiction in your course, you might want to identify the possible jurisdictional bases for these new claims. Finally, she would need to verify that the court had personal jurisdiction over Shockley. Subject matter jurisdiction and personal jurisdiction are discussed in Chapters Two and Three.

[11] The discussion in the next section of this chapter reveals some of the problems Lane might encounter in seeking to amend the complaint at this point in the suit. These problems would apply equally to joinder of Shockley.

and had been replaced by a younger manager. On the advice of Lane, Dubidoux had previously filed a charge with the EEOC alleging age discrimination. The administrative process had recently ended, and Dubidoux's claim was ripe for filing in court.

While investigating Dubidoux's case, Lane discovered that her client's complaint was not limited to one of age discrimination. In recent years, Dubidoux had struggled with chronic illness and, as a result, had incurred substantial medical costs under Full Moon's health insurance plan. Lane suspected that Dubidoux's termination may have resulted, at least in part, from Full Moon's efforts to control its health care expenses by terminating employees with costly medical problems. So Dubidoux's complaint would need to allege two separate causes of action, reflecting the fact that her termination may have been the product of two unlawful motives.[12]

First, consider the procedural issues Lane had to address in deciding whether, and how, to join Dubidoux as co-plaintiff.

Question 10.7

1. What procedural steps must Lane take to join Dubidoux as co-plaintiff?

2. Does Lane's attempt to add Dubidoux satisfy the requirements of Rule 20 governing joinder of plaintiffs? Make sure that you consider the likely arguments of both Lane and Tweedy.

3. If the court permits Dubidoux to join as co-plaintiff in the Olmans' suit for age discrimination, will Dubidoux also be permitted to assert the claim that her termination was motivated by her high health care costs? Or does Dubidoux's second claim fail because it does not satisfy Rule 20's requirement that a co-plaintiff's claim arise out of the same "transaction or occurrence" underlying the Olmans' claims of age discrimination?

Regardless of how Lane resolved the procedural issues posed by the possible joinder of Dubidoux, she had to consider the strategic advantages and disadvantages of joinder. She saw several potential advantages. Like Otis, Dubidoux had a long employment record with Full Moon and had contributed substantially to the success of the store that she managed. And like Otis, Dubidoux had worked under regional manager Bruce Belcher. As a result, the claims of Otis and Dubidoux were mutually reinforcing. Besides, Dubidoux was a person who would likely have a lot of jury appeal.

But there were several disadvantages to joining Dubidoux as co-plaintiff. Most important, Dubidoux's joinder would inject new issues in the case not directly pertinent to the Olmans' claims. As mentioned, Full Moon's termination of Dubidoux might be attributable, in whole

---

[12] *See, e.g., Vaszlavik v. Storage Technology Corp.*, 183 F.R.D. 264, 271 (D. Colo. 1998) (discussing the distinct cause of action available to older employees who have been terminated to reduce health care costs).

or in part, to her medical history. The Olmans' claims had nothing to do with their medical history. A jury might find it difficult to sort out the varying claims. Second, because Dubidoux had been employed in a different city and state (Savannah, Georgia) than the Olmans, Lane anticipated that Full Moon would argue that Dubidoux's claims should be litigated in a federal court in Georgia rather than in Florida.[13] At a minimum, Full Moon's argument would delay Lane's prosecution of the Olmans' claims. Finally, joinder of Dubidoux at this point in the Olmans' suit would require that the trial court change the scheduling order that had governed the case so far.[14] For example, the parties would have to conduct new discovery pertinent to Dubidoux's claims, which would inevitably delay the scheduled trial date.

The possible addition of Dubidoux as co-plaintiff also raised an ethical consideration for Lane. Under the rules of professional responsibility, Lane had to consider whether it was in *each* of her clients' best interests to join them as co-plaintiffs. According to Model Rule 1.7(a), a lawyer may not represent multiple clients if there is "a significant risk that the representation of one or more clients will be materially limited by the lawyer's responsibilities to another client." This rule required that Lane consider whether any of her clients would be disadvantaged by joining Dubidoux to the pending suit. It also required that Lane carefully confer with each of her clients and explain the potential risks, ethical and strategic, involved with joinder.

Lane and her clients eventually agreed that joining Dubidoux as co-plaintiff was inadvisable. There was simply too much divergence between the Olmans' situation and that of Dubidoux. Joining Dubidoux would complicate the jury's task and might detract from efficient proof of the Olmans' case. And her joinder would certainly disrupt the trial court's litigation plan—even assuming that Judge Sarah Goodenough would agree to revisit her plan. As a consequence, Lane told her clients she could likely provide more effective and more ethical representation by litigating their claims in separate suits. Her clients agreed.

So Lane decided she would forego amending the complaint and allow the case to retain its original party structure. Still, by carefully considering her amendment options, she had complied with her ethical obligations to competently and zealously represent her clients.

3. Amending the Pleadings: The Importance of Timing

a. The Potential Impact of Rules 15 and 16

As mentioned above, any attempt to add new parties to the suit would undermine the case management plan already worked out by the existing parties and approved by the trial court. This raises an important issue regarding amendment of pleadings. How willing are courts to permit amendment of the pleadings when the parties have advanced far in the pretrial process?

---

[13] If you have already studied the materials in Chapter Four, you should be able to articulate Full Moon's venue objection. How would you respond if you represented the Olmans and Dubidoux?

[14] This order is found at the end of Chapter Eight.

The U.S. Supreme Court has stated that permission to amend pleadings under Rule 15 should be "freely given."[15] According to the Court, amendment should normally be permitted unless the *opposing* party can show either that it will be unduly prejudiced or the movant has acted in bad faith. "Prejudice" does not mean that the opposing party will risk greater liability if a new claim is added. Instead, prejudice refers to the adverse *procedural* consequences that result from the movant's failure to allege the new matter earlier in the suit. For example, the party opposing an amendment might show that amendment of the pleadings will now cause it to incur substantially greater expense in responding to the new allegations than it would have incurred at an earlier date. Or the opposing party might show that the movant's delay now prevents it from obtaining discovery that would have been available had it known of the amended allegations earlier in the suit.

Lane knew that if she sought to amend the complaint to add a new plaintiff or defendant, Full Moon would argue "prejudice" within the meaning of Rule 15. The court would then decide whether Full Moon had met its burden of proving sufficient prejudice to overcome Rule 15's policy of liberal amendment. Lane recognized that the Rule sometimes conveys a misleading impression of courts' willingness to permit amendment of the pleadings. In particular, Rule 15 standing alone fails to take into account the *court*'s interest in seeing that the parties comply with the litigation plan issued at the outset of a suit.

As discussed in Chapter Eight, Rule 26(f) requires that parties confer early in the suit and develop a plan and schedule for litigation. After the parties confer, the trial court is required by Rule 16(b) to issue a case management order. Rule 16(b)(3)(A) specifically provides that this order must "limit the time to . . . file motions." And Rule 16(b)(4) states that this order "*may be modified only for good cause.*"[16]

In most cases, the case management order will contain a deadline for amending pleadings. Violation of this deadline provides an additional ground to object to a proposed amendment. If a party moves to amend after this deadline has passed, he or she bears the burden of showing "good cause" for deviating from the case management order. In other words, the case management order effectively *reverses* the burden typically imposed by Rule 15(a), which requires that the party *opposing* an amendment show he will be "prejudiced."

If you reexamine the case management order in *Olman v. Full Moon*, you will find that it states that motions to amend are "distinctly disfavor[ed]" after the date of the order's *issuance*.[17] In other words, the order expresses the court's preference that all amendments be made *before* discovery. The order's restriction on amendment seems somewhat at odds with the "liberal"

---

[15] *See Foman v. Davis*, 371 U.S. 178 (1962) ("In the absence of any apparent or declared reason—such as undue delay, bad faith or dilatory motive on the part of the movant, repeated failure to cure deficiencies by amendments previously allowed, undue prejudice to the opposing party by virtue of allowance of the amendment, futility of amendment, etc.—the leave sought should, as the rules require, be 'freely given'.").

[16] Emphasis added.

[17] The case management order, we might note, is derived from one used by a judge for the U.S. District Court for the Middle District of Florida.

amendment policy of Rule 15(a). It also seems a bit unrealistic. Discovery—which often does not commence till after the order's issuance—may be necessary to determine which claims are factually supportable. To "disfavor" amendments made before discovery is conducted places a greater emphasis on expedited litigation, while undermining the goal of informed pleading.

Nonetheless, such deadlines are now commonly included in case management orders, and the majority of courts enforce them unless a party seeking to make an untimely amendment shows "good cause."[18] This emphasizes a point made earlier in this Guide[19]—Court orders are a source of procedural "law" that can be as important as the rules themselves.[20]

Consequently, the case management order would have created a serious impediment to Lane's efforts to amend the complaint at this point in the suit. This procedural impediment reaffirmed her strategic and ethical decision to decline to bring new parties into the suit.

b. Beating the Statute of Limitations and Rule 15(c)

One final point regarding the timing of amendments merits attention. On occasion, delay in seeking an amendment may be fatal because the applicable statute of limitations has expired. As discussed earlier, each claim in a suit is subject to a particular statute of limitations. If a party seeks to amend his or her complaint and add a new claim *after* its limitations period has expired, the opposing party may challenge the amendment on the ground the claim must fail.[21]

Rule 15(c) provides a means of circumventing the statute of limitations defense in appropriate circumstances. If the new claim to be added arises out of the "conduct, transaction, or occurrence set forth or attempted to be set forth in the original pleading," it "relates back" to the date of the original pleading. That means any new claim the Olmans added to the suit through amendment would not run afoul of the governing statute of limitations if (1) it arose out of the factual allegations set forth in their original complaint and (2) the *original* complaint was filed before the statute of limitations applicable to the new claim expired.

To affirm your understanding of the "relation back" doctrine, consider the hypothetical question below.

---

[18] *See, e.g., O'Connell v. Hyatt Hotels of Puerto Rico,* 357 F.3d 152, 154 (1st Cir. 2004) ("Rule 16(b)'s 'good cause' standard, rather than Rule 15(a)'s 'freely given' standard, governs motions to amend filed after scheduling order deadlines.").

[19] See *A Note Concerning: Sources of Procedural Law,* found at the end of Chapter One.

[20] It's also an important reminder of the power district courts have over pretrial matters under the Federal Rules.

[21] Rule 8(c) specifically identifies a "statute of limitations" defense as an affirmative defense that should be pleaded.

Question 10.8

1. Assume that Lane moved to amend the complaint to add a new claim on behalf of Otis. This claim alleges that, upon Otis's termination, Full Moon failed to pay him for unused vacation time as required by his employment contract. Under the applicable statute of limitations, the period for filing this claim expired one month *after* Lane filed the original complaint. Is the claim untimely under Rule 15(c)?

2. Assume that Lane moved to amend the complaint to add Shockley as a defendant and assert a claim for tortious interference with Otis's business relationship with Full Moon. If the statute of limitations for this claim had already expired at the time the motion to amend was filed, why does Rule 15(c) *fail* to provide Otis with a means for circumventing this limit?

C. Some Concluding Joinder Issues: What Might Have Been

Rarely does a single case require the application of *all* rules of joinder. The dispute between the Olmans and Full Moon, for example, does not provide occasion for using several important joinder devices you will study in Civil Procedure. Before leaving the subject of joinder, however, we would like to provide a very brief introduction to a few other rules that *might* have applied if the facts in *Olman* were different. These include Rules 14 (impleader), 19 (necessary and indispensable parties), 24 (intervention), and 23 (class actions).

1. Impleader

Rule 14 provides a procedural mechanism by which a defending party can "implead" nonparties who may be liable for all or part of the liability judgment the plaintiff obtains against the defending party. By authorizing the defending party to implead such a "third party," Rule 14 helps the defending party reduce the impact of a judgment. The defending party may be able to obtain its *own* judgment from the third party obligating it to reimburse damages paid to the plaintiff.

One common application of Rule 14 occurs when the defending party is being sued based on the principle of "respondeat superior." For example, employers are often held liable for the wrongdoing of their employees that occurs within the scope of employment. Rule 14 may permit an employer to implead the culprit-employee and obtain its own judgment requiring the employee to reimburse the employer for damages paid to the plaintiff. The key legal question in determining whether impleader is authorized is: Under applicable law, does the employer have a *right* to reimbursement?

If an employer has the right to reimbursement, it may assert that right in the pending suit in one of two ways.[22] First, if the employee is already a defendant in the suit (e.g., the plaintiff

[22] The employer also has the right to seek reimbursement later in a separate suit.

has sued both the employer and the employee), the employer can simply crossclaim against the employee under Rule 13(g). In Chapter Seven, we briefly mentioned Full Moon's possible use of Rule 13(g) for this purpose to assert a claim against Belcher. Second, if the employee has not been sued, Rule 14 permits the defendant-employer to serve a "third-party" complaint on the employee and add him to the suit as a "third-party defendant."

Now let's consider Rule 14's potential relevance in the Olmans' suit.

In Chapter One, we discussed how age discrimination statutes render an "employer" liable for age discrimination perpetrated by managers like Belcher. This raises a question: Since Full Moon is being sued by the Olmans for what might have been the wrongdoing of Belcher, could Full Moon seek reimbursement for any judgment it has to pay the Olmans? If Full Moon had the right to reimbursement, it could either (1) crossclaim against Belcher if he was already a co-defendant in the suit, or (2) implead Belcher if he was not a party to the suit.

Alas for Full Moon, it could use neither option. The reason is that, while Full Moon might be found liable for wrongful acts of Belcher, age discrimination statutes do *not* give it a substantive right to seek reimbursement. According to courts that have addressed this issue, because age discrimination law expressly creates "employer" liability, by implication it does not impose liability on employees or supervisors whose conduct renders their employer liable.[23] This form of employer-only liability is common in employment discrimination laws.

As a consequence, Full Moon would have to pay any judgment the Olmans obtained for age discrimination and could not seek any reimbursement from Belcher. Because Full Moon had no substantive right against Belcher, neither Rule 13(g) nor Rule 14 applied.

Recall that Otis Olman originally sued Full Moon for common law fraud as well. The alleged fraud was apparently committed by Belcher. According to applicable state tort law, if Full Moon were forced to pay a judgment based solely on Belcher's misconduct, Full Moon *would* have a right of reimbursement or "indemnification."[24] As a consequence, when Full Moon was served with the Olmans' complaint, it had the right to seek reimbursement from Belcher. If Belcher were also named as a defendant (the original facts), Full Moon could assert a crossclaim for reimbursement from Belcher under Rule 13(g). On the other hand, if only Full Moon had been named as defendant, it could have impleaded Belcher under Rule 14. Both strategies were ultimately mooted, you may recall, when the trial court dismissed Otis's fraud claim.

2. Compulsory Joinder of Parties

Rule 20 gives the plaintiff the right to choose who will be parties to the suit. For example, Otis Olman could choose whether to include Fiona or Dubidoux as co-plaintiffs, and he could choose whether to sue Full Moon, Belcher, Shockley, or some combination of these. Rule 20 permits the joinder of multiple plaintiffs or defendants, but it does not mandate joinder.

---

[23] *See, e.g., Stults v. Conoco, Inc.*, 76 F.3d 651, 655 (5th Cir. 1996).

[24] *See, e.g., Stuart v. Hertz Corp.*, 351 So.2d 703, 705 (Fla. 1977).

In some suits, however, joinder is not permissive. According to Rule 19, some persons may have to be joined in a suit. If, because of problems with service of process or subject matter jurisdiction, these persons cannot be joined, the court must consider whether, "in equity and good conscience," the suit should proceed.[25]

Rule 19 does not prescribe a specific formula for determining whether someone should be joined as a party. Instead, the court must consider several factors. Two of the more important ones are (1) whether failure to join an absentee will jeopardize his or her interests and (2) whether failure to join an absentee will expose an existing party to a substantial risk of incurring multiple or inconsistent obligations.[26] If the absentee cannot be properly joined, the court is required to consider alternatives to dismissal that will protect the interests of both the absentee and existing parties.[27] If the court cannot develop measures to protect those interests, Rule 19(b) requires dismissal.

Recall that the Olmans sought monetary damages from Full Moon. They did not want their old jobs back. Given the limited relief sought by the Olmans, it is highly unlikely that Full Moon could have successfully argued that either it or some absentee would be prejudiced if the suit remained limited to the existing parties. But consider the possible consequences had Otis Olman sought nonmonetary relief.

Assume that the original complaint demanded that Otis be reinstated as store manager. Upon receiving the complaint, Tweedy met with Full Moon personnel and considered the company's options. The company was now party to a four-year contract with Shockley permitting him to continue as store manager unless Full Moon had "good cause" to terminate him. When Full Moon informed Shockley about Otis's demand that he be reinstated as store manager, Shockley said that he would be "very unhappy" if he were forced to give up his position. Full Moon then explored with Shockley the possibility of reaching some sort of settlement with Otis that would address both men's concerns. In particular, Full Moon raised the possibility of transferring Shockley back to his former position as manager of the store's extreme sporting goods department, but at his new salary level. Shockley did not care for this proposal. Further, he pointed out that Full Moon had just hired a new manager of the extreme sporting goods department. Although the new manager, Caliope Wacker, had no contract with Full Moon (she was an "employee at will" who had no legal right to continued employment), she would probably be very unhappy if she lost her position in the store.

Assume that, at present, the only parties to the suit are the Olmans and Full Moon. In light of these facts, consider the following question:

---

[25] *See* Rule 19(a)(1), (b).

[26] *See* Rule 19(a)(1).

[27] *See* Rule 19(b). Specifically, Rule 19(b) directs the court to consider factors like "the extent to which a judgment rendered in the person's absence might prejudice that person or the existing parties;" and "the extent to which any prejudice could be lessened or avoided" by "protective provisions in the judgment; . . . shaping the relief; or . . . other measures." Rule 19(b)(1)-(2).

Question 10.9

1. Does Full Moon have persuasive grounds for arguing that Shockley is a necessary party? That Caliope Wacker is a necessary party?

2. If for some reason Shockley and Wacker cannot be made parties to the Olmans' suit, are they indispensable? Or can you think of any action the court might take to ensure that neither their interests nor those of Full Moon would be jeopardized if the suit proceeded in their absence?

3. By the way, how does Full Moon go about asserting its contention that either Shockley or Wacker should be joined under Rule 19? (Hint—consider Rule 12(b).)

3. Intervention

Another procedural mechanism for changing the cast of parties selected by the plaintiff is intervention under Rule 24. According to Rule 24, an absentee can move to intervene in a suit "upon timely application." Rule 24(a) addresses the situation where the prospective intervenor has a "right" to participate in the suit. To establish his right to intervene, an absentee must prove three things: (1) that he has an "interest" related to the transaction that is the subject of the suit; (2) that his absence from the suit "may as a practical matter impair or impede [his] ability to protect that interest"; and (3) existing parties do not "adequately represent" the absentee's interest. An absentee who cannot satisfy these criteria may still seek court permission to intervene under Rule 24(b). Permissive intervention may be granted if the absentee's "claim or defense" shares a "common question of law or fact" with the main action.

Now consider how Rule 24 might apply in the hypothetical scenarios presented in the following question.

Question 10.10

1. Assume, again, that Shockley and Wacker find themselves in the circumstances described in the previous section. Do they have persuasive grounds for seeking to intervene in the Olmans' suit as a matter of right? Do they have grounds for seeking permissive intervention?

2. Now consider the earlier discussion regarding Lane's decision not to join Dubidoux as co-plaintiff. Assume that, in response to Lane's decision, Dubidoux retains other legal counsel. She now asks new counsel to file a motion to intervene in the Olmans' suit. Does she have persuasive grounds for seeking to intervene as a matter of right? For seeking permissive intervention?

3. Finally, consider the situation of Belcher, whose alleged wrongdoing constitutes a critical part of the Olmans' claim that they were the victims of age discrimination. As explained earlier, Belcher is not liable for age discrimination under applicable law, only his former employer is. Assume that Belcher was never named as a party in the Olmans' suit. But after learning more about the Olmans' allegations, he decides it is important that he appear in the case "to defend his good name." Does he have persuasive grounds for seeking intervention as a matter of right? For seeking permissive intervention?

4. Class Actions

The dispute between the Olmans and Full Moon represents a typical employment discrimination suit brought by an individual. Imagine, however, that Lane had reason to believe that the Olmans were not the victims of isolated incidents. Rather, assume that Lane's investigation revealed an apparent pattern of age discrimination throughout all of Full Moon's stores in the southeast region, encompassing dozens of older employee victims. Perhaps the pattern even extended throughout all of Full Moon's stores across the country, encompassing hundreds of potential plaintiffs. Joinder of a small number of co-plaintiffs, such as Otis, Fiona, and Dubidoux, can be accomplished using Rule 20, but at some point, joinder of too many individual plaintiffs under Rule 20 would become unwieldy or impracticable. Can dozens, hundreds, or even thousands of plaintiffs pursue their related discrimination claims against Full Moon in a single civil action?

Rule 23 generally permits a party to sue (or be sued) as a representative member of a class of similarly situated persons. Interestingly, Rule 23 would not apply to the Olmans' federal ADEA claims because the ADEA prescribes an alternative class procedure to enforce its provisions.[28] But the Rule would apply in class actions to enforce other types of claims against Full Moon, including state-law claims of age discrimination and federal claims challenging other forms of employment discrimination. For example, Rule 23 generally governs class actions under Title VII of the federal Civil Rights Act, which prohibits discrimination on the basis of race, color, religion, sex, or national origin.[29] Because Rule 23 governs most federal-court actions alleging employment discrimination against a class, we will focus our brief discussion on the hypothetical application of Rule 23 to such claims.[30]

---

[28] *See* 29 U.S.C. § 626 (incorporating into the ADEA the special classwide enforcement provisions of the Fair Labor Standards Act, found at 29 U.S.C. § 216(b)); *see also Hoffman-LaRoche v. Sperling*, 493 U.S. 165, 169-70 (1989) (applying the classwide enforcement provisions of the Fair Labor Standards Act to the ADEA).

[29] *See* 42 U.S.C. § 2000e-2(a).

[30] Importantly, when the EEOC elects to pursue classwide relief on behalf of a group of aggrieved individuals, the EEOC is not required to satisfy the class certification requirements of Rule 23. *See General Tel. Co. of Northwest v. EEOC*, 446 U.S. 318, 323 (1980).

a. The Prerequisites to Class Certification

Before a civil action can be pursued on behalf of a class of similarly situated individuals under Rule 23, the court must determine that class treatment is appropriate. The court does so in a "class certification" order that defines the class, identifies the class claims or defenses, and appoints counsel for the class.[31] Rule 23(a) provides these prerequisites for certification of any class:

1. The class is so numerous that joinder of all members is impracticable;
2. There are questions of law or fact common to the class;
3. The claims or defenses of the representative parties are typical of the claims or defenses of the class; and
4. The representative parties will fairly and adequately protect the interests of the class.

For the first prerequisite, *numerosity*, the Rules do not specify any determinative threshold. Some federal courts have suggested that sufficient numerosity is presumed when the number of potential class members attains a certain size (usually 40).[32] Other courts, stressing that numerosity depends on the impracticality of joining individual class members, have refused to identify any specific formula or number.[33]

The second prerequisite to class certification, the *commonality* of legal or factual questions among class members, was addressed at length by the Supreme Court in *Wal-Mart Stores, Inc. v. Dukes*, a nationwide class action alleging that the largest employer in the country had engaged in sex discrimination in violation of Title VII.[34] The Court held that commonality under Rule 23(a)(2) requires more than simply reciting a single question of law or fact, no matter how inconsequential, that might be common to all class members. For example, the common question, "Do all of us plaintiffs indeed work for Wal-Mart?" is not sufficient.[35] Rather, the class members' claims must hinge on a common contention, such that the determination of that contention "will resolve an issue that is central to the validity of each one of the claims in one stroke."[36] In other words, commonality requires not just common questions, but common *answers* that will move the litigation efficiently toward resolution.

---

[31] *See* Rule 23(c)(1).

[32] The Second and Eleventh Circuits have suggested that 40 members might be adequate to presume numerosity. *See Robidoux v. Celani*, 987 F.2d 931, 936 (2d Cir. 1993); *Cox v. American Cast Iron Pipe Co.*, 784 F.2d 1546, 1553 (11th Cir. 1986).

[33] *See, e.g., Trevizo v. Adams*, 455 F.3d 1155, 1162 (10th Cir. 2006); *Paxton v. Union Nat. Bank*, 688 F.2d 552, 559 (8th Cir. 1982).

[34] 131 S. Ct. 2541 (2011).

[35] *Id.* at 2551.

[36] *Id.*

The *typicality* requirement focuses on the similarity between the class representative's claims or defenses and those of other class members. The factual situations of each class member need not be identical or perfectly aligned with that of the class representative. They must, however, be sufficiently similar to ensure that pursuit of the class representative's interests will simultaneously advance the interests of the other class members. Typicality will be satisfied where "the claims or defenses of the class and the class representative arise from the same event or pattern or practice and are based on the same legal theory."[37]

The final prerequisite considers the *adequacy of representation* by the class representative. This inquiry can be subdivided into two components: First, will the class representative's interests conflict with or diverge from the interests of the other members?[38] Second, is the proposed class counsel sufficiently qualified, experienced, and knowledgeable to handle the class litigation?[39]

Question 10.11

Consider how a federal court would apply the four prerequisites of Rule 23(a) in ruling on motions for class certification in the following hypothetical cases:

1. The Olmans, represented by Lane, sue Full Moon and allege classwide discrimination on the basis of age in violation of the Florida Civil Rights Act. The complaint doesn't assert claims under the federal ADEA. The complaint alleges that Full Moon's regional manager for the southeast region, Belcher, makes all promotion and termination decisions in the region and has engaged in an unlawful pattern of basing those decisions on age. Lane has moved for certification of a class defined as follows: "All current or former employees of Full Moon who (i) worked at a Full Moon retail store located in Florida for any length of time between January 1, 2019 and August 1, 2022; (ii) were either (a) terminated or (b) denied a promotion for which he or she applied; and (iii) were over the age of 40 years old at the time of such termination or denial of promotion." Assume that this proposed class will include 35 individuals.

2. Fiona, represented by Lane, sues Full Moon and alleges classwide employment discrimination on the basis of sex in violation of Title VII. The complaint alleges that Full Moon has a practice of favoring men over women in promotions to management positions at all of its stores across the country.

---

[37] *See Ault v. Walt Disney World Co.*, 692 F.3d 1212, 1216 (11th Cir. 2012).

[38] *See Amchem Prods. v. Windsor*, 521 U.S. 591, 625 (1997).

[39] *See In re Flag Telecom Holdings Ltd. Securities Litig.*, 574 F.3d 29, 35 (2d Cir. 2009). A class-certification order must appoint class counsel pursuant to Rule 23(g), which directs the court to consider the work done by counsel in investigating the claims at issue, counsel's experience in handling class actions and complex litigation, counsel's knowledge of the law applicable to the action, and the resources that counsel can commit to the representation. Fed. R. Civ. P. 23(g).

> The complaint alleges that this discrimination is the result of Full Moon's "tap on the shoulder" procedure for making promotions, where regional managers approach preferred candidates for management-level promotions, without posting openings or accepting applications. Historically, nearly all of Full Moon's regional managers have been men, and the complaint alleges that men are statistically more likely to approach other men for promotion, while overlooking qualified female candidates. Lane has moved for certification of a class defined as follows: "All female employees or former employees of Full Moon who held any nonmanagerial position at any Full Moon retail store for any length of time between January 1, 2019 and August 1, 2022." She estimates that this proposed class would include approximately 5,000 individuals.

b. Types of Classes

All class actions must meet the four initial prerequisites of Rule 23(a). But these prerequisites are only the first hurdle. Before certifying a class, the court must also determine which of the three *types* of class it will certify under Rule 23(b) and determine whether the requirements for that type of class have been satisfied.

Rule 23(b)(1) authorizes class actions where separate individual lawsuits would create a risk of inconsistent judgments that establish "incompatible standards of conduct for the party opposing the class" or where individual actions would, as a practical matter, limit the ability of the other members to protect their own interests. Rule 23(b)(2) authorizes class actions when the opposing party has "acted or refused to act on grounds that apply generally to the class," such that injunctive or declaratory relief as to the whole class is appropriate. As a general matter, Rule 23(b)(2) classes are appropriate when the class seeks injunctive or declaratory relief that is indivisible and applicable to all members of the purported class rather than seeking individualized remedies.[40]

Rule 23(b)(3) authorizes class actions seeking individualized relief for class members, often including monetary damages, and contains additional protections for the class members. Before certifying a Rule 23(b)(3) class action, the court must determine that common questions of law or fact "predominate" over any individual questions and class resolution of the claims would be superior to other possible methods for adjudicating the controversy. In addition, in Rule 23(b)(3) class actions, the court must ensure that the class members are provided with notice of the suit (including individual notice where class members can be identified) and an opportunity to opt out of the class. Potential class members who choose to opt out will not be bound by any judgment and may pursue an individual action should they choose to do so.[41]

---

[40] *See Wal-Mart Stores, supra* at 2557.

[41] It is on this point that the special class action procedures for federal ADEA claims differ significantly from Rule 23. For ADEA class actions, individuals must affirmatively *opt in* to the class by written consent to become class members and be bound by any judgment in the litigation. *See Hipp v. Liberty Nat. Life Ins.*, 252 F.3d 1208, 1216 (11th Cir. 2001) (*citing* 29 U.S.C. § 216(b)).

Those individuals falling within the class definition who do not opt out will be bound by any judgment in the case, whether favorable or unfavorable.

Question 10.12

Consider again the two hypothetical cases described in Question 10.11. Recall that under the Florida Civil Rights Act, a plaintiff's available remedies include reinstatement or other appropriate injunctive relief, back pay, full compensatory damages, and punitive damages. Under Title VII, a plaintiff's remedies for discrimination on the basis of sex are more limited. They include reinstatement or other appropriate injunctive relief and back pay. In addition, Title VII plaintiffs may be awarded limited compensatory or punitive damages, but only if the employer is unable to prove that it would have taken the challenged employment action even in the absence of any discriminatory motive.

What type of class certification should Lane pursue if she brings each of the two hypothetical class actions described in Question 10.11? Is the court likely to grant certification? For either case, might she be able to structure the complaint's request for relief in a manner that makes class certification more likely?

Chapter Eleven
Summary Judgment

Rule References: 5, 7, 11, 52, *56*, 78

A. Full Moon Moves for Summary Judgment

From the outset of the Olmans' suit, Bart Tweedy began thinking ahead to the time when he would move for summary judgment. One of the reasons Tweedy often recommended that his clients choose federal court over state court was the improved prospects of obtaining summary judgment.[1]

Judge Sarah Goodenough's case management and scheduling order had set a deadline of September 29, 2023—one month after discovery closed—for filing dispositive motions. As the discovery phase neared its end, Tweedy began a systematic review of discovery product and began work on a motion for summary judgment. Tweedy was optimistic he could succeed in having at least some of the Olmans' claims resolved.

B. The Standard for Summary Judgment

The main purpose of summary judgment is to avoid a useless trial.[2] When the evidence is such that no rational jury could find against the party seeking summary judgment, that party should prevail without having to incur the time and expense associated with trial. Summary judgment does not address the question of who *will* win at trial. Rather, the issue is whether the nonmovant *can* win. If the evidence leads to but one rational view of the facts, and those facts mean that the nonmovant can't win at trial, there is no need for a trial. It is this reality that Rule 56 enforces. And entry of summary judgment doesn't infringe the losing party's constitutional right to a jury trial because the role of the jury is to find the facts. When the critical facts are indisputably established by the evidence, the jury's role doesn't come into play.[3]

---

[1] Since the Supreme Court announced the "*Celotex* trilogy" of decisions in 1986, federal courts have shown greater willingness to grant summary judgment. *See Matsushita Elec. Indus. Co. v. Zenith Radio Corp.*, 475 U.S. 574 (1986); *Anderson v. Liberty Lobby, Inc.*, 477 U.S. 242 (1986); *Celotex Corp. v. Catrett*, 477 U.S. 317 (1986). You will examine some of those cases during your study of civil procedure. The increased availability of summary judgment extends to suits alleging claims of age discrimination; federal courts now grant summary judgment in an appreciable number of ADEA actions. *See* Andrew J. Ruzicho, et al., 2 Litigating Age Discrimination Cases § 9:3 (2015).

[2] *See* J. Friedenthal, M. Kane, & A. Miller, Civil Procedure § 9.1, at 449 (2015).

[3] *See United States v. Fritz*, 608 Fed. Appx. 259, 260 (5th Cir. 2015) ("The function of a jury is to try the material facts; where no such facts are in dispute, there is no occasion for jury trial. Thus the right to trial by jury does not prevent a court from granting summary judgment."). For a contrary view arguing that summary judgment is unconstitutional, see Suja Thomas, *Why Summary Judgment Is Unconstitutional*, 93 Va. L. Rev. 139 (2007).

Summary judgment can also serve other purposes. When some but not all issues are summarily adjudged, the scope of a trial can be limited and simplified. Further, the exchange of evidence that occurs during the resolution of a summary judgment motion helps the parties better prepare for trial and may encourage settlement.

Rule 56 permits a party to seek full or partial summary judgment, and the court can resolve individual claims, defenses, or issues. In practice, a defending party like Full Moon often seeks summary judgment on specific claims, with the hope that the plaintiff's suit can be whittled down to a few counts if not fully resolved. Rule 56(a) is the heart of the rule. It states that summary judgment can be granted when there is "no genuine dispute as to any material fact" and "the movant is entitled to judgment as a matter of law." Based on this standard, Full Moon could win some form of summary judgment on the Olmans' claims by proving either of two things. First, Full Moon could show that the Olmans had *failed* to produce sufficient evidence to support a jury verdict in their favor on particular claims. Alternatively, it could show that one of its *defenses* to liability was established by indisputable evidence.

The key insight of the U.S. Supreme Court's summary judgment decisions is this: if the function of summary judgment is to test whether there should be a trial, the allocation of responsibility for presenting evidence should generally be the same at both stages. In other words, if Otis Olman was required to present evidence at trial in support of his discrimination claims, he had the same responsibility at summary judgment. This responsibility is called the *burden of production*, or the burden of coming forward.[4] The party with this burden must present some admissible evidence from which a rational factfinder *could* find in its favor. Failure to meet this burden means that party loses. Satisfaction of the burden means that party survives summary judgment and can present its case to the jury.[5]

At the same time, Tweedy knew that as the movant, he would have the initial responsibility to show that the motion should be granted. How he met that responsibility depended on the assignment of the burden of production on the claim or defense in dispute. If Full Moon had the burden of production on that claim or defense, it had the duty to submit affirmative evidence in support of its motion. For example, Full Moon had the burden of producing evidence supporting its affirmative defense that Fiona Olman signed an enforceable release. If Full Moon met its burden of production, Fiona would need to submit evidence showing there was a genuine factual dispute concerning the release's enforceability.

---

[4] The burden of production should be distinguished from the burden of persuasion. We discuss the latter burden in Chapter Twelve.

[5] A party may also seek summary judgment in a case where the judge serves as the factfinder. *See, e.g., Phillips Oil Co. v. OKC Corp.*, 812 F.2d 265 (5th Cir. 1987). It remains unclear whether the standard for summary judgment in a nonjury case differs from that in a case tried to a jury. In *Phillips Oil, supra,* the court asked but did not resolve the question of whether the standard might be more lenient in a nonjury case. *Id.* at 273 n.15. Given the judge's ultimate fact-finding role in a nonjury case, arguably the judge can draw inferences from the evidence presented at summary judgment and resolve factual issues before the case moves into its formal fact-finding stage. *See generally* Shira A. Scheindlin, *Judicial Fact-Finding and the Trial Court Judge*, 69 U. Miami L. Rev. 367 (2015).

On the other hand, Otis had the burden of production for his claim of age discrimination. All Full Moon had to do to satisfy its modest procedural responsibility as movant was to point out that Otis *lacked* evidence sufficient to support a rational jury verdict in his favor. Full Moon could accomplish this by pointing to the absence of recorded evidence supporting a favorable finding on a required element of Otis's claim. At that point, Otis had to satisfy his burden of production and could not "rest on his pleadings." To do this, he had to identify evidence sufficient to support a rational jury verdict in his favor. If Otis failed to produce such evidence, the court would enter summary judgment against him. If he produced evidence he thought sufficient to support a favorable verdict, Full Moon could respond in one of two ways. It could show that Otis's proffered evidence actually fell short of what was required to support a verdict in his favor, or it could submit counterevidence conclusively refuting the evidence on which he relied.

In short, because Otis would eventually have to produce sufficient evidence at trial to support a verdict that he was the victim of age discrimination, he was required do so at summary judgment as well.

In many cases, a party seeks summary judgment after the discovery process is completed. This timing reflects the fact that a court must provide the nonmovant adequate opportunity to discover evidence needed to support its claims. If the nonmovant has failed to discover such evidence during discovery, a court can fairly conclude that the evidence doesn't exist.

But there is no per se requirement that a party wait until discovery is completed to move for summary judgment. If there is evidence showing a party's entitlement to summary judgment before discovery is completed or, for that matter, before discovery is undertaken, Rule 56 permits a party to move for summary judgment without delay. To better appreciate the parties' options for seeking summary judgment, consider the following question.

Question 11.1

1. According to Rule 56, could Tweedy have moved for summary judgment immediately after Full Moon was served with the Olmans' complaint?

2. According to Rule 56, could Eleanor Lane have served a motion for summary judgment at the same time she served the complaint on Full Moon?

3. Assume Tweedy had moved for summary judgment at the same time he served Full Moon's answer. In that motion, he argues that Otis lacks evidence that would support a jury verdict that he was the victim of age discrimination. Assume that Lane realizes that, at this early stage of litigation, Full Moon's argument is correct. What can Lane do to avoid entry of summary judgment?

C. Full Moon's Grounds for Summary Judgment

1. Challenging Fiona's Suit Based on the Affirmative Defense of Release

All of Fiona's claims would fail if the release she signed when she left Full Moon was enforceable. Tweedy had brought this release to Lane's attention earlier in the suit when he served a Rule 11 motion demanding that she dismiss Fiona's claims. Lane responded by contending that the release was unenforceable because it failed to advise Fiona of her right to seek the advice of an attorney before signing it. Federal law required that the release specifically advise Fiona to consult an "attorney," but the release prepared by Full Moon merely advised her to consult with an "advisor." Lane also argued that Fiona signed the release under sufficient duress to preclude its enforcement.

Tweedy had questioned whether Lane's legal quibble, as he thought of it, would defeat the release. But, after receiving Lane's response to the Rule 11 motion he sent her, he had decided not to file the motion with the court. Instead, he had chosen to conduct discovery into the circumstances surrounding Fiona's signing of the release, with the hope that discovery would reveal information conclusively affirming the release's enforceability.

During her deposition in discovery, Fiona had admitted that (1) Full Moon's Human Resources officer had advised her to consult with an attorney before signing the release and (2) she actually considered speaking with an attorney but decided not to. So Tweedy believed that Full Moon had adequately fulfilled its statutory obligation to advise Fiona to consult an attorney and, in any event, Fiona had consciously decided not to avail herself of this statutory safeguard. Tweedy now moved for summary judgment and supported his motion with the signed release and a transcript of Fiona's deposition.

Question 11.2

To reaffirm your understanding of the distinction between a Rule 56 motion for summary judgment and a Rule 12(b)(6) motion to dismiss for failure to state a claim, explain why a Rule 56 motion was the proper method for Tweedy to seek the disposition of Fiona's claims.

2. Challenging Otis's Claims That Full Moon Acted with Ageist Motive

Otis had asserted claims of age discrimination under both federal and state law. To succeed on these claims, he needed to prove that age-based animus had a "determinative influence" on Full Moon's decision to replace him as store manager. The ultimate rationale of Full Moon's decision makers in replacing Otis with Shockley was critical to the success of his claims. Court precedent made clear that Otis could not prevail by simply showing that age was one of *several* motives influencing Full Moon's decision. Instead, Otis had to show that *but-for* Full Moon's ageist motive, he would not have suffered adverse employment action.[6]

Courts have often expressed reluctance to resolve discrimination claims by summary judgment. An opinion illustrating this reluctance is *Carlton v. Mystic Transportation, Inc.*[7] In *Mystic Transportation,* the Second Circuit observed:

> Because this is a discrimination case where intent and state of mind are in dispute, summary judgment is ordinarily inappropriate. . . . [A] trial court should exercise caution when granting summary judgment to an employer where . . . its intent is a genuine issue.[8]

Yet, as Tweedy knew, employers often obtain summary judgments in age-discrimination suits notwithstanding the courts' general preference for letting juries decide issues of intent or motive.[9]

To win summary judgment, Tweedy needed to show that Otis's allegations of ageist motive lacked sufficient evidentiary support. To do this, he had developed substantial evidence showing that Full Moon was motivated by *economic* factors when it replaced Otis as store manager. Otis's salary of $100,000 was much higher than the going rate for managers of sporting goods store, and profits from the Jacksonville store were increasingly attributable to sales of extreme sporting goods. Full Moon would argue that Shockley was best suited to lead the Jacksonville store as it continued to emphasize the sale of such goods. Further, Shockley had agreed to work for a guaranteed salary of only $70,000, well within the salary range that Full Moon established when it began its corporate downsizing.

Summary judgment proceedings in employment discrimination suits often introduce complexities not encountered in other forms of litigation. In particular, the Supreme Court has developed special procedures for resolving questions of motive when defendants seek summary judgment in employment-discrimination cases. These special procedures are referred to as the *McDonnell Douglas*[10] standard, a standard that would apply in assessing Full Moon's motion for summary judgment.[11]

---

[6] *See Gross v. FBL Financial Serv. Inc.*, 557 U.S. 167, 179 (2009). In *Gross*, the Court rejected the argument that an ADEA plaintiff can prevail by showing that age was "a motivating factor" and distinguished Title VII precedent governing sex and racial discrimination where a plaintiff can prevail in a case of mixed motives.

[7] 202 F.3d 129 (2d Cir. 2000).

[8] *Id.* at 134.

[9] *See, e.g., Collins v. Baltimore City Bd. of School Com'rs,* 528 Fed. Appx. 269 (4th Cir. 2013); *Minton v. American Bankers Insur. Group,* 2003 WL 21303330 (11th Cir. Feb. 6, 2003).

[10] *See McDonnell Douglas Corp. v. Green,* 411 U.S. 792 (1973).

[11] *See, e.g., Kilgore v. Trussville Development, LLC,* 2016 WL 1138412 at *6 (11th Cir. Mar. 24, 2016).

Lower courts contour the *McDonnell Douglas* standard to the type of discriminatory action alleged by the plaintiff. In a case like Otis's alleging discriminatory demotion of an existing employee, the plaintiff's burden of production is satisfied by evidence showing:

1. The plaintiff was at least 40 years old;
2. The plaintiff was demoted;
3. The plaintiff was replaced by a substantially younger person; and,
4. The plaintiff was qualified to perform the job given to the younger person.[12]

If the plaintiff produces evidence that would support a favorable jury finding on each element, the employer is required to produce its own evidence showing that it had a legitimate, nondiscriminatory reason for demoting the plaintiff. If the employer produces such evidence, the plaintiff must respond by producing evidence that the employer's alleged reason is pretextual.[13]

Our goal is to introduce you to the basics of summary judgment procedure rather than the complexities of employment discrimination law. For that reason, you need not be overly concerned with understanding the technical aspects of discrimination law such as the *McDonnell Douglas* standard. Instead, keep a few things in mind. First, when Full Moon presented evidence supporting its argument that it replaced Otis for economic reasons, Otis had to respond to that evidence or suffer entry of summary judgment. Next, in his response, Otis would present evidence showing that Full Moon's economic explanation was a *pretext*.[14] According to the Supreme Court, when an employer gives a pretextual reason for taking action against an employee, a jury can infer that the pretext was intended to conceal a discriminatory reason.[15] Thus, to survive summary judgment, Otis would rely on positive evidence of age discrimination—such as expressions of ageist sentiments—as well as evidence casting doubt on Full Moon's economic explanation.

3. Challenging Otis's Claim of Retaliation

Otis's second principal charge was that his firing occurred in retaliation for the letter he sent to the Full Moon president, Bertie Lurch, in which he accused the company of age discrimination. To prevail on his retaliation claims, Otis had to show that (1) he engaged in some form of statutorily protected activity, (2) he suffered adverse employment action, and (3) the adverse action was taken in retaliation for Otis's protected action. Otis had sufficient evidence to support a verdict on element two; his firing was obviously an adverse employment action. Likewise, Otis had sufficient circumstantial evidence to support element three; Lurch's firing

---

[12] *See Damon v. Fleming Supermarkets of Florida, Inc.*, 196 F.3d 1354, 1360 (11th Cir. 1999).

[13] *See id.* at 1360-62.

[14] *See, e.g., Hinga v. MIC Group, L.L.C.*, 609 Fed. Appx. 823, 826 (5th Cir. 2015) (discussing application of the *McDonnell Douglas* standard at summary judgment).

[15] *See Reeves v. Sanderson Plumbing Products, Inc.*, 530 U.S. 133, 147-48 (2000).

of Otis within a few weeks of receiving his letter permitted the jury to infer that Lurch acted in retaliation.[16] But Otis might be vulnerable on element one, requiring that Otis engaged in statutorily protected activity.

Recall that the party who bears the burden of persuasion at trial—here Otis—must present evidence that would support a jury finding in his favor. And this requires sufficient evidence to support *each and every element* of a cause of action. Harkening back to our table analogy, where the table will stand only if each leg is supported, you can see how Tweedy could topple the retaliation table by showing that any one of its legs (i.e., elements of the cause of action) was unsupported. The protected-activity element was the weakness in Otis's claim for retaliation. If Tweedy could show that Otis was incapable of meeting his burden of production on this element, it didn't matter that Otis could support the other elements.

To attack the sufficiency of evidence showing Otis engaged in protected activity, Tweedy would focus on one issue: What did Otis know at the time he sent his letter to Lurch opposing age discrimination in the company?[17] As discussed earlier, a letter objecting to unlawful discrimination is protected only if the protester had an objectively reasonable belief that discrimination had occurred based on what he knew *at the time he objected*.[18] This meant that Otis couldn't rely on evidence of discrimination he later uncovered during discovery, even though this evidence would be very useful in the trial of Otis's claim of age discrimination. Rule 56(c)(2) affirms that a party can rely only on "admissible evidence" to support its position in summary judgment, and one admissibility requirement is that evidence be *relevant* to the issue. Because later-discovered evidence of discrimination was irrelevant to the issue of whether Otis had objectively reasonable suspicions of age discrimination when he wrote to Lurch, Tweedy could properly object to the admissibility of such evidence at summary judgment.[19] As you can see, while Rule 26(b)(1) permits discovery of information regardless of whether it would be "admissible in evidence,"[20] Rule 56 restricts the ultimate use of information by imposing an admissibility requirement.

---

[16] *See Higdon v. Jackson*, 393 F.3d 1211, 1220 (11th Cir. 2004) ("A close temporal proximity between the protected expression and an adverse action is sufficient circumstantial evidence of a causal connection for purposes of a prima facie case.").

[17] The sending of the letter constituted an act of objection that would support a claim of protected activity. *See Paquin v. Federal Nat. Mortg. Ass'n*, 119 F.3d 23, 31 (D.C. Cir. 1997) (holding that an employee's letter protesting unlawful firing is protected activity under the ADEA). But more is required, as discussed in the text.

[18] *See, e.g., Clover v. Total System Services, Inc.*, 176 F.3d 1346, 1352 (11th Cir. 1999) ("For opposition clause purposes, the relevant conduct does not include conduct that actually occurred—or that was averred in an EEOC complaint by the alleged victim—but was unknown to the person claiming protection under the clause. Instead, what counts is only the conduct that person opposed, which cannot be more than what she was aware of. Additional conduct or allegations unknown to the opposing person are not relevant to the opposition clause inquiry.").

[19] *See* Fed. R. Evid. 402 (affirming admissibility of "relevant evidence").

[20] Rule 26(b)(1) states, "Information within this scope of discovery need not be admissible in evidence to be discoverable."

Tweedy would need to be vigilant in monitoring Lane's use of evidence at summary judgment. Plaintiffs asserting retaliation claims tend to overlook the distinction between evidence that's relevant to a retaliation claim and evidence that's relevant to the larger claim of employment discrimination.[21] Tweedy needed to ensure that the court was not improperly influenced by Lane's introduction of irrelevant evidence when ruling on his motion for summary judgment.

Chapter One recounts Otis's remarks to Lane in which he explained his reasons for believing that Full Moon had engaged in age discrimination. In ruling on Full Moon's motion for summary judgment, the court would have to assess (1) Otis's reasons for believing Full Moon had engaged in age discrimination at the time he wrote his letter to Lurch and (2) whether Otis's belief was "objectively reasonable." How would the court assess reasonableness? The court would have to determine whether a person *knowledgeable of discrimination law and case precedent*, who possessed the information known to Otis when he wrote Lurch, would have reasonably perceived age discrimination.[22] In other words, the law of retaliation presumed that Otis was familiar with age-discrimination decisions in which courts have elaborated on the type of evidence sufficient to support a claim of discrimination. If Otis honestly believed Full Moon was discriminating, but that belief was not objectively reasonable in light of case law, Otis's letter objecting to age discrimination was not "protected activity" under the ADEA.

Question 11.3

Assume that a business adopts a grooming policy that permits its female employees to wear shoulder-length hair but denies such permission to male employees. Current male employees complain to management about the policy and are soon terminated. These employees sue their former employer and allege claims of sex discrimination and retaliation. The employer moves for summary judgment on the retaliation claim and argues that the plaintiffs lacked an objectively reasonable belief that the company's grooming policy was discriminatory when they complained. The employer relies on several decisions, including one by the federal circuit court whose precedent binds the trial court, holding that differing hair-length rules for males and females don't violate employment discrimination statutes. The Supreme Court has never ruled on the specific issue, but in one opinion challenging a policy that distinguished between males and females in employee benefits, the Court broadly stated, "Such a practice does not pass the simple test of whether the evidence shows treatment of a person in a manner which but for that person's sex would be different."

1. Should the court grant the employer's motion for summary judgment of the plaintiffs' retaliation claim?

---

[21] *See Clover*, 176 F.3d at 1352.

[22] *See id.* at 1351 ("The objective reasonableness of an employee's belief that her employer has engaged in an unlawful employment practice must be measured against existing substantive law.").

2. Assume that, during discovery, the plaintiffs discover a memo in which the store's manager states that its new grooming policy is "a less obvious way to get rid of male employees and replace them with females." Does discovery of this memo improve the plaintiffs' odds of surviving the employer's summary judgment motion?

3. Note the potential dilemma that employees face when they suspect their employer has engaged in employment discrimination. If they object to conduct they sincerely believe is discrimination, but that conduct doesn't rise to the level of illegality under case precedent, they have no cause of action for retaliation even if their employer targets them because of their objection. Is the "objective reasonableness" requirement fair to employees—especially those who lack the ability to access and interpret legal precedent? Can you think of a valid concern addressed by this requirement?

D. Full Moon Seeks Summary Judgment of Otis's Age Discrimination Claims

For the remainder of this chapter, we focus on Full Moon's efforts to obtain summary judgment on Otis's claim of age discrimination. As you have already learned, motions filed in federal court must include the movant's supporting argument. In many cases, the parties will also file a substantial amount of supporting evidence obtained during discovery. This filing requirement reflects Rule 56(c)'s mandate that the parties rely on evidence that has been made part of the case record. Evidence that has not been properly filed and made part of the record will not be considered by the trial court or by an appellate court later asked to review the trial court's ruling.[23]

Tactical Tip ✍

Making the Record

Rules of procedure and rules of evidence are central to the practice of civil litigators. Summary judgment illustrates this. Even the most compelling information unearthed during discovery is useless unless a litigator properly introduces that information into the record. And the litigator's task doesn't end there. According to Rule 56(c)(3), if a party fails to properly *cite* to record evidence in its summary judgment argument, the court is not obliged to consider that evidence: "The court need consider only the cited materials, but it may consider other materials in the record." *See also Jackson v. Cal-Western Packaging Corp.*, 602 F.3d 374, 379 (5th Cir. 2010) (ruling that, because the plaintiff "did not identify [supporting] evidence in

[23] Rule 56(c)(3) states, "The court need consider only the cited materials, but it may consider other materials *in the record*." (emphasis added).

> his opposition to summary judgment, we will not consider his argument"). The point is, courts expect the parties' counsel to know and use those procedural rules designed to create the official record that tells the story of a dispute.

Much of the evidence filed by Tweedy and Lane would be the product of discovery, including deposition transcripts, answers to interrogatories, admissions, and documents. According to Rule 5(d)(1), discovery product should not be filed until it will be "used in the proceeding." Summary judgment often provides the first occasion for use of discovery product.

Rule 56(c) also permits the parties to file affidavits to support or resist summary judgment. *Affidavits* are sworn statements made by a person "competent to testify" that are offered as evidence in support of a party's position.[24] In these affidavits, a party may affirm allegations already recited in their pleadings. Why might a party submit an affidavit that reiterates what is already alleged in the pleadings?

Pleadings, you may recall, have little if any evidentiary value and are generally not admissible at trial. For one thing, pleadings are usually signed by the parties' lawyers, but not by the parties themselves.[25] They are seldom "verified or accompanied by an affidavit" of the party, and thus they don't formally attest to the truth of the allegations.[26] Because a party's pleadings lack the reliability of testimony given under oath, a party can't "rest on the pleadings" and in most cases can't rely on them at all in responding to a summary judgment motion.[27]

To provide testimonial evidence in support of party's position on summary judgment, that party can file either (1) the transcript of a witness's deposition testimony (including the party's own testimony) or (2) an affidavit. This use of affidavits might at first glance seem dubious. Affidavits are usually drafted by lawyers to provide testimony specifically crafted to support their clients' position. Further, there is no opposing lawyer present to cross-examine the affiant and expose doubts about his or her credibility, as there is during a deposition.

The common use of affidavit testimony reflects the fact that summary judgment is *not* the occasion to resolve issues of credibility.[28] Provided that an affiant is competent to testify about an issue in dispute, his or her credibility should not be assessed by the court when it rules on a summary judgment motion.[29] This works to the advantage of the party opposing summary

---

[24] Rule 56(c)(4) states that affidavits "must be made on personal knowledge, set out facts that would be admissible in evidence, and show that the affiant or declarant is competent to testify on the matters stated."

[25] *See* Rule 11(a) (requiring that every pleading be signed by the attorney of record, but not requiring the signature of the represented client).

[26] *See id.*

[27] *See* Rule 56(c).

[28] *See Anderson v. Liberty Lobby, Inc.*, 477 U.S. 242, 255 (1986).

[29] There is one important exception. A party is usually not permitted to defeat summary judgment by giving affidavit testimony that contradicts earlier sworn testimony, like that given at a deposition. Only

judgment and demanding a right to trial by jury. That party's evidence and affidavits are construed in his or her favor, and the court must normally assume that a jury would find the nonmovant's supporting witnesses credible.

So both Tweedy and Lane would file memoranda arguing their positions and support their arguments with references to the discovery product and affidavits made part of the case record. In addition, many federal courts require by local rules that the moving party file a separate document, often called a "Statement of Uncontested Facts," identifying the salient facts that are not in dispute.[30] As you can imagine, there is often dispute as to what facts are "uncontested."

They could also request a hearing before the trial judge, but they had no right to demand one.[31] Federal courts typically have discretion whether to hold a hearing before ruling on a motion.[32] To some extent, it makes sense for a court to dispense with a hearing when ruling on a motion for summary judgment. After all, the court is not permitted to assess the credibility of a witness's statements made under oath in a deposition or affidavit; and all doubts about the resolution of contested matters must be resolved in favor of the nonmovant.[33] Finally, the court's decision is largely driven by the content of written materials filed by the parties. But the infrequency of hearings in federal court contrasts with the practice in many state courts, where the lawyers' oral advocacy skills can make a difference in the court's decision.

Below are excerpts from Full Moon's memorandum in support of its motion for summary judgment, together with an illustrative affidavit.[34] As you read this memorandum, recall that the ultimate issue for the court to decide is this: Does the record contain sufficient evidence to support a jury finding that age discrimination was the but-for cause of Otis's replacement as store manager?

---

if the party provides an explanation for the apparent discrepancy will the contradictory affidavit testimony be accepted. *See, e.g., Cleveland v. Policy Management Sys. Corp.*, 526 U.S. 795, 804 (1999).

[30] *See, e.g.*, N.D. Ill. Local Rule 56.1(a).

[31] *See, e.g., Cruz v. Melecio*, 204 F.3d 14, 19 (1st Cir. 2000) (holding that it is not a denial of due process to deny a hearing before deciding a motion for summary judgment).

[32] *See* Rule 78(b).

[33] *See, e.g., Davis v. Shah*, 2016 WL 1138768, at *7 (2d Cir. Mar. 24, 2016) (stating that a court ruling on a summary judgment motion must "resolv[e] all ambiguities and draw[] all permissible factual inferences in favor of the non-moving party").

[34] Each party's legal argument would contain specific citations to the record evidence supporting its assertions. We have omitted such citations in this excerpt.

IN THE UNITED STATES DISTRICT COURT
FOR THE MIDDLE DISTRICT OF FLORIDA,
JACKSONVILLE DIVISION

OTIS AND FIONA OLMAN,

Plaintiffs,

v. Case No. 8-23-CV-00637

FULL MOON SPORTS, INC.,
& BRUCE BELCHER

Defendants.

DEFENDANT'S MOTION FOR SUMMARY JUDGMENT AND SUPPORTING MEMORANDUM OF LAW

. . . .

II. Plaintiff Otis Olman has failed to present sufficient evidence to support a jury verdict that he was replaced as store manager because of his age.

Summary judgment must be granted when it is evident that the nonmoving party is unable to prove the essential elements of his case. *Celotex Corp. v. Catrett*, 477 U.S. 317, 321-22 (1986). When a plaintiff like Otis Olman alleges he was the victim of disparate treatment based on age, his case must fail "unless the employee's protected trait played a role in the [decision-making] process and had a *determinative influence* on the outcome." *Hazen Paper Co. v. Biggins*, 507 U.S. 604, 610 (1993) (emphasis added). And as the Supreme Court has made clear, Olman has the burden of persuasion throughout this proceeding: "The burden of persuasion [to show age was a determinative influence] does not shift to the employer to show that it would have taken the action regardless of age, even when a plaintiff has produced some evidence that age was one mitigating factor in that decision." *Gross v. FBL Financial Services, Inc.*, 557 U.S. 167, 180 (2009).

The decision-making process leading to Olman's replacement as store manager has been extensively probed by the parties during discovery. The factors influencing that process are undisputed, and they show that Olman was replaced so that the Jacksonville store might be more profitable. There is no record evidence supporting Olman's speculation that his age somehow influenced the decision to replace him as store manager.

Full Moon owns and operates a chain of retail sporting goods stores throughout the United States. In 2022, due to declining profits and losses in many of its stores, Full Moon was compelled to implement a nationwide reorganization, reduction in force, and reduction in salaries and benefits. One of the factors contributing to the company's lackluster economic performance was the salary scale implemented by prior corporate management, which often resulted in salaries for store managers and assistants some 15-25% higher than those paid by competitor companies. To implement economic change, Full Moon established a Reorganization Committee (the "Committee") that made decisions from corporate headquarters in Atlanta, Georgia. The Committee consisted of four corporate officers, whose ages ranged from 33 to 54 years. Three of the Committee members were over the age of 40. By resolution of Full Moon's Board of Directors, the Committee had final authority to implement change related to the company's reorganization and reduction in force. Company president, Bertie Lurch, was a member of the Committee. Lurch was 48 years old at the time the Committee voted to replace Olman as store manager. The Committee's chairperson was Chloé Michaela, who was 45 years old at that time.

One of the Committee's decisions was to close unprofitable or marginally profitable stores. The Jacksonville store managed by Olman was among those considered for closure. But the Committee eventually decided to keep the store open, while shifting emphasis to the sale of extreme sporting goods. The Committee hoped this marketing shift might begin generating adequate profits to avoid the store's closure and further layoffs of store employees.

Another Committee decision was to cap the base salary of all store managers at $70,000, while giving managers the opportunity to share in store profits. The Committee decided that current store managers making more than $70,000 should, whenever feasible, be replaced or reassigned to a different store at a reduced salary. In the Committee's considered business judgment, it was undesirable to retain a manager at the same store while substantially reducing his or her salary. After implementation of the Committee's policy, only a few stores nationwide retained managers earning over $70,000. Most of these stores had generated strong profits in recent years, and none of their retained managers earned a base salary greater than $90,000.

All regional managers were informed of the Committee's decision and instructed to file a report with the Committee concerning implementation of the new policy at individual stores. Shortly after managers received this instruction, the Committee received a report from Bruce Belcher, regional manager for stores in the southeastern United States, including the Jacksonville store managed by plaintiff Otis Olman. Belcher informed the Committee that Olman was currently receiving a salary of $100,000 a year. Belcher also informed the Committee that sales in Olman's store had held steady during the past three years, but only because of a substantial increase in the sale of extreme sporting goods.

The Committee reviewed sales figures for the Jacksonville store, which indicated that in the past three years the sale of extreme sporting goods had gone from accounting for less than 5% of store profits to accounting for some 40% of store profits. Absent those profits attributable to the sale of extreme sporting goods, the Jacksonville store would probably have been closed.

Belcher advised the Committee that, in accordance with its policy, Olman did not qualify for renewal as store manager. But Belcher recommended that Olman be retained by Full Moon in some capacity. Belcher commended Olman for his long service to the company and his popularity among a certain niche of store customers. Because Olman had specifically told Belcher that he did not want to be considered for a position as manager of another Full Moon store, Belcher recommended that Olman be retained as department manager of the Jacksonville store's camping section at a reduced salary. Finally, Belcher recommended promotion of the store's current manager of the extreme sporting goods department, Sid Shockley, to the position of overall store manager. He also recommended that Shockley receive a base salary of $70,000 along with profit-sharing incentives.

Three of the Committee's members were deposed by Olman during discovery. *All* testified that their decision to replace Olman as store manager was based on his high salary, as well as the emergence of extreme sporting goods as the store's most profitable sales category. All testified that their decision to replace Otis was unaffected by consideration of his age. In fact, no Committee member was even aware of the ages of Olman or his replacement, Shockley. Committee members also testified that Olman's salary of $100,000 was simply unsustainable in the company's new salary scale for managers.

Thus, the record evidence is undisputed: Full Moon, acting through its Reorganization Committee, made a series of personnel decisions that were intended to make its stores more profitable. In the case of the Jacksonville store managed by Olman, this entailed cutting back on Olman's unjustifiably high salary and replacing him with a store manager with a proven record in the marketing of extreme sporting goods.

Case precedent makes clear that an employer can make prudent personnel decisions based on economic considerations without violating the ADEA. For example, in *Hazen Paper Corp. v. Biggens*, 507 U.S. 604 (1993), the Supreme Court unanimously held that an employer does not violate the ADEA when it bases its personnel decisions on economic factors (pension level in *Hazen Paper*), even if those factors happen to correlate with employees' age. The Court observed that "there is no disparate treatment under the ADEA when the factor motivating the employer is some other feature other than the employee's age." *Id.* at 611. As the Court explained, the ADEA is concerned with "older workers . . . being deprived of employment on the basis of inaccurate and stigmatizing stereotypes." *Id.* But "when the employer's decision is wholly motivated by factors other than age, the problem of inaccurate and stigmatizing stereotypes disappears. This is true even if the motivating factor is correlated with age, as pension status typically is." *Id.*

Hazen Paper thus affirms that the decision to replace Olman as store manager in order to improve the store's profitability did not violate the ADEA. As a leading case on salary-based personnel decisions observes, the *Hazen Paper* rationale "applies with equal force to cases where workers are discharged because of salary considerations." *See Anderson v. Baxter Healthcare Corp.*, 13 F.3d 1120, 1125 (7th Cir. 1994). Although the older employee in *Anderson* was terminated (not offered alternative employment at a reduced salary as was Olman), the Seventh Circuit nonetheless upheld his termination under the ADEA: "Anderson could not prove age discrimination even if he was fired simply because [the employer] desired to reduce its salary costs by discharging him." *Id.* at 1126. The Seventh Circuit's application of the ADEA has been followed by other courts. *See, e.g., Snow v. Ridgefield Medical Center*, 128 F.3d 1201, 1208 (8th Cir. 1997) (entering summary judgment on employee's ADEA claim that "she was terminated because she had been employed at RMC longer than the other then-current employees, and thus earned a comparatively higher salary"). As one court has aptly stated, "Employers do not violate the law by discriminating against overpaid, unnecessary employees." *See Hennessey v. Good Earth Tools, Inc.*, 126 F.3d 1107, 1109 (8th Cir. 1997).

Because the record evidence overwhelmingly demonstrates that the Committee's decision to replace Olman as store manager was motivated by economic concerns, Olman's claim of age discrimination must fail. Aware that the theory of his case is foreclosed by precedent, Olman has attempted throughout discovery to find a shred of evidence that would show the Committee's economic justification was "pretext." Olman's pretext argument ultimately comes down to several isolated statements allegedly made by his replacement, Sid Shockley, or by regional manager, Belcher. Olman argues that these comments about Olman's age somehow tainted the Committee's decision-making process hundreds of miles away in Atlanta, Georgia, even though there is no record evidence the Committee ever knew of these comments.

During discovery, Olman came up with the following evidence he claims is proof that the Committee in Atlanta acted based on ageist motives:

1. Olman testified that Shockley often referred to him as the "old man"; and referred to older customers as the "boomers."

2. Olman's wife, Fiona Olman, and another store employee who lost her job during Full Moon's downsizing, testified they heard Shockley refer to Olman repeatedly as the "old man."

3. Bruce Belcher, regional manager, testified that he had no recollection of Shockley's ever referring to Olman as the "old man." He did recall one specific conversation with Shockley, some six months before the decision to replace Olman as store manager was made, in which Shockley expressed the opinion that he could improve store sales if he were given greater authority to expand the store's marketing of extreme sporting goods. Shockley also told Belcher that Olman seemed to have a "problem" with the culture of extreme sports enthusiasts, particularly their dress and speech.

4. Shockley testified that he did occasionally refer to Olman as the "old man," an expression he acquired when serving in the Navy and intended to signify that Olman was the "boss" or store "commander." Shockley testified that he was never told that Olman or anyone else thought "old man" was a disparaging, ageist term. Shockley also affirmed the conversation about which Belcher testified, in which Shockley expressed the belief that the store's sales would improve if Olman would give greater support to extreme sporting goods sales.

5. Finally, Olman testified that he could not recall a specific occasion on which he complained to Belcher about Shockley's ageist remarks, although he is sure he informally complained at some point. The record confirms that Otis first formally complained about Shockley's remarks *after* he received notice of his replacement as store manager. At that time, Full Moon sent a formal letter of reprimand to Shockley warning him that future words or actions reflecting ageist sentiments would result in his termination.

The fundamental flaw in Olman's pretext contention is that there is no evidence (1) that any member of the Committee had or expressed ageist sentiments (not surprising since three of the four committee members were over 40); or (2) that any member of the Committee was ever aware of the ageist statements attributed to Shockley or Belcher. The Supreme Court has recognized that an inference of ageist motivation can be drawn when the person "principally responsible" for the employment decision has expressed ageist sentiments. *See Reeves v. Sanderson Plumbing Products, Inc.*, 530 U.S. 133, 151 (2000). But there is no record evidence in this case that would support an inference that anyone responsible for Olman's replacement was motivated by ageism.

Courts also recognize that a nondecision maker may taint an employment decision if that person has "influence or leverage over the official decisionmaker." *See Staub v. Proctor Hospital*, 562 U.S. 411 (2011). As explained by one court, "If the [formal decision makers] acted as the conduit of [an employee's] prejudice—his cat's paw—the innocence of the [decision makers] would not spare the company from liability." *See Shager v. Upjohn Co.*, 913 F.2d 398, 405 (7th Cir. 1990).

But in Olman's case there is no evidence that the Committee was the "cat's paw" of Shockley or Belcher, the only persons alleged to have expressed ageist sentiments. The uncontroverted record evidence shows that the Committee made a purely economic decision to replace Olman as store manager. Olman earned a salary $30,000 greater than the base salary cap established for store managers. His replacement, Shockley, agreed to manage the Jacksonville store for a salary within the salary cap, and Shockley specialized in the sale of merchandise—extreme sporting goods—that was key to the store's continuing success. Finally, Full Moon's decision not to retain current store managers like Olman at a reduced salary has been recognized as a "legitimate reason" for an employment decision. *See Bay v. Times Mirror Magazine, Inc.*, 936 F.2d 112, 118 (2d Cir. 1991). Thus, Full Moon's decision to replace Olman as store manager was precisely the type of employment decision that courts have found consistent with the ADEA.

Nor do the alleged ageist remarks of regional manager, Belcher, somehow taint the lawful decision of the Reorganization Committee. This Circuit has repeatedly affirmed that ageist statements made by a person having no role in employment decision making do not provide credible evidence to justify a trial by jury. *See, e.g., Standard v. A.B.E.L. Services, Inc.*, 161 F.3d 1318, 1329-30 (11th Cir. 1998) (affirming summary judgment for employer where brother of decision maker had stated that "older people have more go wrong"); *Mauter v. Hardy Corp.*, 825 F.2d 1554, 1558 (11th Cir. 1987) (holding that statement by vice president of company uninvolved in decision making that company "was going to weed out the old ones" failed to present a genuine issue of material fact). Indeed, even statements made by one actually involved in company decision making are not adequate to support an inference of age discrimination when the statements are "isolated remarks" that do not relate "directly, in time and subject, to the company's decision to terminate older employees." *See Minton v. American Bankers Insur. Group, Inc.*, 2003 WL 21303330 (11th Cir. 2003) (disregarding decision maker's isolated remarks that company needed "fresh new blood").

In sum, Full Moon has presented uncontroverted evidence that its decision to replace Olman as store manager was motivated by economic concerns. The isolated statements of employees uninvolved in Full Moon's final decision making are not sufficient to raise a genuine issue whether Full Moon's decision was a pretext.

. . . .

Respectfully submitted,

____

Harrison Ames, Esq.
Bart A. Tweedy, Esq.
Lord, Howe & Mercy, P.A.
Counsel for Full Moon Sports, Inc.
[Further detail omitted]

[Certificate of Service omitted]

IN THE UNITED STATES DISTRICT COURT
FOR THE MIDDLE DISTRICT OF FLORIDA,
JACKSONVILLE DIVISION

OTIS AND FIONA OLMAN

Plaintiffs,

v. Case No. 8-23-CV-00637

FULL MOON SPORTS, INC.
& BRUCE BELCHER

AFFIDAVIT OF CHLOÉ MICHAELA

I, Chloé Michaela, being first duly sworn and deposed, say:

1. I have personal knowledge of the facts set forth herein.

2. This affidavit is submitted in support of defendant, Full Moon Sports, Inc.'s motion for summary judgment for the purpose of showing that there is no genuine as to any material fact, and that Full Moon Sports, Inc., is entitled to judgment as a matter of law.

3. I am Vice President of Sales for Full Moon Sports, Inc., and have served in that capacity since 2020. I am 45 years old.

4. I was Chairperson of Full Moon's Reorganization Committee from 2022-2023, which committee made all final decisions concerning the transfer, termination, demotion, promotion, and compensation of all store managers in the Southeast region of the United States.

5. I participated in all above-referenced decisions, including the decision to replace plaintiff, Otis Olman, as manager of the Full Moon Sports Outdoor Center in Jacksonville, Florida, and to place in that position, Sidney Shockley.

6. At no time during the consideration and making the above-mentioned decisions was I aware of the ages of Otis Olman or Sid Shockley.

7. At no time during the consideration and making of the above-mentioned decisions were the ages of Otis Olman or Sid Shockley mentioned by committee members.

8. At no time during the consideration and making of the above-mentioned decisions was the committee informed of alleged age-discriminatory statements having been made by Sid Shockley, former regional manager, Bruce Belcher, or any other person connected with the Jacksonville store.

9. The decision to replace Otis Olman as store manager was necessitated by company-wide guidelines, including guidelines related to Olman's compensation level and store profits.

10. The decision to replace Otis Olman as store manager was not influenced by the recommendation of Bruce Belcher, even though Belcher conveyed favorable impressions of Olman to the committee.

11. Had the committee been informed of any alleged age-discriminatory comments or behavior by any company personnel, it would have taken immediate action to ensure that no committee decisions were affected by age-discriminatory beliefs, opinions, or motives.

12. At no time during committee deliberations did Full Moon president, Bertie Lurch, express any comments about the age of Otis Olman, his fitness to serve as manager of the Jacksonville store, or Olman's attitudes or opinions regarding Full Moon's corporate downsizing.

____
Chloé Michaela

Signed and sworn to before me on this 28th day of September, 2023.

[Further Notary Public information omitted.]

Question 11.4

Recall that a court should not make determinations about witness credibility on a motion for summary judgment. Could a juror review the evidence cited by Full Moon and still have "reasonable" doubts about the company's actual motivation in replacing Otis? Does the fact that Full Moon cites substantial evidence of its economic motivation preclude a jury's believing that ageism had a "determinative influence" on the company's decision, which is the critical legal issue under the ADEA?

E. The Olmans' Response to Summary Judgment

Before responding to Full Moon's summary judgment motion, Lane considered whether she might file her own motion on behalf of the Olmans. Nothing in the Rules prohibits both parties from seeking summary judgment. But Lane did not believe she had good grounds for seeking summary judgment. First, Full Moon had already abandoned its counterclaim alleging that Otis converted store property. Discovery had made clear that this counterclaim was based on misinformed speculation. When Tweedy learned that Full Moon's counterclaim lacked factual support, he obtained Otis's permission to voluntarily dismiss it under Rule 41(a)(1).[35]

As for the Olmans' remaining claims, Lane believed they were well supported but knew she lacked evidence sufficient to win on summary judgment. But she took Full Moon's summary judgment motion very seriously. She believed summary judgment posed the greatest threat to her clients' chance of success in litigation. Provided that the Olmans could survive summary judgment, they would present attractive figures to a jury. They were plain spoken, and jurors would probably relate to two middle-aged folks who lost their jobs because a large corporation wanted to maximize profits by cutting the salaries of its long-term employees. It also helped that the jurors, like the Olmans, would be Floridians and residents of the same county. Sympathies would more likely lie with fellow Floridians than with an out-of-state corporation.

Lane *had* to get this case to a jury. Here is how she assessed her risks on summary judgment.

1. Responding to the Liability Release

Fiona's case presented the greatest problem. Her deposition testimony appeared to bolster Full Moon's argument that she was sufficiently notified of her right to consult an attorney

---

[35] Rule 41(a) provides a means for the parties, or in some circumstances, the plaintiff alone, to voluntarily dismiss a claim. A plaintiff may voluntarily dismiss a claim on its own, so long as no answer or motion for summary judgment has been filed. *See* Rule 41(a)(1)(A)(i). Once either of these documents has been filed, a voluntary dismissal is permissible only if all parties agree. *See* Rule 41(a)(1)(A)(ii). In this case, both Full Moon and Otis agreed to voluntarily dismiss the conversion counterclaim. The stipulation of dismissal they filed with the court specified that the dismissal was with prejudice. This meant that Full Moon could not later reassert the claim. If the stipulation had not so provided, the default presumption was that the dismissal would have been without prejudice. *See* Rule 41(a)(1)(B). The most common use of voluntary dismissals occurs when the parties agree to settle their dispute.

before signing the release. Likewise, Fiona's admission that she actually considered speaking with an attorney suggested that she knowingly declined to avail herself of this opportunity.

Yet Lane thought she might still attack the release's enforceability based on the "totality of circumstances" test that many jurisdictions use to assess whether an employee has "knowingly and voluntarily" waived her rights under the ADEA.[36] Among other things, Fiona had been utterly surprised by Full Moon's decision to terminate her and demote her husband. This blow to their personal finances had precipitated an episode of depression. Her immediate reaction to Full Moon's offer had been to take the severance pay the company offered and distance herself from Full Moon by signing the release—which she did within a few days of receiving it. Lane thus believed she could argue that Fiona signed the release under economic and emotional duress. This, combined with the fact that the release used squirrelly language referring to an "advisor" rather than an "attorney," might persuade a court that the release's validity presented a question for the jury to decide.

2. Responding to Full Moon's Contention That Otis Was Demoted for Economic Reasons

Full Moon's economic justification for Otis's replacement was worrisome. During depositions, every member of the Reorganization Committee had emphasized the centrality of economic reasons for replacing higher-paid store managers. Committee members stated that the policy decision to replace higher-salaried managers like Otis was made before they received any input from regional managers like Belcher. And this policy had been implemented with very few exceptions. Thus, if the court focused on the final decision makers in Atlanta when assessing Full Moon's motives, the company would likely win its motion for summary judgment.

So Lane's strategy was to shift focus away from the Committee and onto Belcher (and Shockley). The Supreme Court has recognized that the concept of proximate cause used in tort law applies to statutory claims as well. In *Staub v. Proctor Hospital*,[37] the Court held that a final decision maker's actions may result from unlawful motive even if the decision maker lacks such a motive. Based on the "cat's paw" theory of liability,[38] if a lower-level manager acts with unlawful motive in making an employee recommendation, and that recommendation causes the final decision maker to take adverse job action against the employee, the employer is liable for discriminatory conduct. So if Lane could show that the Committee's decision to replace Otis with Shockley resulted from discriminatory action by Belcher, Otis would prevail—and at least survive summary judgment.

Below are excerpts from the Olmans' memorandum opposing Full Moon's motion for summary judgment. We have included only those excerpts relevant to Otis's claim of age discrimination under the ADEA.

---

[36] *See Griffin v. Kraft General Foods*, 62 F.3d 368, 373-74 (11th Cir. 1995); *Wells v. Xpedx, a Div. of International Paper Co.*, 2006 WL 3133984, at *7 (M.D. Fla. Oct. 31, 2006).

[37] 562 U.S. 411 (2011).

[38] The name is derived from a French fable in which Bertrand the monkey persuades Raton the cat to pull chestnuts from a fire—burning Raton's paw—but eats the recovered chestnuts without giving Raton a share. In other words, the cat is a dupe for the monkey.

IN THE UNITED STATES DISTRICT COURT
FOR THE MIDDLE DISTRICT OF FLORIDA,
JACKSONVILLE DIVISION

OTIS AND FIONA OLMAN,

Plaintiffs,

vs. Case No. 8-23-CV-00637

FULL MOON SPORTS, INC.,
& BRUCE BELCHER

Defendants.

MEMORANDUM IN OPPOSITION TO DEFENDANT'S MOTION FOR SUMMARY JUDGMENT

. . . .

In ruling on Full Moon's motion for summary judgment, the court "must draw all reasonable inferences in favor of the nonmoving party, and it may not make credibility determinations or weigh the evidence." *Reeves v. Sanderson Plumbing Products, Inc.*, 530 U.S. 133, 150 (2000). Application of this standard requires that the Court deny Full Moon's motion for summary judgment on Otis Olman's age-discrimination claims.

Full Moon attempts to create a wall between its Reorganization Committee and the ageist sentiments of regional manager Belcher and his chosen replacement for Olman, Sid Shockley. According to Full Moon, its Committee made the final decision to replace Olman with a younger manager, and regional manager, Belcher, had no influence on that decision.

But a more complete review of the record evidence refutes Full Moon's depiction. This review shows that (1) Olman's replacement was not the inevitable result of economic factors and (2) Belcher used his influence with the Committee to bring about a change in management motivated by undisguised ageism. Here is the critical evidence that, if believed by a jury, would support a verdict finding Full Moon liable under the ADEA:

1. Otis Olman worked for Full Moon for twenty years before being terminated. In 2011, he accepted Full Moon's offer to become manager of its Jacksonville store, which had enjoyed "mediocre" sales under prior management. As Full Moon's own witnesses agree, Olman transformed the Jacksonville store into a profitable, successful business.

2. In 2019, Full Moon was acquired by another company and replaced both its president and southeast regional manager. The new president and regional manager were, respectively, Bertie Lurch and Bruce Belcher.

3. In 2019, Olman received an attractive business offer that would have required his leaving Full Moon's employment. But Lurch and Belcher induced Olman to remain with the company by offering to increase his salary from $85,000 to $100,000 a year. Although Olman expressed concerns about his job security under Full Moon's new management, Belcher stated unequivocally to Olman that "a guy with your track record shouldn't worry about his future with Full Moon. Jacksonville is your store as long as you want it to be. You can retire here."

4. That same year, Sid Shockley was hired to manage the new extreme sporting goods department of the Jacksonville store. Shockley had no prior retail sales experience. From the inception of his hiring, Shockley required careful training by Olman. As Shockley acknowledged during his deposition, "He taught me everything I know about retail sales. I owe it all to him."

5. Although Shockley "owed it all" to Olman, he continually expressed his age prejudice against Olman. He constantly referred to Olman as the "old man" both within and outside Olman's presence. On several occasions, Shockley expressed the view that the Jacksonville store could improve its sales if it turned attention away from older customers—called "boomers" by Shockley—and marketed to the "younger" customer base interested in extreme sports. Shockley also claimed a younger manager could better appeal to the store's younger clientele.

6. Olman declined to formally complain about Shockley's ageist sentiments and hoped that he would mature. On one occasion, however, he felt compelled to warn Shockley about his slovenly dress and excessively slang speech. When Olman told Belcher about the warning he had given to Shockley, Belcher laughed and said, "Lighten up Otis. Stop being an old fart."

7. Former store employee, Rachel Ortiz, testified that she had socialized with Belcher, Shockley, and other store employees on several occasions. According to Ortiz, at one social gathering Shockley openly expressed his disdain for Olman and asked Belcher, "When are you going to do something about the old man?" On another occasion, Ortiz recalls hearing Belcher say to Shockley, "Be patient, the old guy will probably retire soon."

8. In November 2022, Belcher informed Olman of the company's reorganization plans and asked him to consider relocating to another store. Belcher asked Olman if he was ready to retire, or perhaps assume management of another store.

9. In response to Belcher's request, Olman informed him that he did not want to retire or move to another store and displace some other store manager.

10. Belcher promised Olman he would "look out" for his interests and do his best to see that Olman was retained as manager of the Jacksonville store. Belcher conveyed the clear impression that he had considerable influence over the decisions to be made by corporate headquarters in Atlanta, Georgia.

11. Despite Belcher's assurances, Olman soon learned that he was being replaced as store manager by Shockley. He also learned that the company had disregarded his advice to

Belcher—that Full Moon should retain its store employees who had worked longer and were both more productive and more loyal.

12. At no time leading up to Olman's demotion did Belcher ever inform him that the company intended to cap the salaries of all store managers, that Olman's salary was too high, or that Olman might retain his position as store manager if he agreed to accept a salary reduction.

13. After learning that he would no longer be store manager, Olman contacted Rex Ornstein, an advertising agent for Full Moon and Olman's former regional manager, to seek advice. Ornstein told Olman that "The extreme generation is young. We're not. Maybe it's time to move on." At the time, Ornstein worked at Full Moon's headquarters in Atlanta and was familiar with the company's culture.

14. A few weeks after learning of his demotion, the termination of his wife, and the termination of numerous other, older employees at the Jacksonville store, Olman wrote a letter to Full Moon's president complaining about what he perceived as a pattern of age discrimination in the company's reorganization and downsizing. In response to the letter, Lurch terminated Olman.

15. As a result of Full Moon's reorganization and downsizing in 2022-2023, a far greater number of managers over the age of 40 were replaced than younger managers. In particular, 55% of the managers affected by downsizing were over 40.

This evidence reveals a genuine issue of fact concerning Full Moon's motive in replacing Olman, and especially the motive of Belcher, the person who supervised Olman, who had greatest familiarity with his qualifications to continue as store manager, and who had responsibility for making recommendations to the Reorganization Committee.

First, there is ample evidence that Belcher "consciously refused to consider retaining [Olman] because of his age, or . . . regarded age as a negative factor in such consideration." *See Castro v. School Bd. of Manatee Cty.*, 903 F. Supp. 2d 1290, 1300 (M.D. Fla. 2012). Belcher was obviously aware that Shockley openly disparaged Olman as an "old man" who was ill equipped to appeal to a "younger" generation of customers. Rather than censure Shockley's open declarations of ageism, Belcher recommended that he replace Olman as store manager. And Shockley's expressions of ageist sentiments were mirrored by those of Belcher. Belcher repeatedly referred to Olman as an "old guy" and "old fart." And when Belcher approached Olman to discuss the company's planned reduction in force, he began the discussion by stating, "Maybe you're ready to retire." Such comments provide strong circumstantial evidence of ageist motive because they were made at the time Belcher was preparing his recommendation to Full Moon's Reorganization Committee. *See, e.g., Jackson v. Cal-Western Packing Co.*, 602 F.3d 374, 380 (5th Cir. 2010) (emphasizing that ageist comments that were "proximate in time" to an employment decision constitute evidence of ageist motive).

Further, there is evidence that Full Moon tolerated a "corporate atmosphere hostile to older employees." *See Madel v. FCI Marketing, Inc.*, 116 F.3d 1247, 1252 (8th Cir. 1997). As shown, there was a "pervasive use of age-based epithets" in the Jacksonville store. *See id.* And there is evidence that a preference for younger managers had become part of Full Moon's larger corporate culture. When Olman contacted Rex Ornstein, his former regional manager and current company executive located in Atlanta, Ornstein told Olman, "The sporting goods business has changed, and Full Moon has changed, too. The extreme generation is young. We're not. Maybe it's time to move on. I plan to retire next year."

Full Moon contends that the "decision to replace Olman was *dictated* to regional manager Belcher, who had no choice but to implement the Committee's instruction." But the record belies this claim. Full Moon concedes that its policy decision to cap the salaries of store managers was not implemented uniformly without exceptions. A number of store managers with salaries in excess of $70,000 were retained after the company's reorganization.[39] Exceptions were made for these store managers after the Committee received recommendations from regional managers like Belcher. This meant that Belcher had the power to recommend Olman's retention—as he falsely promised Olman he would do. Particularly given Olman's excellent employment record after serving Full Moon for 20 years, Belcher was in a strong position to advocate Olman's retention as store manager. At a minimum, Belcher could have informed Olman of the company's desire to cap the salary of most managers at $70,000 and discussed whether Olman was willing to continue as store manager at a reduced salary. But Belcher did nothing to "look out" for Olman's interests. Instead, he successfully advocated the promotion of young Shockley, who shared Belcher's view that Olman was too old to continue managing the Jacksonville store.

An employer is liable for the actions of subordinate managers if its final decision makers act "as a rubber stamp . . . for a subordinate employee's prejudice, even if the [Committee] lacked discriminatory intent." *See Russell v. McKinney Hosp. Venture,* 235 F.3d 219, 227 (5th Cir. 2000). Courts must consider "not only . . . the formal decisionmaker, but also . . . lower-level employees who had influence or leverage over the decisionmaker." *Crisp v. Sears Roebuck & Co.,* 628 Fed. Appx. 220, 223 (5th Cir. 2015). In Olman's case, there is ample evidence that Belcher had "influence or leverage" over Full Moon's Committee. Obviously a committee of high-level corporate executives in Atlanta had to rely on the recommendation of Belcher, the only person who had direct experience with Olman and the Jacksonville store. Not surprisingly, the Committee did exactly what Belcher recommended: It replaced Olman with Shockley.

Finally, there is evidence that at least one influential Committee member may not have acted as the innocent "cat's paw" in following Belcher's recommendation. The company's *president,* Bertie Lurch, served on the Committee. And he is the same president who precipitously fired Olman as soon as Olman suggested that corporate downsizing might be influenced by age discrimination. Lurch's rash action might well be interpreted by a jury as the mark of a guilty conscience.

The Supreme Court has emphasized that "credibility determinations, the weighing of the evidence, and the drawing of legitimate inferences from the facts are jury functions, not those of a judge." *See Reeves, supra* at 150. Under this standard, "the plaintiff need produce very little evidence of discriminatory motive to raise a genuine issue of fact." *See Lindahl v. Air France,* 930 F.2d 1434, 1438 (9th Cir. 1991) (applying *McDonnell Douglas* standard). Olman's evidence greatly exceeds the "very little" required under case precedent to survive summary judgment.

---

[39] One notorious example of Full Moon's willingness to depart from its alleged policy capping managers' salaries at $70,000 is the retention of Mickey Nosocks as manager of Full Moon's store in Ashville, North Carolina. Nosocks—son of company director Tony Nosocks—currently receives a salary of $100,000. Yet the Ashville store's sales record in 2022 was no better than that of the Jacksonville store. Mickey Nosocks was 41 at the time of Full Moon's downsizing.

Question 11.5

1. As you can see, Lane portrayed the evidence and case law much differently than Tweedy did. What are the principal disagreements between the parties about the facts?

2. Lane's primary focus is to show that Belcher was a conduit for ageist prejudice in the Reorganization Committee's decision to replace Olman. What particular evidence does she cite to show that Belcher may have acted with ageist motive? Do you think this evidence sufficient to persuade a "reasonable" juror? Did it persuade you? Or is Lane asking the court to engage in pure speculation and go beyond the reasonable implications of the evidence?

3. Lane also refers to Lurch's membership on the Committee and asks the court to infer that evidence of his retaliatory response to Otis's letter also supports an inference of ageist motive. Do you find this tack persuasive? Or is Lurch's alleged retaliatory motive irrelevant to his motive in affirming Otis's replacement?

4. If Full Moon departed from its salary plan in compensating Mickey Nosocks, who was 41 at the time of the downsizing, does this departure—apparently motivated by nepotism—enhance Olman's claim of age discrimination? Does the fact that Nosocks was 41 years old, and thus a member of the age group protected by the ADEA, negate any inference of ageist motive? *See O'Connor v. Consolidated Coin Caterers Corp.*, 517 U.S. 308, 312 (1996) (suggesting that the ADEA bans discrimination motivated by age even though both the favored and unfavored employee are 40 or over).

F. Judge Goodenough's Ruling[40]

Once the parties' summary judgment briefing was completed, Judge Goodenough was faced with the task of reviewing their submissions and supporting evidence. In many and perhaps most courts, this review is conducted by the judge's clerk, at least in the first instance. The clerk will carefully review the parties' legal arguments, their citations to record evidence, and their representations of case law. The clerk will often draft an opinion or memorandum for the judge that will provide the basis for further discussion between them. Eventually, the judge will finalize her views and issue a decision.

Judges vary in the length and detail of their opinions. Rule 56(a) states that a court ruling on a motion for summary judgment "should state on the record the reasons for granting or denying the motion." Below are excerpts from the order and memorandum written by Judge Goodenough, which focus on Otis Olman's claim of age discrimination.

---

[40] Depending on local rules, Full Moon might have the right to file a reply to the Olmans' response or might have the option of seeking permission to reply. Such a reply could be valuable if Full Moon needed to challenge the Olmans' use of record evidence or their interpretation of law. At the same time, this response might prompt the Olmans to seek permission to file their own reply—sometimes called a "surreply."

IN THE UNITED STATES DISTRICT COURT
FOR THE MIDDLE DISTRICT OF FLORIDA,
JACKSONVILLE DIVISION

OTIS AND FIONA OLMAN,

Plaintiffs,

v. Case No. 8-23-CV-00637

FULL MOON SPORTS, INC.,
& BRUCE BELCHER

Defendants.

ORDER

This cause comes before the Court for consideration of Defendant's Motion for Summary Judgment. The Court hereby orders as follows:

1. Defendant's motion for summary judgment on all claims of plaintiff Fiona Olman (counts six and seven) is GRANTED;

2. Defendant's motion for summary judgment on plaintiff Otis Olman's claims of age discrimination under the Age Discrimination in Employment Act ("ADEA") and the Florida Civil Rights Act (counts one and three) is GRANTED; and

3. Defendant's motion for summary judgment on plaintiff Otis Olman's claims of retaliation under the ADEA and the Florida Civil Rights Act (counts two and four) is DENIED.

. . . .

MEMORANDUM

. . . .

Plaintiff Otis Olman next claims that Full Moon acted with discriminatory motive when it replaced him as manager of the Jacksonville store and promoted Shockley to his position. Olman has adduced credible evidence that he was over the age of 40, that he was qualified to serve as manager of the Jacksonville store, and that he was replaced by a person under the age of 40. Full Moon, in turn, has responded with credible evidence that it replaced Olman and numerous other store managers in the southeast region to reduce salary costs and improve the economic performance of stores. Under the *McDonnell Douglas* standard governing this motion, Olman must produce credible evidence that Full Moon's economic explanation is a "pretext" to survive summary judgment.

Olman's evidence of pretext comes down to the following. First, he cites evidence that (a) Olman's regional manager, Belcher, and the employee who replaced Olman, Shockley, expressed ageist sentiments prior to Olman's replacement, (b) Belcher took no action to censure Shockley but instead recommended his promotion to store manager, and (c) Belcher's age-based recommendation to the Reorganization Committee led to the decision to replace Olman with Shockley. Second, Olman argues that the retaliatory action taken against him by company president, Lurch, evidences ageism on the part of Lurch, who participated in the decision to replace Olman.

This Court finds that the evidence of ageist remarks by Belcher and Shockley fall short of providing a reasonable basis for inferring that Belcher acted with ageist motive in failing to recommend Olman's retention as manager. Initially, it merits emphasis that the supervisor who is pivotal to Olman's argument—Bruce Belcher—is the same person who renewed Olman in 2019 at a substantial salary of $100,000. As other courts have observed, when the same person charged with discrimination has previously taken favorable job action regarding the plaintiff the inference of ageism is unlikely. *See, e.g., Hennessey v. Good Earth Tools, Inc.*, 126 F.3d 1107, 1109 (8th Cir. 1997); *Horwitz v. Board of Educ.*, 260 F.3d 602, 611 (7th Cir. 2001).

In addition, the evidence suggesting that Belcher acted with ageist motive largely consists of remarks that were not made "proximate to or related to the employment decision." *Jackson v. Cal-Western Packing Co.*, 602 F.3d 374, 380 (5th Cir. 2010). The sole remark made proximate to the time when the decision was made to replace Olman was Belcher's inquiry about Olman's interest in retiring. But a single stray remark, especially by someone who lacks final decision-making authority, is not sufficient to prove a claim of age discrimination. *See, e.g., Gonzalez v. El Dia, Inc., 304 F.3d 63, 69-70*; *Weichman v. Chubb & Son*, 552 F. Supp. 2d 271, 284 (D. Conn. 2008). This is true even assuming Belcher's inquiry about retirement is construed as an expression of ageist sentiment rather than a sincere inquiry into Olman's employment interests.

Nor does the Court agree that Lurch's possible retaliatory action—which will be examined later at trial—provides evidence that he acted with ageist motive in replacing Olman. Lurch, a 48-year-old man himself, may have acted rashly and even illegally in terminating Olman after receiving a letter complaining of age discrimination. But retaliation against an outspoken employee differs from age discrimination.

In sum, Olman has failed to produce evidence rebutting Full Moon's defense that it replaced him based on lawful, nondiscriminatory factors. While this Court (a member of the age group protected by the ADEA) sympathizes with Olman, and questions the wisdom of corporate policy that penalizes the very employees who have helped an employer attain economic success, the ADEA provides no authority to second-guess that policy.

. . . .

DONE and ORDERED at Jacksonville, Florida, this 25th day of October, 2023.

Hon. Sarah Goodenough

Question 11.6

1. Are you persuaded that Judge Goodenough has properly applied the summary judgment standard of Rule 56?
2. To what extent does the judge's opinion appear to be influenced by her intuitive views of human motive and behavior? Should she act based on these views, or is that the reason we have trial by jury?

Chapter Twelve
Trial

Chapter Rule References: 16, 43, 45, 47, 48, 49, *50*, 51, 54, 58, *59*

A. Preparing for Trial

It is paradoxical that while civil trials are relatively rare events,[1] in many respects they drive the entire litigation process. It is usually not possible to determine at the pleading stage which cases will go to trial. Thus, good lawyers, like those representing the litigants in the *Olman* suit, will prepare each case as if it will go the distance. If they failed to do so, by the time it became clear a trial was necessary, they might find it was too late to use the various discovery tools to prepare adequately.

Judge Sarah Goodenough's decisions on prior dispositive motions left only two claims for trial: Otis Olman's retaliation claims under the ADEA and the Florida Civil Rights Act. It was on these claims that the lawyers focused their attention. For Otis to win under either federal or state law, he needed to establish:

1. He engaged in statutorily protected expression;

2. He suffered adverse employment action; and

3. The adverse action against him was causally related to his protected expression.[2]

Otis would have the burden of production and persuasion at trial on these claims. Although more commonly known, the burden of persuasion is rarely dispositive in a civil case. The reason is that the party in such a case must win by a preponderance of the evidence, meaning that the scales of justice tip in its favor. Thus, the only time when the assignment of the burden of persuasion comes into play to dictate the winner in a civil case is when those scales are exactly evenly balanced. In other words, it matters only when the jury simply cannot decide between two versions of events. In that instance, and that instance only, the assignment of the burden of persuasion would be dispositive, with the person assigned the burden losing.[3]

The burden of production is a different story because it is quite important at various stages of civil litigation. If a party has the burden of production on an issue, it means he or she must produce evidence from which a rational factfinder could rule in his or her favor. A failure to

---

[1] Fewer than 2% of cases filed in federal court reach trial. *See* Chapter One.

[2] *See* 29 U.S.C. § 623(d); Fla. Stat. § 760.10(7) (2004); *Weeks v. Harden Mftg. Co.*, 291 F.3d 1307, 1311 (11th Cir. 2002).

[3] Of course, the assignment of the burden of persuasion, while not often dispositive, can certainly be important when developing trial strategy or deciding which motions to file.

produce such evidence is fatal. We have previously discussed the burden of production in connection with Full Moon's motion for summary judgment.[4]

While the entire litigation process to this point had been largely a preparation for trial, the period after summary judgment was a time of heightened activity. After ruling on Full Moon's motion, Judge Goodenough scheduled a final pretrial conference for October 27, 2023.[5] The trial was set to commence on November 7, 2023.

Eleanor Lane and Bart Tweedy knew the final pretrial conference was an enormously significant event in the case. This conference would establish the specific rules of the trial. During the conference, Judge Goodenough would resolve most disputes between the parties on a range of issues, including the admissibility of evidence and the legal instructions she would give to the jury. To put her and the parties in the best position to consider issues that could arise at trial, Judge Goodenough issued a final pretrial order that required the parties to do a number of things before the conference, including the following:

- The parties were to inform the court how long they each anticipated trial would take.
- Lane and Tweedy were to work together to prepare the instructions that Judge Goodenough would give to the jury.[6] To the extent possible, Judge Goodenough wanted instructions on which both parties agreed. If they were unable to agree on a particular instruction, each party was to submit its own version for the court's consideration.
- Each party was to submit a list of witnesses it expected to call at trial. If either party objected to a witness listed by the other party, the objection needed to be stated and briefed. The party offering the witness would then need to respond.
- Each party was to submit a list of documents it expected to introduce into evidence at trial. If either party objected to a document listed by the other party, the objection needed to be stated and briefed.[7] The party offering the document would then need to respond.
- Each party was to identify those portions of deposition transcripts it wished to read into evidence at the trial.[8] As with documents and witnesses, all objections to such designations needed to be stated at this point.

---

[4] *See* Chapter Eleven.

[5] *See* Rule 16(e) (requiring a district court to hold a final pretrial conference "as close to the start of trial as is reasonable").

[6] *See* Rule 51.

[7] The objections to both documents and witnesses would most often be based on the Federal Rules of Evidence. They could, however, also be based on procedural defects such as a failure to disclose matters as part of the Rule 26(a) process. *See, e.g.*, Rule 37(c)(1).

[8] *See* Rule 32 (concerning the use of depositions in court proceedings).

- The parties were to agree on any stipulations of fact to be read to the jury. The jury would be required to accept such stipulations as true.

Lane and Tweedy worked diligently to prepare the materials Judge Goodenough requested. They did not see Judge Goodenough's requirements as mere make-work, as the requirements were designed to make the trial as efficient as possible.[9] They essentially had to map out their entire trial strategy. After complying with Judge Goodenough's order, Lane and Tweedy appeared at the final pretrial conference, where the judge ruled on their various objections and confirmed the trial date.

Following the conference, Lane and Tweedy continued their intensive trial preparation. For example, each prepared a trial notebook that contained all the materials they would likely need during trial. These materials included notes they would use when examining witnesses and making statements to the jury; documents to be introduced; proposed jury instructions; and the motions each expected to make during trial. Lane was old-fashioned and felt more comfortable with paper, so she used actual notebooks. Tweedy, on the other hand, opted to use a laptop computer to compile his "notebook."

Lane and Tweedy also worked closely with the witnesses they would call at trial. They knew that a case could be won or lost based on a witness's performance on the stand. Thus, each of them spent many hours with their witnesses going over the form of the questions the lawyers would ask and the substance of their answers. They wanted to make sure their witnesses felt comfortable with the questions they would be asked at trial. They also confirmed that their witnesses understood how their testimony fit into the overall trial and appreciated their obligation to tell the truth.

Tactical Tip ✍

The Importance of Preparation

Most cases are won or lost long before an attorney steps through the doors of a courtroom. The preparation done from the moment a lawsuit starts pays dividends at trial. From pleading the proper claims, to using discovery devices effectively, to preparing witnesses to take the stand, the lawyer who has thought about the trial before it starts will be in a far better position than one who has not. Thus, keep your eyes on the ultimate trial from the beginning of the case and prepare thoroughly if you want to best serve your client.

---

[9] Judges usually require that the lawyers who will actually try the case be present at the final pretrial conference. Thus, if Tweedy's superior, Harrison Ames, intended to try the case, he would have to appear. Ames had decided, however, that Tweedy should try the case. Tweedy was most familiar with the facts, and Full Moon had confidence in him. Plus, Ames recognized that the retaliation case was one that could easily go against Full Moon if the jury disliked Bertie Lurch. Ames figured it was just as well to let Tweedy shoulder the risk of loss.

The night before trial was to begin, Lane and Tweedy were tired but excited. After all, they had waited a long time to reach this stage of the adversarial process.

B. The Trial

1. Structure of a Trial and the Role of Procedure

A trial is a fascinating experience. But you will only get a brief glimpse of it in the Guide. Much of your learning about trial will come in classes on Evidence and Trial Advocacy. There, you will learn about a variety of matters, such as the objections lawyers can make to the introduction of evidence, the phrasing of questions when examining a hostile witness, and even where the lawyers should stand in the courtroom when asking questions of the witnesses.

In Civil Procedure, the typically brief introduction to trial emphasizes how procedural rules are used to guard against improper or untrustworthy results. The rules do this by ensuring that (1) the jurors are unbiased,[10] (2) the jury is accurately informed about the law, (3) the trial process and the jury verdict are relatively free of harmful defects, and (4) the jury makes rational decisions based on the evidence and the law. We will touch on how these concerns arose in the *Olman* trial, although we focus principally on the third and fourth concerns.

To appreciate how procedure works at trial, you need to understand the basic structure of the trial. The trial is the epitome of the adversarial process itself. A neutral decision maker—the jury, in the *Olman* case—is presented with two competing stories. For each action a plaintiff takes, the defendant gets its turn as well. So, for example, the plaintiff is allowed to make an opening statement to the jury, after which it is the defendant's turn. And after the plaintiff calls a witness and asks questions, the defendant is allowed to ask its own questions of the witness.

One of the more common structures of civil jury trials is listed below.[11] We have placed in **bold** those steps in which procedure plays a significant role and upon which our discussion is focused.

---

[10] The Olmans' case will be tried by a jury, as requested by them. But in an appreciable number of civil suits, the parties either dispense with a jury trial or have no right to obtain one. In these "bench" trials, the judge serves as the factfinder. From time to time, we make reference to certain Rules and practices concerning bench trials.

[11] The process is more streamlined in a bench trial. There would obviously be no need to have jury selection or a verdict. In addition, motions testing the sufficiency of the parties' evidence differ because of the judge's role as factfinder. Some judges dispense with opening statements or closing arguments, although most find these parts of the trial informative and so retain them. At the conclusion of a bench trial, the judge will issue a written opinion. That opinion will include the judge's legal conclusions, but it must also set forth his or her findings of fact. *See* Rule 52(a). As we will see, there is no similar requirement that a jury state its factual findings.

The Structure of a Civil Trial
Jury selection
Opening statements
Plaintiff's case
Direct examination
Cross-examination by defendant
Motions testing the sufficiency of plaintiff's case
Defendant's case
Direct examination
Cross-examination by plaintiff
Motions testing the sufficiency of each party's case
Closing arguments
Jury instructions
Jury deliberation
Jury verdict
Postverdict motions
Entry of final judgment

2. Selecting a Jury and the Beginning of Trial

The first step in a jury trial is to select the members of the community who will serve as the finders of fact.[12] Members of the trial jury are selected from a group called the *venire*, who are citizens called to the courthouse for "jury duty." The venire must be randomly drawn from a fair cross section of the relevant community.[13] In the Olmans' case, the relevant community consisted of several counties in the eastern part of the Middle District of Florida.

[12] Otis was entitled to a jury trial of his retaliation claims as a matter of statutory law. *See* 29 U.S.C. § 626(c)(2) (ADEA retaliation); Fla. Stat. § 760.11(5) (FCRA retaliation). In the absence of a statutory right, entitlement to jury trials in civil cases in federal courts is governed by the Seventh Amendment to the U.S. Constitution.

[13] *See* 28 U.S.C. § 1861. The detailed procedures by which the venire is assembled and may be challenged are set forth in the United States Code. *See* 28 U.S.C. §§ 1861-1867.

Miss, you can't just "sign up" to be on the next celebrity murder jury.

Once a proper venire is assembled, the question becomes how to select the actual trial jury.[14] The problem in some sense stems from the reality that neither Lane nor Tweedy really wanted an unbiased jury. Rather, if truth be told, they preferred a jury biased in their own client's favor. Jury selection is designed in part to counteract these desires by giving the judge power to eliminate persons who are obviously biased (*cause* challenges) and by giving the lawyers power to unilaterally eliminate an additional number of persons they suspect are disinclined to favor their client (*peremptory* challenges). The result of this process—called *voir dire*—hopefully approximates a collection of citizens who enter the case without a preconceived opinion as to which party should prevail, and who are capable of fairly considering all the evidence. However, much of voir dire is essentially guesswork.

"Kick Juror #4."

Jurors who appear to be biased are removed for cause. Judges tend to construe cause challenges narrowly. Any jurors who know the parties, the witnesses, the lawyers, or sometimes the judge will be struck for cause. In addition, any jurors who have personal knowledge of the

[14] The jury would consist of between 6 and 12 citizens. Rule 48. The jury would need to reach a unanimous verdict unless the parties stipulated otherwise.

events at issue in the case will be struck. Beyond these more bright-line characteristics, Judge Goodenough would have broad discretion in determining whether a potential juror should be struck for cause. If a party believed that a particular person should be removed for cause, it needed to request that the court take such action.

Once all cause challenges have been decided, the parties can strike up to three jurors from the panel for almost any reason or, in fact, no reason at all.[15] These challenges are known as *peremptory challenges*. Peremptory challenges permit a party to exclude jurors it suspects are not favorably inclined to its position, even though the jurors have not demonstrated "cause" for being struck by the judge. The problem in exercising peremptory challenges is that lawyers usually have precious little information on which to base this decision. The information they do have will generally come from one of three sources. First, the lawyer will have a preconception of juror characteristics or attitudes that predispose the juror to favor one party.[16] Second, the lawyer will have limited information found in a questionnaire that each juror must complete, including a juror's residence, age, occupation, and history of criminal convictions. Finally, each lawyer will have the opportunity to obtain some information from jurors during voir dire.[17] But the reality is that many peremptory challenges are the product of nothing more than intuition.

Task 12.1

1. What characteristics and attitudes would you want in a juror if you represented Otis? Why? What if you represented Full Moon?

2. What questions would you want Judge Goodenough to ask potential jurors if you represented Otis? Why? What if you represented Full Moon?

[15] *See* 28 U.S.C. § 1870 (granting each party in a civil case three peremptory challenges). But a party cannot base a peremptory challenge on the race, ethnicity, or gender of the juror. *See Edmonson v. Leesville Concrete Co.*, 500 U.S. 614 (1991) (race); *JEB v. Alabama*, 511 U.S. 127 (1994) (gender).

[16] In most cases, lawyers' preconceptions are based on stereotypes about how certain types of jurors might react to the parties and the evidence. However, in a growing number of high-stakes cases, lawyers employ professional jury consultants to help them develop more accurate (at least they hope) predictors of which types of jurors are desirable or undesirable. There are differing views as to the effectiveness of jury consultants in selecting jurors. One limitation to the potential effectiveness of professional jury consultants is that lawyers may not be permitted in voir dire to obtain the information needed to determine whether a juror "fits" the profile developed by a consultant. *See generally*, Shari Diamond, *Scientific Jury Selection: What Social Scientists Know and Do Not Know*, 73 JUDICATURE 178, 181 (1990).

[17] *See* Rule 47(a), which gives the judge discretion over whether to permit the lawyers to question potential jurors or to do so herself or himself. This practice varies by judge, but many federal judges are inclined to ask the questions themselves to make the voir dire process more efficient. When judges conduct voir dire, they permit the parties to submit questions for the judge's consideration.

After the jury was selected and Judge Goodenough gave them preliminary instructions concerning the nature of the case and the trial process itself, the parties were finally ready to try the case. Judge Goodenough called on Lane to give an opening statement for the plaintiff. An opening statement is important because it is usually the first chance an attorney has to speak to the jury about the substance of the case. The opening statement is not an argument; instead, it is meant to be a road map for the jury to follow when listening to the evidence that will be presented at trial.

Lane had two overarching goals for her opening. First, she wanted the jury to know the theme of her case, and therefore be able to fit the evidence they would hear into that theme. Second, she wanted to introduce Otis as a human being. Lane accomplished the latter goal by spending time in her opening describing Otis's background, family, and interests, as well as his contributions to the "Full Moon family."

As for her theme, Lane did not try to hide the ball. She told the jury that this case was about a corporate decision to get rid of an employee for standing up for what he perceived to be unlawful activity. She told the jury they would hear from Otis and learn that he discovered what Full Moon was actually doing in "restructuring" its retail operation: implementing the now unlawful philosophy of "out with the old and in with the new." She explained that the evidence the jury would see and hear would demonstrate that, as soon as Full Moon learned Otis was going to make a claim that age discrimination was at work, it fired him. This retaliation, she explained, was unlawful even if Full Moon was not in fact engaging in age discrimination. Finally, Lane promised that when all the evidence was in, she would address them again, during which she would review the evidence and describe the specific award she wanted the jury to make to Otis.

It was then Tweedy's turn to speak to the jury. He, too, knew it was critically important to have a theme. And he knew it was necessary to personify Full Moon. Thus, he began by introducing the jury to Full Moon's president, Bertie Lurch, who was sitting at counsel table and would be present for the entire trial. Tweedy knew that Lurch was going to be a crucial witness at trial. If the jury believed him, Full Moon would win. If it did not, Full Moon would lose. Thus, Tweedy wanted the jury to see him as a person, not merely the "face" of a large corporation.

For his theme, Tweedy started out by making it clear to the jury that the case was not about age discrimination. He explained that, as Judge Goodenough would instruct them at the conclusion of the trial, Full Moon had not discriminated against Otis based on his age when it terminated him. Instead, the case turned on whether Full Moon fired Otis because Otis complained about what he incorrectly perceived to be ageist motivations in corporate decisions. On this point, Tweedy explained that the evidence would show Full Moon fired Otis for two reasons unrelated to retaliation. First, the evidence would show that Otis was no longer able to work in a constructive manner in the restructured Jacksonville store. Second, at the time of its decision, Full Moon believed (erroneously, as it later turned out) that Otis had been involved in the theft of merchandise from the store. Thus, Tweedy would ask the jury to return a verdict in favor of Full Moon at the conclusion of the trial.

3. Otis's Case-in-Chief

It was now time for Otis to put on his case. Lane's goal was to make the case as simple as possible for the jury. In essence, she wanted the jury to see the case as nothing more than an example of Newton's law—that every action produces an equal and opposite reaction. In this case, the action was Otis's sending his letter to Full Moon complaining about its ageist motives during the reduction in force.[18] The reaction was the letter from Lurch firing Otis. Lane wanted the jury members to follow their common sense and conclude that there was a cause-and-effect relationship between Otis's complaints and his firing.

To keep the case simple, Lane called only a few witnesses. Otis was the first witness. Through Otis, she was able to convey all the important details of her case. She had Otis describe for the jury his background with Full Moon, including all the positive reviews he had received over the years. She then took Otis through the events leading up to his termination. In particular, Lane made sure to have Otis explain why he believed that Full Moon's actions at the Jacksonville store had been the result of unlawful ageism. Then she had Otis lay out the time line concerning his communication with Full Moon about ageism and his receipt of Lurch's letter terminating his employment a few weeks later. For this last point, she used a visual aid to underscore the temporal proximity between these critical events.

After Lane examined Otis, Tweedy had the opportunity to cross-examine him. Unlike what one often sees on television, he was not hostile toward Otis on the stand. Tweedy knew that a juror was much more likely to identify with a witness than with a lawyer. So Tweedy treated Otis with respect at all times. In addition, he did not use cross-examination solely to try to undermine Otis's story (the popular view of cross-examination). He used the examination as a means to build Full Moon's defenses. Of course, Otis was not going to try to be helpful, but to the extent he had helpful information, Tweedy tried to bring that out. The main point Tweedy tried to make was that Otis had no actual knowledge about what went into Full Moon's decision to terminate him. In other words, he tried to underscore for the jury that Otis's claim amounted to speculation based solely on the timing of the termination letter.

When cross-examining Otis, Tweedy was careful to ask questions that didn't elicit responses damaging to Full Moon's case. Tweedy did this by confining his questions to those he had already asked at Otis's deposition, and to which Otis had already responded under oath. If Otis answered differently now, Tweedy would be able to "impeach" him with his prior deposition testimony.[19] This illustrates the importance of asking carefully crafted deposition questions during discovery.

After Otis testified, Lane called two former employees of Full Moon's Jacksonville store. The purpose of this testimony was to preemptively address the claims that Full Moon would make

---

[18] This letter is found in Chapter One.

[19] Rule 32(a)(2) permits a party to use the deposition of any witness to "contradict or impeach" testimony at trial.

during its case about Otis's alleged inability to work within the new corporate structure. The direct testimony was brief, as was cross-examination. Similar to his goal in cross-examining Otis, Tweedy wanted to show that these witnesses had limited knowledge. This reinforced his contention that Otis's case was based on supposition.

Lane's final witness was an expert to discuss Otis's damages.[20] As you will recall, in his retaliation claims, Otis sought lost wages (both back and future pay), the doubling of back pay under the federal statute, compensatory and punitive damages under the state statute, interest, costs and attorneys' fees.[21] Of these damage elements, the one on which the jury needed expert testimony was damages for lost wages. The expert provided the jury with calculations concerning Otis's back and future pay. Other calculations were either questions of law to be decided by the trial judge (e.g., interest on the judgment) or questions requiring no expert assistance (e.g., punitive damages).

After the damages expert finished her testimony on both direct and cross, Lane rested Otis's case. By resting, Lane essentially communicated to the judge that she believed she had done everything necessary for Otis to prevail in the trial.

The declaration that the plaintiff has rested his case often prompts action by the defendant—the filing of a motion for judgment as a matter of law under Rule 50(a).[22] Rule 50(a) provides a means by which a party can test whether its adversary has satisfied the burden of coming forward with sufficient evidence to prevail. In other words, the Rule asks whether the party *may* win if a rational jury considers the evidence presented in the case. It does not test whether the party *will* win. Thus, the motion for judgment as a matter of law operates in many respects like a summary judgment motion, except for the fact that it is made during trial rather than before.

The next question addresses the Rule 50(a) motion made by Full Moon.

Question 12.1

Based on the summary of the evidence introduced thus far at trial and the language of Rule 50(a), answer the following questions:

1. What provision in Rule 50(a) allows Full Moon to make a motion for judgment as a matter of law at the conclusion of Otis's case? Why would it be improper for Otis to make such a motion at this point in the trial?

---

[20] It would have been possible for Judge Goodenough to bifurcate or divide the trial into phases, one concerning liability and the other damages. *See* Rule 42(b) ("For convenience, to avoid prejudice, or to expedite and economize, the court may order a separate trial of one or more separate issues, claims, crossclaims, counterclaims, or third-party claims."). Judge Goodenough had determined, and neither party had contested, that the better course was to proceed in a single trial.

[21] *See* Complaint, Counts Two and Four, found in Chapter Six.

[22] The motion for judgment as a matter of law used to be called a "motion for a directed verdict," and still is in some state rules of civil procedure. Many lawyers and judges still use the older terminology even in federal court.

2. What would be Full Moon's argument that "there is no legally sufficient evidentiary basis for a reasonable jury to find for" Otis on his claims?

3. What counterargument would you make on behalf of Otis?

Judge Goodenough had excused the jury so she could address the motion she expected Full Moon to make. Full Moon submitted a brief written motion for judgment as a matter of law, but the majority of its reasoning was addressed through oral argument. Lane argued against the motion. As was common for judges, Judge Goodenough did not rule on the motion but rather "took it under advisement." In other words, she waited to rule on the motion until later. She then directed Tweedy to begin Full Moon's case.

A Note Concerning: The Jury

The jury system has a long pedigree in Anglo-American law. For example, the Seventh Amendment to the U.S. Constitution guarantees citizens the right to a trial by jury in federal courts if they had such a right when the amendment was adopted and there is more than $20 at stake.

In recognition of the jury's important historical role, many facets of the system are designed to give the jury freedom to make its factual conclusions. At the same time, however, the legal system is also concerned with fundamental fairness. Thus, we are reluctant to allow decisions to be made by juries that are not rational.

How should the legal system balance the right to a jury trial with the right not to be the victim of an irrational verdict? We have struck a balance by monitoring closely the inputs to the jury (e.g., by using rules of evidence and instructions as to the law) and by comparing that input with the output of a verdict. If the output could have rationally been reached based on the input, then we generally uphold the jury determination. Notice, however, that we will not look behind the reason for jury's decision making absent extraordinary circumstances, such as an external influence like bribery or intimidation. In other words, we treat the jury as a "black box" by not looking behind the jury room door.

There is currently a debate about the wisdom of adopting additional practices to increase the chance that jurors will act based upon the evidence. For example, some state-court rules and some federal judges allow jurors to take notes during the trial. Other judges do not allow note-taking, based largely on the belief that note-taking will distract jurors from what is taking place in the trial. A similar debate exists concerning the wisdom of allowing jurors to pose questions to witnesses (via the judge). As these debates illustrate, courts are continuing to struggle with the long-running question of how to balance a commitment to rational judgment with the desire to have the jury bring the "sense of the community" into the courtroom.

4. Full Moon's Case-in-Chief

Tweedy had given a great deal of thought to Full Moon's case. In many ways, he had reached the same basic conclusion about trying the case as had Lane. Tweedy had concluded that a simple and direct case was in Full Moon's interest. It is not always the case that parties will reach the same conclusion about basic case presentation. Indeed, in many situations, one party will conclude it is in its best interest to make matters seem complicated or even confusing. Here, however, Tweedy wanted to forcefully drive home the direct evidence he had of Full Moon's motivations for firing Otis and contrast that direct evidence with Otis's circumstantial case. Tweedy made the tactical judgment to present only two witnesses at trial.

The first witness Tweedy called was the most important: Bertie Lurch. Lurch was the lynchpin of Full Moon's case. Through him, Tweedy brought out Full Moon's version of the chronology of events leading to Otis's termination. He had Lurch describe Full Moon's corporate restructuring and the ill will that this business move seemed to cause between Otis and Shockley. He explained that he was sorry that things had not worked out with Otis. Otis had been a good employee, and Lurch had hoped that Otis would fit into the new corporate structure, but that had not come to pass.

Tweedy then asked Lurch to explain to the jury why he sent the termination letter to Otis. Lurch gave two reasons: (1) growing tension in the Jacksonville store and (2) information Lurch had acquired about missing inventory and what appeared to be Otis's involvement in those losses. Tweedy asked specifically whether Otis's complaint of ageism had played any role in the decision to terminate his employment. Lurch said it had not. As to the timing of the termination letter, he said this was coincidental. The fact was, Lurch explained, at the same time Otis was complaining about age discrimination, he was making it more and more difficult for store personnel to work together.

It was now Lane's turn to cross-examine. Lane did not spend long with Lurch on the stand. She had two main goals. First, she went over in detail Otis's employment history with Full Moon. Her point was to discredit Lurch's testimony about why he terminated Otis. To believe Lurch's explanation, the jury would need to believe that Otis acted in a manner never displayed before. Lane's second point was to use Lurch as a means to remind the jury about the temporal proximity of the termination letter and Otis's complaints. It really did not matter to Lane that he reiterated his position that there was no causal relationship between the two events.

Full Moon's next witness was Sid Shockley. Tweedy had thought long and hard about putting Shockley on the stand. To be frank, he did not really care for him. In the end, however, Tweedy concluded that it might be a good thing if the jury found Shockley a bit hard to stomach. This reaction could actually be useful in corroborating Lurch's testimony that Otis was not getting along with Shockley in his role as the new store manager.

Tweedy largely limited Shockley's testimony to his tension with Otis after he was promoted to manager. On cross-examination, Lane focused on the help Otis had been to Shockley when he first began working at the store, and once again, she took the opportunity to remind the jury of the relevant sequence of events.

After Shockley testified, Tweedy rested his case. He made a strategic decision to rely on his cross-examination of Lane's damages expert rather than call his own expert. Although Tweedy had an expert prepared to testify, he concluded that Lane's expert had not been particularly strong. In addition, he did not want to send a message to the jury that the case was about *how much* to award Otis. Rather, Tweedy wanted the jury to focus on whether to give Otis anything at all. He explained his approach to Full Moon, and the company agreed with his decision.

After Full Moon rested its case, Judge Goodenough again excused the jury. She knew that both parties would likely have motions for her to consider. Once again, the motions would be made pursuant to Rule 50(a) and assert that no rational jury could rule in favor of the opposing party.

Question 12.2

Based on the summary of the evidence introduced thus far at trial and the language of Rule 50(a), answer the following questions:

1. Why are both Otis and Full Moon now allowed to make motions under Rule 50(a)?
2. How would it be possible for Judge Goodenough to deny *both* motions? What would such a decision indicate?
3. Regardless of the merits of a Rule 50(a) motion at the end of trial, why might a court be tempted to deny the motions? Consider the consequences if the court grants such a motion and is later reversed on appeal. Does this suggest a reason why a court might deny the motion and submit the case to the jury?

After listening to arguments, Judge Goodenough denied both parties' motions. She concluded that Otis had made out a prima facie case (i.e., he had met his burden of production) by submitting evidence that he opposed conduct of Full Moon with a reasonable belief that its conduct was unlawful. Moreover, she ruled that the circumstantial evidence of the timing of Full Moon's action was sufficient for the jury to conclude that Full Moon's firing was in retaliation for Otis's opposition.[23] At the same time, she ruled that Full Moon had presented sufficient evidence to support a jury verdict in its favor. She told the attorneys to be ready for closing arguments in the morning.

---

[23] *See, e.g., Farley v. Nationwide Mutual Ins. Co.*, 197 F.3d 1322, 1337 (11th Cir. 1999) (plaintiff has produced sufficient evidence of retaliation if "the decision-maker became aware of the protected conduct, and . . . there was close temporal proximity between this awareness and the adverse employment action").

5. The Jury Deliberates and Reaches Its Verdict

Both Lane and Tweedy spent the evening getting ready for their closing arguments. Each planned to return to the themes they had laid out in their openings and developed throughout the trial. Both of these experienced attorneys knew that, like most civil cases that go to a jury, this case could go either way.

After Lane and Tweedy completed their closing arguments, Judge Goodenough instructed the jury.[24] These instructions were quite important for controlling the jury. Among other things, the instructions (1) summarized the parties' claims and defenses; (2) summarized the applicable burdens of proof; (3) explained how various forms of evidence (e.g., direct and circumstantial) were to be used; (4) explained the jurors' right to assess the credibility of witnesses and resolve contradictory testimony; and (5) explained how jurors were to assess damages in the event they found the defendant liable. As mentioned earlier, Lane and Tweedy had worked to develop joint instructions and Judge Goodenough resolved any remaining disagreements.[25]

The judge also told the jury about the questions they were to answer on the verdict form. She had the option of having the jury answer several specific questions about the factual issues in the case.[26] For example, Judge Goodenough could have submitted "special interrogatories" to the jury, keyed to the specific elements of Otis's retaliation claims. The use of such special interrogatories is most common in complex or lengthy trials.

Judge Goodenough believed that special interrogatories were not needed in the Olmans' case, given the relative simplicity of the issues in dispute. Instead, she used a general verdict form asking the jury to simply find for Olman or Full Moon on the two retaliation claims. She did, however, include a few interrogatories she thought necessary to decide damages properly.[27] Under applicable law, the jury needed to decide whether Full Moon had acted in willful or reckless disregard of Otis's legal rights. If it did, Otis would be awarded "double back pay" under the ADEA, and possibly additional punitive damages under state law.

The general verdict form given to the jury to complete as part of its deliberations is set forth next.

---

[24] *See* Rule 51 (concerning court's instructions to the jury).

[25] In many cases, the court's task is assisted by the development of "standard" or "pattern" jury instructions. These instructions are often developed by committees appointed by courts (e.g., the federal circuit courts or state supreme courts), and officially approved for use. Pattern jury instructions are tailored to address specific issues (e.g., the elements of a cause of action, the meaning of a particular burden of proof), although they must be modified to reflect the circumstances of a particular case. For example, the U.S. Court of Appeals for the Eleventh Circuit has adopted pattern jury instructions to be used for claims of employer retaliation. *See* https://www.ca11.uscourts.gov/sites/default/files/courtdocs/clk/FormCivilPatternJuryInstructionsRevisedAPR2024.pdf, at Instruction 4.22 (last visited July 31, 2024).

[26] *See* Rule 49 ("The court may require a jury to return only a special verdict in the form of a special written finding on each issue of fact.").

[27] *See* Rule 49(b) (authorizing use of a general verdict form with specific interrogatories).

**IN THE UNITED STATES DISTRICT COURT
FOR THE MIDDLE DISTRICT OF FLORIDA,
JACKSONVILLE DIVISION**

OTIS AND FIONA OLMAN,

Plaintiffs,

v. Case No. 8-23-CV-00637

FULL MOON SPORTS, INC.,
Defendant.

VERDICT FORM

We the Jury unanimously find as follows:

I. Retaliation under the Age Discrimination in Employment Act

1. With respect to this claim, we the Jury unanimously find in favor of:

The Plaintiff Otis Olman ______

or

The Defendant Full Moon Sports, Inc. ______

If your verdict is in favor of the Defendant, proceed to Part II below. If your verdict is in favor of the Plaintiff, proceed to Question 2 in Part I.

2. If your verdict is in favor of Plaintiff, to what total amount of damages for *back pay and benefits* is Plaintiff entitled?

____
(Insert dollar amount)

3. If your verdict is in favor of Plaintiff, to what total amount of damages for *front pay and benefits* is Plaintiff entitled?

____
(Insert dollar amount)

4. If your verdict is in favor of Plaintiff, do you find that Defendant knowingly violated Plaintiff's rights under the Age Discrimination in Employment Act or showed reckless disregard for those rights?

______
(Yes)

______
(No)

II. Retaliation under the Florida Civil Rights Act

1. With respect to this claim, we the Jury unanimously find in favor of:

The Plaintiff Otis Olman _____

or

The Defendant Full Moon Sports, Inc. _____

If your verdict is in favor of the Defendant, STOP. If your verdict is in favor of the Plaintiff, proceed to Question 2 in Part II.

2. If your verdict is in favor of Plaintiff, to what total amount of *compensatory* damages is Plaintiff entitled?

____
(Insert dollar amount)

3. If your verdict is in favor of Plaintiff, to what total amount of *punitive damages* is Plaintiff entitled?

____
(Insert dollar amount)

SO SAY WE ALL

____

Jury Foreperson

Dated: ________________________

After being instructed, the jury began its deliberations. Thus began a period of anxious waiting for the parties and their lawyers. While the jury is out, there is not much for the parties to do. They usually stay at the courthouse so they will be present when the jury reaches a verdict. The Olmans, Lane, Lurch, and Tweedy were all waiting when the court clerk informed them that the jury had reached a verdict. The jury had deliberated only two hours.

Once the parties, lawyers, and Judge Goodenough were in place, the jury returned to the courtroom. Judge Goodenough confirmed with the jury foreperson that the jury had reached a verdict. The judge then asked the foreperson to read the jury's answers to the questions on the verdict form. As the parties watched and listened intently, the jury foreperson stated that the jury ruled in favor of Otis on both retaliation counts. The jury also awarded significant damages to Otis. Otis received $300,000 in damages for front and back pay ($100,000 in back pay and $200,000 in front pay) for his retaliation claim under the ADEA. The jury also found that Full Moon had acted "willfully" in violating the ADEA, which meant the court would double the back pay award. Consequently, Otis's total recovery under the ADEA claim was $400,000. The jury awarded Otis no additional damages under his state law claim, apparently based on its conclusion that damages under the ADEA fully compensated Otis and punished Full Moon. In this respect, the jury may have been following the court's instruction not to award Otis duplicative damages. In addition, the jury did not award punitive damages to Otis on his state-law claim.

C. Posttrial Matters before Judge Goodenough

The jury had returned a verdict. The clerk of court would now convert this verdict to a "final judgment" and enter it on the court's docket.[28] Below is the judgment that was filed the next day.[29]

---

[28] *See* Rule 58(b)(1)(A) (subject to some exceptions, the clerk must "promptly prepare, sign, and enter the judgment" upon return of a general verdict).

[29] Before the U.S. Supreme Court abrogated the forms accompanying the Federal Rules, form 70 specified the content of an acceptable final judgment. While abrogated, form 70 continues to provide practical guidance to courts.

**IN THE UNITED STATES DISTRICT COURT
FOR THE MIDDLE DISTRICT OF FLORIDA,
JACKSONVILLE DIVISION**

OTIS AND FIONA OLMAN,

Plaintiffs,

v. Case No. 8-23-CV-00637

FULL MOON SPORTS, INC.,

Defendant.

JUDGMENT ON JURY VERDICT

This action came on for trial before the Court and a jury, the Honorable Sarah Goodenough, United States District Judge, presiding, and the issues having been duly tried and the jury having duly rendered its verdict, IT IS ORDERED AND ADJUDGED:

That Plaintiff Otis Olman recover under his claims of retaliation under the Age Discrimination in Employment Act from the Defendant Full Moon Sports, Inc. the sum of $300,000 as damages for front and back pay, with interest thereon at the rate of ___% as provided by law;

That said amount of damages reflecting back pay of $100,000 under the Age Discrimination in Employment Act be doubled; and

That Plaintiff Otis Olman recover from Defendant Full Moon Sports, Inc. his costs of this action, including reasonable attorneys' fees.

Dated at Jacksonville, Florida,
this 10th day of November, 2023.

____

Robert Smith
Clerk of Court

Entry of judgment is an important, albeit routine step in litigation. For one thing, 30 days after entry, Otis could begin taking steps to collect the judgment.[30] Almost always, however, judgment enforcement is stayed by the court until it resolves posttrial motions.[31] A party wanting to assert a posttrial motion must usually file it within 28 days of the entry of judgment.[32] Two posttrial motions typically filed in a civil suit are (1) the renewed motion for judgment as a matter of law under Rule 50(b), and (2) the motion for a new trial under Rule 59. Both motions can be used to "control" the jury even after a verdict has been rendered.

Tweedy first drafted a renewed motion for judgment as a matter of law.[33] Consider the following question:

Question 12.3

1. What would Tweedy have to argue to prevail in his renewed motion for judgment as a matter of law? Would the standard governing this motion differ from that applied by Judge Goodenough to resolve the motion for judgment as a matter of law Tweedy made at the close of all evidence?
2. If Tweedy had not made a Rule 50(a) motion, would he now be permitted to make a motion under Rule 50(b)?

MOTION FOR JUDGMENT NOTWITHSTANDING VERDICT

[30] *See* Rule 62(a) ("Except as stated in Rule 62(c) and (d), execution on a judgment and proceedings to enforce it are stayed for 30 days after its entry, unless the court orders otherwise.").

[31] *See* Rule 62(b) (authorizing court to stay enforcement of a judgment while certain posttrial motions are pending).

[32] *See* Rules 50(b) and 59(b). Unless the court otherwise orders, a motion for attorneys' fees must be filed within 14 days of the entry of final judgment. *See* Rule 54(d)(2)(B).

[33] What the Rules now refer to as the "renewed motion for judgment as a matter of law" was formerly known as the "judgment notwithstanding the verdict," or "JNOV." Once again, many lawyers and judges continue to use the older terminology.

Tweedy also filed a motion for new trial under Rule 59. The motion for new trial essentially addresses two situations, although one needs to study case law to figure this out.[34] First, the motion can be used to correct flaws in the procedures leading to the verdict. For example, if Judge Goodenough concluded that she had erroneously admitted or excluded a piece of evidence or had given an improper instruction to the jury, she could use the Rule 59 motion to fix the problem. As discussed in Chapter Thirteen, Tweedy's Rule 59 motion included a challenge to improper comments Lane had made during her closing argument, which the court had permitted over Tweedy's objection. Lane had liberally referred to Full Moon and Lurch as "corporate predators" that had "preyed on their most senior employees to earn a buck," even though age discrimination was not an issue at trial. Lane had even told the jury that she was "personally revolted" by Lurch's "vengeful and mean-spirited" treatment of Otis, and that she had "never seen such shabby treatment of an older employee during my years of practice."

The second use of the new trial motion is to challenge a flawed verdict. Tweedy could argue that the jury's verdict was against the great weight of the evidence. The argument was different than the one Tweedy made in the renewed motion for judgment as a matter of law. In the latter motion, Tweedy claimed that no rational jury could have reached the verdict they actually reached. If Judge Goodenough agreed, Full Moon would go from losing to winning. In contrast, in his motion for new trial, Tweedy argued that, while a rationally functioning jury *could* reach the verdict delivered, it is so unlikely that the court should no longer have faith in the verdict. The result of granting this motion is to grant a new trial with a new jury. As Tweedy thought of the result, it was like calling a "do-over."

Question 12.4

1. Can Tweedy make motions under both Rules 50(b) and 59 consistent with his obligations under Rule 11?

2. If Judge Goodenough independently realizes she made an error during the trial, can she unilaterally order a new trial? What does Rule 59 say about the court's authority to order a new trial sua sponte?

3. If Judge Goodenough decides to grant the renewed motion for judgment as a matter of law, can she ignore the motion for new trial as moot? Why not? What should Judge Goodenough do in this situation?

Judge Goodenough considered both of Full Moon's postverdict motions, as well as Lane's opposition. She denied both motions. The only remaining matter for consideration by the

[34] Rule 59 is not itself helpful in defining the grounds on which a new trial may properly be granted. *See* Rule 59(a)(1)(A) (a new trial may be granted following a jury trial "for any reason for which a new trial has heretofore been granted in an action at law in federal court").

court was Lane's motion for attorneys' fees. Under Rule 54(d), Lane was obligated to file her motion within 14 days of the entry of final judgment. She had, and the judge would later hear argument on the motion. But the pending fee motion did not affect the "finality" of the judgment.[35] Thus, argument on the merits in *Olman v. Full Moon* had come to an end in the trial court. As we discuss in the next and concluding chapter, however, still more litigation was to come.

[35] A judgment is deemed final even though attorneys' fees have not yet been determined. *See Budinich v. Becton Dickinson Co.*, 486 U.S. 196 (1988) (a judgment is final and appealable, even though attorneys' fees remain in dispute).

Chapter Thirteen
Final Resolution

Rule References: 61, 62

A. Considering Appeal

1. The Olmans' Perspective

Although the Olmans were pleased with Otis's victory at trial, they were still dissatisfied with Judge Sarah Goodenough's pretrial termination of most of their claims. The heart of their case against Full Moon—that they were the victims of age discrimination—had never been considered by the jury. As Otis remarked to Eleanor Lane, "I feel like we won on a technicality." The Olmans asked Lane whether they could appeal the judge's decisions disposing of their discrimination claims.

Lane explained that the Olmans now had the right to appeal.[1] But they would need to make a decision soon because appellate rules gave them only *30 days* to file their "notice of appeal" once final judgment entered and posttrial motions resolved.[2]

Lane then discussed the pros and cons of appealing. Fiona Olman, of course, might win the right to try her case of age discrimination and recover the damages resulting from her termination. But Lane was not enthusiastic about Fiona's chances of winning on appeal. Her argument did rely, to some extent, on a legal "technicality"—whether Full Moon's failure to specifically advise her to consult an "attorney" invalidated the waiver she signed. And an appellate court would likely defer to the trial court's finding that, based on the "totality of the circumstances," Fiona had knowingly and voluntarily signed the release.[3] The Eleventh Circuit is often viewed as a moderate to conservative court, and unless Fiona's case was randomly assigned to a more favorable panel, she faced an uphill battle.[4]

---

[1] As discussed earlier, the judge's pretrial decisions on Full Moon's motion to dismiss and motion for summary judgment were not "final judgments" and so were not immediately appealable. *See* 28 U.S.C. § 1291 (granting appellate jurisdiction over "final decisions" of district courts). The court's entry of final judgment on the jury's verdict brought finality to these pretrial decisions. As also mentioned earlier, the finality of the judgment was not affected by Otis's pending motion for attorneys' fees. There are other limited exceptions to the final judgment rule. One of the most important is found in 28 U.S.C. § 1292(a)(1), which permits appeals from nonfinal orders that grant or refuse injunctive relief.

[2] *See* Fed. R. App. P. 4(a)(1)(A). Filing the notice of appeal preserves the right to appeal. The notice of appeal itself contains no legal argument. The actual appellate briefs are usually filed months later, after the parties have reviewed the record and completed their legal research.

[3] This standard is explained in Chapter Eleven.

[4] Circuit courts almost always hear cases as three-judge panels. Thus, a given panel's membership can often be decisive on appeal.

Lane believed Otis had stronger arguments to make on appeal. She thought Judge Goodenough had erred in granting summary judgment on Otis's age discrimination claims. She believed she could persuade the appellate court that Full Moon's motives in downsizing raised a question of fact for a jury to decide, particularly since the jury had apparently found Bertie Lurch to be untrustworthy.

But Lane also knew that the appellate court was not limited to the reasoning adopted by the district court; it could affirm the district court's grant of summary judgment on any basis supported by the record.[5] And Lane was troubled by the weakness of Otis's remaining claim of damages. The jury had already compensated him for all lost income and benefits. He might still recover under state law for the psychic damages Full Moon caused him and possibly receive extra punitive damages. But these damages were far more speculative than his lost earnings.[6]

If Otis appealed, Lane explained, Full Moon would surely file its own cross-appeal and seek to have Otis's judgment reversed. If Full Moon prevailed in its cross-appeal, Otis would no longer be entitled to the $400,000 awarded by the jury, and Lane would no longer be entitled to recover her attorneys' fee from Full Moon.

The prospect of forfeiting Otis's hard-won verdict was sobering to the Olmans. Given the weakness of Fiona's legal claim and the uncertainty of Otis's remaining damages claim, they decided not to *initiate* an appeal. On the other hand, if Full Moon filed its own appeal, they would cross-appeal. At a minimum, a cross-appeal would improve the Olmans' leverage in the postjudgment settlement negotiations that were sure to come.

2. Full Moon's Perspective

Bertie Lurch took Full Moon's loss at trial personally. And although Bert Tweedy didn't say it, he believed Lurch should take it personally. Had Lurch only paused and sought legal advice when he received Otis's letter complaining of age discrimination, Full Moon would not be facing a $400,000 judgment.[7]

---

[5] *See, e.g., Lucas v. W.W. Grainger, Inc.*, 257 F.3d 1249, 1256 (11th Cir. 2001). For example, the appellate court might not agree with the district court's specific reasons for finding Otis's evidence of pretext insufficient, but it might find other deficiencies with that evidence. Or, although unlikely in this case, it might find that Otis had not even established a prima facie case of age discrimination under *McDonnell Douglas*.

[6] Lane also considered appealing the court's pretrial dismissal of Otis's fraud claim against Full Moon and Bruce Belcher. But Lane thought Otis would have great difficulty proving damages resulting from the alleged fraud. At the outset of the suit, Otis believed he had lost out on a lucrative business deal in Key Largo as a result of the defendants' fraud. But Otis subsequently learned that his potential business partner—Izzy Able—had a poor business record that included a recent bankruptcy. Consequently, it would be difficult to prove Otis was damaged by his failure to join with Able in a business venture.

[7] In reality, this figure would be much higher. Full Moon would also need to consider both the attorneys' fees to which Otis was now entitled and the addition of interest on the amount of the judgment. And these considerations do not take into account the money Full Moon would pay to Tweedy's firm.

Full Moon expressed interest in appealing Otis's judgment. Tweedy's firm was willing to handle the appeal, but he was not overly encouraging about the company's chances of success. Tweedy explained to Lurch that most appeals fail. Appellate judges are fond of saying that if you want to win on appeal, make sure you win at trial.

Tweedy thought the chances of having the jury's verdict reversed were slim. His assessment was based on his review of the evidence presented at trial, taking into consideration the highly deferential standard of appellate review applicable to jury verdicts. The jury's factual determinations would be overturned on appeal only if no reasonable jury could have arrived at those determinations.[8] This standard of review is functionally equivalent to the test applied by district courts when ruling on motions for judgment as a matter of law, which was discussed in Chapter Twelve.[9] Full Moon's best chance on appeal was to identify an error of law committed by Judge Goodenough. Legal determinations are reviewed under a *de novo* standard of appellate review, meaning the appellate court revisits the issue without giving any deference to the district court's determination.[10] But even when the appellant identifies a legal error in the proceedings below, the appellate court often affirms the judgment if it concludes that the error had no effect on the outcome.[11]

Tweedy believed the judge may have committed a potentially harmful error during trial, when she permitted Lane to make a very colorful and inflammatory closing argument attacking Full Moon. Tweedy had properly objected to these comments during Lane's closing argument,[12] and Judge Goodenough had instructed the jury to "disregard" the improper comments. But the judge had denied Tweedy's motion for a mistrial and later denied his later request for a new trial. Yet again, the standard of review limited Full Moon's prospects on appeal: the trial court's denial of a new trial based on Lane's improper comments would be reversed only if Full Moon could show that the court's decision amounted to an "abuse of discretion."[13]

---

[8] *See, e.g., Parker v. Scrap Metal Processors, Inc.*, 386 F.3d 993, 1010 (11th Cir. 2004) ("We review a jury's verdict to determine whether reasonable and impartial minds could reach the conclusion the jury expressed in its verdict. . . . The verdict must stand unless there is no substantial evidence to support it.") (citation and internal quotation marks omitted).

[9] *See Zamora v. City of Houston*, 798 F.3d 326, 330 (5th Cir. 2015) (denial of motion for judgment as a matter of law is *de novo*, but the appellate court applies the same legal standard as the district court).

[10] *See Salve Regina College v. Russell*, 499 U.S. 225, 231 (1991).

[11] For example, while statements of law included in the jury instructions are reviewed *de novo*, the appellate court will reverse the jury's verdict because of an errant instruction only if it is "left with a substantial and ineradicable doubt as to whether the jury was properly guided in its deliberations." *See Smith v. City of New Smyrna Beach*, 588 Fed. Appx. 965, 983 (11th Cir. 2014) (citation and internal quotation marks omitted.).

[12] To raise an issue on appeal concerning trial misconduct, lawyers must usually have made a "contemporaneous objection" when the conduct occurs.

[13] *See, e.g., Hilger v. Velazquez*, 613 Fed. Appx. 775, 776 (11th Cir. 2015) ("District courts have considerable discretion to control the scope and tone of counsels' closing arguments. . . . Thus, absent an abuse of discretion, the decision of the trial court, which has had the opportunity to hear the offensive remarks within the context of the argument and to view their effect on the jury, should not be disturbed.") (citations and internal quotation marks omitted).

"The jury will disregard the witness's last statement."

Tweedy believed that even though the jury's verdict was otherwise supported by record evidence, an appellate court might reverse the verdict if it concluded Lane's conduct unduly biased the jury against Full Moon.[14] This, Tweedy advised Full Moon, was its best argument in seeking to have the judgment reversed on appeal.

Tweedy explained to his client that an appeal might have substantial costs. Unless Full Moon prevailed on appeal, it would have to pay the legal fees of both Tweedy and Lane.[15] Tweedy estimated his firm's fee for the appeal would be in the range of $100,000 to $150,000, and Lane's fee would be at least half that amount. Further, throughout the appeal, interest would be accumulating on the judgment. There was also the risk that an appeal would increase the adverse publicity Full Moon was receiving from its defeat.

Yet Tweedy was not surprised when Full Moon directed him to file the simple one-page notice of appeal. Nor was he surprised when the Olmans responded with their own cross-appeal. The parties' appellate counsel would now begin the painstaking process of assembling and reviewing the record evidence and drafting their initial appellate briefs.

---

[14] *See generally* Charles B. Gibbons, Federal Rules of Evidence with Trial Objections C3 (2003). Lane's comments might also have violated Model Rule of Professional Conduct 3.4(e), which prohibits argument not supported by evidence and argument expressing a lawyer's "personal opinion" about the justness of a client's position. But a violation of professional rules of conduct, standing alone, seldom results in the reversal of a final judgment.

[15] As discussed earlier, a prevailing plaintiff is entitled to recover his or her attorneys' fees under the ADEA. This entitlement includes fees incurred on appeal.

IN THE UNITED STATES DISTRICT COURT
FOR THE MIDDLE DISTRICT OF FLORIDA,
JACKSONVILLE DIVISION

OTIS AND FIONA OLMAN,

Plaintiffs,

v. Case No. 8-23-CV-00637

FULL MOON SPORTS, INC.,
& BRUCE BELCHER

Defendants.

NOTICE OF APPEAL

Notice is hereby given that Full Moon Sports Inc., defendant in the above-named case, hereby appeals to the United States Court of Appeals for the Eleventh Circuit from the Final Judgment entered on November 9, 2023. The Notice of Appeal is timely filed pursuant to Rule 4(b) of the Federal Rules of Appellate Procedure.

Respectfully submitted,

____

Harrison Ames, Esq.
Bart A. Tweedy, Esq.
Counsel for Full Moon Sports, Inc.
[Address etc. omitted.]

[Certificate of Service Omitted]

B. Settlement Negotiations Continue

Tweedy and Lane knew there would be continuing settlement discussions now that proceedings in the trial court were completed. You might ask why. After all, Otis had a judgment requiring Full Moon to pay $400,000, plus attorneys' fees and interest.[16] Why would he want to discuss settlement?

There were several reasons. First, so long as appeal remained an option, the ultimate outcome remained uncertain. Otis was in a much better settlement position than before trial, and Full Moon was in a much worse one. But this fact affected settlement values (i.e., how much the parties might pay to resolve the dispute) more than the parties' willingness to consider settlement.

Otis was also influenced by the desire to avoid further attorneys' fees and related expenses.[17] As discussed in the previous section, an appeal costs both sides money. And a successful appeal by Full Moon could lead to further proceedings in the trial court. Those proceedings would cost still more money.

Third, Otis had nonmonetary reasons for ending the dispute. By this point, he and Fiona had been in litigation for years. Their personal costs had been considerable. There was appreciable nonmonetary value in putting the dispute behind them, even if it meant accepting less money than they might recover after an appeal.

Finally, the appellate court would likely require the parties to participate in a formal settlement process anyway. Applicable court rules contemplated the mediation of disputes on appeal. The Eleventh Circuit, like many other courts, usually refers civil disputes such as the Olmans' case to mediation. Consequently, settlement negotiations are often inevitable.

These same factors also influenced Full Moon's willingness to discuss settlement. Therefore, once the parties' notices of appeal were filed, Tweedy spoke with Lurch and then called Lane. Tweedy asked if Lane would be available to sit down and discuss "where the case was going from here." He suggested meeting for lunch at a reasonably nice restaurant in Jacksonville. Tweedy hoped that his willingness to travel to Jacksonville from Atlanta showed he was serious about settlement. He was not concerned with being seen as "too eager." The trial was over. Lane held many important cards, and everyone knew it. Tweedy would do everything

---

[16] When a party has won a monetary judgment, he or she is entitled to enforce that judgment once the trial court disposes of various posttrial motions. The party is now a "judgment creditor" of the losing party, who is called a "judgment debtor." However, the judgment debtor may defer collection of the judgment while the case is on appeal by posting a "supersedeas bond" equal to the value of the judgment plus interest. *See* Rule 62(d). The supersedeas bond accomplishes two things. First, it assures the judgment creditor a source of payment for the judgment if it is upheld on appeal. Second, it assures the judgment debtor that, if it succeeds in having the judgment reversed, it can recover the bond monies it had deposited with the court.

[17] For example, the appellant would likely have to pay the court reporter for a copy of the trial transcript. Transcripts can be quite costly, especially for longer trials.

he could, within reason, to resolve the case without an appeal. If he was unsuccessful, Full Moon had agreed to fund an appeal. So far as Tweedy was concerned, he had nothing to lose by sitting down with Lane.

In light of the risks for her own clients, Lane agreed to meet Tweedy for lunch. At their luncheon meeting, following some small talk, Tweedy broached the subject of avoiding an appeal. He did so by first casually mentioning how nice it was to have a client like Full Moon that paid its bills and was willing to take litigation to the end of the line. He then discussed the strengths and weaknesses of his case on appeal. Lane, of course, responded to these comments by acknowledging some of the weaknesses in Otis's appeal, but reinforcing the reality that he had won at trial.

Discussion continued over lunch. Tweedy finally raised the prospect of settling the case for $100,000, the jury award for back pay. Lane told Tweedy that anything in that range was a nonstarter. The bargaining went back and forth. By dessert, both Tweedy and Lane knew the case was going to settle; it was just a question of the details. Tweedy finally proposed the following to Lane. Within 15 days, Full Moon would pay Otis $300,000, representing the jury's award of back and future pay. Full Moon would also agree to pay Lane's reasonable attorneys' fees, an amount only slightly less than the fee request Lane had filed with Judge Goodenough. Otis would drop his appeal, forgo recovery of the penalty award of double back pay, and forgo recovery of interest. Lane said she would take the proposal to Otis and Fiona and recommend they accept it.

Within 24 hours, the case was settled on the terms laid out at Tweedy and Lane's lunch. The terms of the settlement were embodied in a settlement agreement signed by both parties. After the agreement was signed, the parties also signed and filed with the trial and appellate courts a "notice of dismissal," formally ending the litigation. Among other things, the settlement agreement provided that (1) Full Moon was making no "admissions" by entering into the agreement; (2) the Olmans fully released Full Moon for any liability relating to the events giving rise to the suit; (3) all parties agreed to keep the terms of the settlement confidential; and (4) the Olmans had been specifically advised by counsel prior to signing the agreement. Although Otis initially chafed at the idea that Full Moon was admitting no liability and prohibiting him from discussing the settlement, he ultimately yielded to Lane's advice that such settlement terms were customary.

IN THE UNITED STATES DISTRICT COURT
FOR THE MIDDLE DISTRICT OF FLORIDA,
JACKSONVILLE DIVISION

OTIS AND FIONA OLMAN,

Plaintiffs,

v. Case No. 8-23-CV-00637

FULL MOON SPORTS, INC.,

Defendant.

JOINT STIPULATION TO DISMISS WITH PREJUDICE

Otis Olman, Fiona Olman, and Full Moon Sports, Inc., through their undersigned counsel, jointly stipulate to the entry of an Order dismissing this action with prejudice.

____
Eleanor Lane, Esq.
Lane & Quincy, P.A.
Counsel for Plaintiffs
[Address, phone number, etc. omitted]

____
Harrison Ames, Esq.
Bart A. Tweedy, Esq.
Counsel for Full Moon Sports, Inc.
[Address etc. omitted]

What you have read about *Olman v. Full Moon* is a fairly typical story of a federal lawsuit—other than the fact that the case went to trial. It reflects the importance of understanding the Rules, consulting with your client, thinking strategically, and acting ethically. It also reflects a fundamental reality of litigation that you, as aspiring lawyers, should recognize now. Almost by definition, the results of civil litigation are second-best substitutes. For example, even though he won at trial, Otis Olman would have preferred to return to the time when he and Fiona worked at the Jacksonville store under corporate management that cared about its employees. But litigation could not make that happen. The best it could do was give Otis money to somewhat compensate him for what he had lost. A significant part of your job as a lawyer is to make clients see this reality of modern American litigation.

Postscript

There is, of course, life after litigation. We thought you might be interested in what happened to some of the people involved in *Olman v. Full Moon.*

Otis and Fiona Olman

After the case ended, Otis and Fiona realized that too much of their time had been consumed fighting Full Moon in litigation. Now that the suit had ended and they had received payment of their judgment, they needed to figure out what to do next. One day over breakfast, Fiona suggested they start their own business catering to adventure tourists in Costa Rica. Otis agreed, and the couple has enjoyed just enough business success to survive. But as William Least Heat-Moon observed in *Blue Highways*, "No bosses is better than money."

Bertie Lurch

Lurch's corporate restructuring at Full Moon caught the attention of people at the parent company, Mizar. Lurch was eventually made vice president of Mizar. But he was later indicted for his involvement in corporate-accounting scandals. He is currently awaiting trial in federal court, where he has been charged with criminal securities fraud. He has also been sued by disgruntled investors, who are seeking $25 million in damages.

Sid Shockley

Shockley didn't last long in management. He quit Full Moon because management "wasn't his thing." When last seen, Shockley was surfing the big ones at Teahupoo and vainly striving to stave off aging.

Bruce Belcher

Belcher worked for several years in a Connecticut retail sporting goods company. He was laid off during a corporate downsizing last year. His own claim of age discrimination is now being investigated by the EEOC.

Eleanor Lane

Soon after the *Olman* case ended, Lane saw that Magistrate Judge Mattthew Malarkey was stepping down and the local district court was taking applications to fill his position. Lane applied, got the job, and was sworn in as a U.S. magistrate judge.

Ramona Quincy

After Lane was appointed a federal magistrate, she could no longer continue her partnership with Ramona Quincy. But Quincy continues to engage in litigation practice. Her latest professional quest is to sue marginal law schools that remain in operation only by enticing applicants with promises of lucrative employment upon graduation.

Bart Tweedy

After billing 200-plus hours for many years, Tweedy finally decided that he'd had enough of big-firm practice. Today, he is teaching courses in Civil Procedure and Employment Discrimination at a small law school in the South. Apart from having to deal with inept administrators, Tweedy couldn't be happier. He has plans to publish a textbook in which he draws on his litigation experience to teach his students how procedural law works in the "real world."

APPENDIX: CHARACTERS, CHRONOLOGY, AND CLAIMS

CHARACTERS

Parties

Otis Olman	The primary plaintiff and former manager of the Full Moon Sports Outdoor Center in Jacksonville, Florida. Otis was 53 years old at the time of his termination.
Fiona Olman	Otis Olman's co-plaintiff and wife. She is the former manager of the kayak department of the Jacksonville store. Fiona is 49 years old.
Full Moon Sports, Inc.	Full Moon is a nationwide sporting goods retailer. It employed Otis Olman as manager from 1999 to 2018. Full Moon's principal place of business is in Atlanta. It is incorporated in Delaware.
Bruce Belcher	Belcher is the former regional sales manager for the region in which the Jacksonville store is located.

Lawyers

Eleanor Lane	Counsel for the Olmans; partner in Lane & Quincy, P.A. (Jacksonville, Florida).
Bart Tweedy	Principal counsel for Full Moon; senior associate in Lord, Howe, & Mercy (Atlanta).

Judges

Trial Judge	Honorable Sarah Goodenough, United States District Court for the Middle District of Florida, Jacksonville Division.
Magistrate Judge	Honorable Matthew Malarkey, United States District Court for the Middle District of Florida, Jacksonville Division.

Other Characters

Izzy Able	An entrepreneur who offered Otis Olman a one-half partnership in a kayak business in Key Largo.
Kay Bailey	Chairperson of Full Moon's Corporate Board of Directors.
Samantha Brown	An employee in Full Moon's Human Resources Department and the author of an internal report concerning Full Moon's corporate restructuring.
Ruby Dubidoux	A former manager of Full Moon's Orlando store, who is also represented by Eleanor Lane.
Judy Kaufman	Associate in-house counsel at Full Moon.
Bertie Lurch	President of Full Moon since 2019.
Dr. Lily Meloy	Statistics professor and expert witness for Otis Olman.
Chloé Michaela	Chairperson of Full Moon's Reorganization Committee, which made the decision to replace the Olmans.
Mizar, Inc.	Mizar is a parent corporation that owns many subsidiaries. In 2015, it purchased Full Moon Sports, Inc., and instituted numerous changes in the company.
Rex Ornstein	A former regional manager for Full Moon stores in the Southeast region.
Sid Shockley	Current store manager of the Jacksonville store; replaced Otis Olman.
Dr. Harold Smeltzly	A statistician and an expert consulted, but not used, by Otis Olman.
Noah Stephen	Vice president of information management at Full Moon.

CHRONOLOGY OF KEY EVENTS

2003

Otis Olman joins Full Moon

2006

Otis made manager of Burlington store

2011

Otis made manager of Jacksonville, FL store

2014

Fiona Olman begins work at Jacksonville store

2019

Fiona becomes department manager

Full Moon acquired by Mizar; Bertie Lurch becomes president; Bruce Belcher replaces Rex Ornstein as regional manager

New contract between Full Moon and Otis (March 1, 2015 through March 1, 2019)

Sid Shockley becomes manager of extreme sports department

2022

November

Full Moon announces downsizing plans

Otis demoted; Fiona terminated soon after downsizing announced

December

Otis sends letter to Lurch and is terminated

Eleanor Lane meets with the Olmans

Otis files claim with the EEOC

2023

March

Olmans file suit in federal court

April

Full Moon answers complaint and files motion to dismiss

Court issues case management and scheduling order and grants Full Moon's motion to dismiss the age-discrimination claim against Olman

May-August

Parties conduct discovery

September

Full Moon files motion for summary judgment

October

Court orders summary judgment of Otis's claim of age discrimination

November

Case tried and jury verdict returned

December

Olman and Full Moon settle

SUMMARY OF LEGAL CLAIMS AND ELEMENTS

Age Discrimination: (federal and Florida statutes)

1. Plaintiff-employee is aged 40 or over;
2. Employer took adverse job action against employee;
3. Job action taken "because of" employee's age; and
4. Employee suffered damages.

Retaliation: (federal and Florida statutes)

1. Plaintiff-employee engaged in statutorily protected expression;
2. Plaintiff suffered an adverse employment action; and
3. The adverse action against him was causally related to his protected expression.

Fraud: (Florida common law)

1. Defendant (or agent) made false representation of fact;
2. Defendant knew representation was false when made;
3. Defendant made false representation to induce plaintiff to rely; and
4. Plaintiff justifiably relied on false representation to his detriment.

Conversion: (Florida common law)

1. Defendant wrongfully exercised control;
2. Of plaintiff's property;
3. In a manner inconsistent with the plaintiff's rights in the property.

Tortious Interference with a Business Relationship: (Florida common law)

1. Plaintiff was party to a business;
2. Defendant knew of plaintiff's business relationship;
3. Defendant intentionally and unjustifiably interfered with plaintiff's business relationship; and
4. Defendant's interference caused damage to plaintiff.

Index